Frameworks for Studying Families

About the Author

Chester A. Winton is a professor of sociology at San Jose State University, where he has taught courses in family and sociological theory for 23 years. Dr. Winton is a licensed marriage, family, and child counselor in California, where he has a private family therapy practice. For the past seven years, he served as a child custody evaluator in Santa Clara County.

Dr. Winton has considerable experience teaching, conducting research, and training family therapists throughout the world. He was a visiting lecturer in Sociology at United College, of the Chinese University of Hong Kong, where he lived for one year. In Hong Kong, he was a consultant to the Hong Kong Marriage Guidance Council. He was a visiting scientist at the Tavistock Institute of Human Relations and the Tavistock Clinic, Department of Children and Parents, in London for one year. In Rugby, England, he assisted in the training of clinical supervisors at the National Marriage Guidance Council. He has also been a visiting scholar at the Hebrew University of Jerusalem. While in Israel, he assisted in the training of family therapists who would be working on kibbutzim.

This is Dr. Winton's third book. Previous titles are *Theory Measurement in Sociology* (1974) and *Family Therapy: Etiology and Treatment of Illness* (1981).

Frameworks for Studying Families

Chester A. Winton

San Jose State University

The Dushkin Publishing Group, Inc.

Guilford, Connecticut

For Nancy

The work illustrated on the cover, Family Group (bronze, 1946), is reproduced by permission of the Henry Moore Foundation.

This book is printed
on recycled paper

Printed in the United States of America

Library of Congress Catalog Card Number 94–071688

International Standard Book Number (ISBN) 1–56134–307–2

10 9 8 7

Preface

This book was written to provide a brief, inexpensive, treatment of the major theoretical approaches to marriage and family. During over 20 years of teaching marriage and family courses to undergraduates, I have found that most marriage and family texts do an outstanding job of describing today's increasingly complex and rapidly changing family structure. Few texts, however, attempt to place these developments in any kind of theoretical context. Those that do often make use of only a single theoretical perspective, ignoring others. Other texts contain a broader discussion of theory at the beginning but do not apply this material in later chapters.

Combining two fields of sociological inquiry, theory and family studies, this text presents the basic principles of the major twentieth century sociological theories. It then applies these theories to contemporary family structure and processes. And unlike other texts on sociological theories of the family, this one is brief, affordable, written by a single author, and specifically intended for an undergraduate audience.

Why bother? One reason is that theoretical frameworks provide an analytic context for understanding human social behavior. They allow us to answer the question "So what?," giving meaning to the real world. The frameworks discussed in this book provide alternative perspectives for describing, accounting for, and predicting the social interaction of people in groups. Each one provides a slightly different view of the subject. Together, they may be used as a set of alternative lenses, each of which gives us a slightly different picture of the marriage and family landscape.

Five major theoretical frameworks are covered in this text, each the focus of a separate chapter. In chapter 1, developmental theories, including unilinear family development theory and multilinear evolutionary theory are discussed. Chapter 2 features structural-functional theory, while chapter 3 explores conflict theory. In chapter 4, social exchange theory is covered and chapter 5 examines symbolic interaction theory. In chapter 6, along with a discussion of the life course perspective and postmodern theory, the frameworks are compared and contrasted. There is a discussion of how all the frameworks can be used to make sense of a very complex social world.

Each chapter first discusses the principles of the particular framework. The framework is then applied to analyze interactional dynamics in families using the concepts and perspective of that framework. Five chapters include sections on romantic love and on divorce. This is done to show how different frameworks, applied to the same subject, result in very different views. Romantic love and divorce were chosen as these themes because of their interest to undergraduates and because of their direct impact on the lives of most students.

Each chapter contains a critical analysis of the framework, often including a feminist perspective, which features a review of the framework's shortcomings and liabilities. Where applicable, tables and figures are used to further illuminate the text. A thorough glossary (the words are highlighted in the text) of terms and concepts and an extensive bibliography are provided.

The text is particularly useful in courses in the family because it directly applies sociological theory to the study and understanding of family life, thus demonstrating the relevance of theory to real life. Instructors of sociological theory will also find the text helpful because it presents theory in connection with a major social institution with which all students have some familiarity. This is, in short, a practical book which shows how theory can be used to make sense of and give some order to reality.

Acknowledgments

This book was written with the assistance and support of many people. The author seeks to acknowledge, with gratitude and thanks, the efforts these people made in improving the manuscript from draft to draft.

My wife, Nancy, to whom this book is dedicated, was unwavering in her support and encouragement.

This project began through the confidence Larry Swanson showed in me while he was a field editor for The Dushkin Publishing Group. Larry negotiated the contract through which this book came into existence. Irv Rockwood, publisher at DPG, managed this project and guided it through to completion with enthusiasm and dedication. Wendy Connal at DPG proved an important communication link.

David Estrin served as developmental editor, and he made organizational and structural improvements in early drafts. Later reviews of the manuscript were made by Kris Bulcroft, Associate Professor of Sociology at Western Washington University, Preston M. Dyer, Ph.D., Professor and Director of the Department of Sociology, Anthropology, Social Work and Gerontology at Baylor University, and Julio Quiñones, Professor of Sociology at California State University at Chico. They formed a constructive team. Each made valuable suggestions toward improving the manuscript. My colleague, Carol Ray, made suggestions that improved two sequential manuscript drafts. My colleague, C. Michael Otten, also reviewed a draft of the manuscript.

San Jose State University awarded me a sabbatical leave for the Fall, 1993 semester. The process of bringing this text to fruition would have been considerably longer had it not been for this leave. Computer assistance was received from Joan Block and Joanne Unger in the Sociology Department at San Jose State University. Assistance with reference citations was provided by Jack Kahn, my graduate student assistant.

I would also like to acknowledge the contributions of several scholars and teachers who have each made a contribution in my intellectual development. At the University of California, Riverside, I did my undergraduate studies in sociology under the tutelage of Egon Bittner, Aaron Cicourel, and Robert Nisbet. At the University of California, Berkeley, I learned much from Neil Smelser, Charles Glock, Erving Goffman, William Peterson and particularly from Herbert Blumer, John Clausen, and Kenneth Bock. Each contributed pieces to the mosaic of my sociological knowledge.

Lastly, at The Dushkin Publishing Group, I would like to acknowledge the contributions of Dorothy Fink, who showed extraordinary skill and great interpersonal diplomacy in editing the final manuscript for the publisher. I am also grateful for the proofreading done by Diane Barker and her team and to Marion Gouge, for her editorial assistance in handling permissions, to Pam Carley for finding the Henry Moore cover illustration, and to Charles Vitelli for his excellent interior and cover designs.

Chester A. Winton

Contents

Introduction

The Focus

The social world is very complex, so complex that it sometimes seems impossible to describe or understand. Attempts to make general statements about human social behavior usually lead to thoughts of the exceptions. Indeed, one way to grasp the complexity of the world is by considering its contradictory nature, for what is true in one instance may not be true in another.

On the one hand, it is tempting to claim that people are inherently good; on the other hand, there have certainly been those who have imposed great hardship and suffering upon others. Conversely, it is tempting to generalize that people all act in their own self-interest, yet there are those who are very altruistic. Conflict, though natural, normal, and inevitable in human interaction, does not exclude the possibility of cooperation and harmonious existence. All things do change over time, change is ever-present and inevitable; yet, some elements of society (churches, governments, families, corporations, parents, administrators) seem very resistant to change.

In a social world, there are often subtle rules that demand that we stay within reality and not try to analyze or make sense of it. We tend to take the realities of our social world for granted, and thus we are often blind to the repetitive patterns of human behavior that exist around us. For example, we may never have thought that everyone in the family has an assigned seat at the dining room table and that when the family congregates, everyone sits in his or her place. We may never have considered that there are dominant coalition patterns in a family—certain people usually siding with each other against other family members. When the family is thought of as a collection of people, each of whom has certain jobs to do in a division of labor, it is possible to ask who does more or less work in the family; who is served and who does the serving of other family members? Often people are oblivious to the patterns of behavior that surround them because it is difficult to see and be part of the very world that is being observed.

It is, however, the goal of sociologists to describe these repetitive patterns of human social behavior. Until recently, sociologists also sought to causally account for why certain regularities existed. If causal factors of present social behavior could be determined, this would allow the theorist to predict future behavior with some reasonable accuracy. Seeking the cause of behavioral processes involves linear thinking, assuming that the world is organized in terms of cause and effect. Sociologists more recently use circular reasoning, describing continuous processes of action and reaction, so that there are no ultimate causes.

In this book, we explore how sociologists have attempted to describe and causally account for interactional behavior in families. Even though we limit our analysis to life in families, we do little to reduce the complexity of the social world because there are so many kinds of families. There are small families, and large families; families with children, and families without children; there are intact nuclear families, single parent families, and stepfamilies; there are families in undeveloped societies, and families in highly urbanized and industrialized societies; there are families in all classes and in every kind of ethnic group; there are heterosexual families, and gay and lesbian families. Faced with this diversity and complexity, sociologists have created theoretical frameworks that are used to interpret and make sense of social interaction in families.

Frameworks as Eyeglasses

It may be helpful to think of each framework as constituting *a set of eyeglasses,* with each set of eyeglasses having a different prescription. When people wear one theorist's glasses, they see the world as that theorist sees it. Each framework, each prescription, involves seeing the world differently, with a different focus. What is seen clearly, in sharp focus, with one set of eyeglasses may be blurred using a different theorist's "correction." Each framework also focuses on a different dimension of reality. Because reality is so complex, we cannot take it all in simultaneously. Thus, these coexisting theories concentrate on a different aspect of the real world.

The developmental theorist's glasses focus on change, which is seen as being natural, normal, and inevitable in social systems. Individuals, groups like families, and whole societies are seen as changing to realize their inherent potential. Change usually occurs slowly, but it is ever-present. Change is described as occurring in stages over time. Names are given to the stages and what happens in each stage of development is described.

Structural-functional theorists' glasses focus on stability and resistance to change. These theorists define systems as attempts to maintain equilibrium, to keep the basic structure that exists. When wearing the structural-functional theorist's glasses, a person sees harmony, cooperation, and integration in social systems. Integration is achieved by having people share common cultural values and conform to widely accepted social norms. Using this perspective, the parts of a social system are seen, and the focus is on how the parts contribute to the whole in a process of interrelated and interdependent interaction.

When the conflict theorist's glasses are used, the focus is on the existence of competition, struggle, and conflict in a system, particularly conflict over scarce resources, such as money, time, attention, affection, or power. Conflict is seen as natural, normal, and inevitable in all social systems. Conflict is seen as necessary to the survival of these systems.

The real world contains elements of both change and stability, cooperation and conflict. Each theory has a particular focus. Each invites people to look at one element of the world. By concentrating on one part of the social world, there is a tendency to ignore or to be blind to other aspects of that world. Each theory thus tends to distort reality, for no one theory attempts to see reality in its totality. The real world is so complex, with so many contradictory elements, that no one theory in sociology has been able to describe its full complexity. Diverse theories thus exist and sociologists use the theory which best "fits" the piece of reality that they are trying to describe.

When sociologists look at a social structure that changes greatly over time, they may want to use a developmental perspective, for that theory focuses on change. If they are examining a social structure that seems particularly resistant to change, they may want to use structural-functional theory because that theory focuses on how systems resist change to maintain stability. When observing a highly integrated, cooperative social system, structural-functional theory may be used, while conflict theory may be the better choice to understand a social system with much competition and strife. Sociologists use these theories to help them make sense of the real world, to describe and understand social processes.

Learning How to See

In the process of early socialization, children learn how to see. Seeing does not happen automatically. This becomes apparent when the behavior of blind adults is studied, people who have been blind for their entire lives (Winton, 1970), who have never seen. Suddenly an operation, such as the removal of congenital cataracts, gives them vision for the first time. When these people are shown an apple and asked what it is, they will not know. They can see the apple; that is, an image is impinging on their brain, but they have not learned how to interpret that image. They have not learned what name or label to give to the image that they see.

If the apple is handed to them, however, they will say, "Oh, that is an apple," because they have learned that this round, waxy object is called an apple. Now they have to learn how to see, how to interpret the images that impinge on their brain (Von Senden, 1960). They have to learn that these round objects, sometimes red, sometimes green, sometimes yellow, are called apples; that this is what apples look like. All sighted children must learn how to interpret the visual images that they "see." Indeed, everyone must learn *how* to see.

In this book, the reader will learn how to see the dynamics of interpersonal interaction in families from different theoretical perspectives. Each perspective will impose a different interpretation of family process. In this sense, reality exists to be interpreted. Reality has no meaning except the meaning that is imparted to it. People give meaning to reality, meaning that they learn from others.

People within a group tend to share common interpretations of reality; people outside the group and in other groups often hold different interpretations of that reality. Interpretations of what families should look like and what they should do may be very different for rich and poor; for men and women; for heterosexuals and gays or lesbians; for young and old; for the employed and the unemployed; and for married, single, divorced, or widowed people.

Interpretations are not right or wrong; they exist because they make sense to a person at a particular point in time. However, since a person's life and condition can change, his or her interpretation of reality is also subject to change over time. Perception, therefore, exists as an evolving, dynamic process.

Sociologists who collectively use a theoretical framework constitute an academic group. The reader will learn how different groups view families, given their particular theoretical approach, because in each chapter the student will see family life from a different group's perspective. Taking this visionary journey, students may learn to see families in ways that they have never seen before.

Language Guides Perception

Thinking can be thought of as talking to ourselves. When people talk to themselves, they use a language. That language has a structure that affects and limits what people can and cannot think about. The nature of our thinking is affected by the language that we use when we think.

The basic structure of an English sentence is Subject-Verb-Object. A person may think "There is a boy throwing a ball." The focus is on the person acting. Not all languages, however, have this structure. Eskimo, for example, is said to have the structure Object-Verb-Subject. An Eskimo, seeing the same event, would think, "There is a ball being thrown by a boy," with the focus on the object being acted upon. The language that a person uses for thinking influences how that person thinks and what he or she is capable of thinking about (Hall, 1960).

In English, for example, time is structured using three primary tenses. Events are seen as occurring in the past, the present, or the future. Not all languages structure time in this way. The language of the Hopi Indians, for instance, uses only one tense, and the Hopis see all things as being in a perpetual process of becoming (Hall, 1959: 146). People's perception of time is affected by their language because people think using language.

Linguist Benjamin Whorf (Carroll, 1956) believed that languages provide a code, a framework, by which people experience reality. He saw reality as a kaleidoscope of impressions that must be organized in peoples' minds for the world to make sense. The world is not intrinsically an ordered structure; rather, people impose order and structure upon it. Language, which has order and structure, helps people create order and structure in their world. Thus, the world is categorized along lines presented by the unique content of a particular language.

Languages also have a **lexicon**, a vocabulary that allows people to order their world. People who have been born and raised in Florida tend to use only one word that means "white fluffy flakes that fall from the sky in the winter." Because they only have one word—snow—to categorize this substance, they tend to see all snow as being the same. Skiers on the other hand, have many different words for snow: powder, corn, and hardpack among them. Each of these words enables them to describe the different textures and consistencies of snow. Their vocabulary allows them to focus on the fact that not all snow is the same. Generally, the more important an object is in a culture, the greater the number of words exist to describe that object. In the Eskimo language, there are, of course, many different words for snow, something of great importance in that culture (Hall, 1959, 107). The lexicon of a language gives people who speak that language dimensions for perceiving and experiencing the world. Whorf (Carroll 1956: 252) states that:

> Every language is a vast pattern-system, different from others, in which the personality not only communicates, but also analyzes nature, notices or neglects types of relationship and phenomena, channels his reasoning, and builds the house of his consciousness.

Each of the frameworks presented in this book has its own *vocabulary of concepts*. The different concepts of each theory force us to see the world using those concepts and the ideas they represent. Each theoretical framework presents a "foreign language" that must be learned, and key concepts that must be used to describe and interpret social interaction. This vocabulary focuses our perception and guides our experience of social reality.

In part, by learning the vocabulary of each framework, you will be able to see the world through the lens that each framework provides. It is much the same process that occurs when we teach small children how to speak. By learning how to use language, children are guided in how to view objects and events in their world and how to label and describe those objects and actions in socially accepted ways. By learning the language, they join a community of people who share common ways of speaking, writing, perceiving, and interpreting their universe. So, too, sociologists who regularly employ a particular theoretical framework constitute a community of scholars who share a common language and who see the world in shared ways. In the chapters that follow, you will share their language and their vision.

Part One

Theories of External Control

In Part 1, three theories will be explored: developmental theory, structural-functional theory, and conflict theory. All three theories contain elements of determinism, in which people are influenced by forces outside themselves. These forces, in part, influence the nature of human social behavior.

In developmental and conflict theory the elements of external control exist in the principle that it is the essential nature of social systems to change and to have conflict. Control in structural-functional theory lies in the power of structural forces to influence the thoughts and behavior of people within those structures. In these three frameworks people are seen as having relatively little power over social forces. This focus on external control does not exist in all sociological theories, as we will come to see in Part II.

Chapter 1

Developmental Theory

Chapter 2

Structural-Functional Theory

Chapter 3

Conflict Theory

Chapter One

Developmental Theories

The Focus

The Greek philosopher Heraclitis was reputed to have said that a person never steps in the same river twice. The second time it is not the same river nor is it the same person. Heraclitis's words were meant to illustrate the position that change is always occurring. Everything on earth is in an ever-present process of change.

Since the time of Greek philosophers, people have been trying to describe and account for the process of change. It is a difficult and complex task because change is not always predictable. The process of change does not easily fit into a single theoretical model. Numerous models have been devised to describe and account for the existence of change within social groups. In this chapter, we will explore some of those frameworks.

First we will use the glasses of the unilinear developmental theorist to see change portrayed as progressing along one, and only one, path. After a general discussion of unilinear development theory, we will focus closely on family developmental theory, which explores how families change their structure and interactional patterns through stages over time.

Lastly, we will take a look at change as depicted by multilinear development theorists—change as proceeding along multiple paths, so that individual families or societies are seen as taking different routes as they change over time.

Unilinear Developmental Theories

Social evolutionary theorists of the nineteenth century used the development of the human organism as their model to discuss the development of institutions and societies over time. The model that they used, in which a person can be seen as aging through stages over time, is adapted from the biological sciences. As part of its inherent potential, the human organism has the capacity to develop to old age. It continues to the realization of this potential through a series of stages, from infancy to childhood to adolescence to young adulthood to middle age and, finally, to old age.

Figure 1.1

The Unilinear Developmental Model

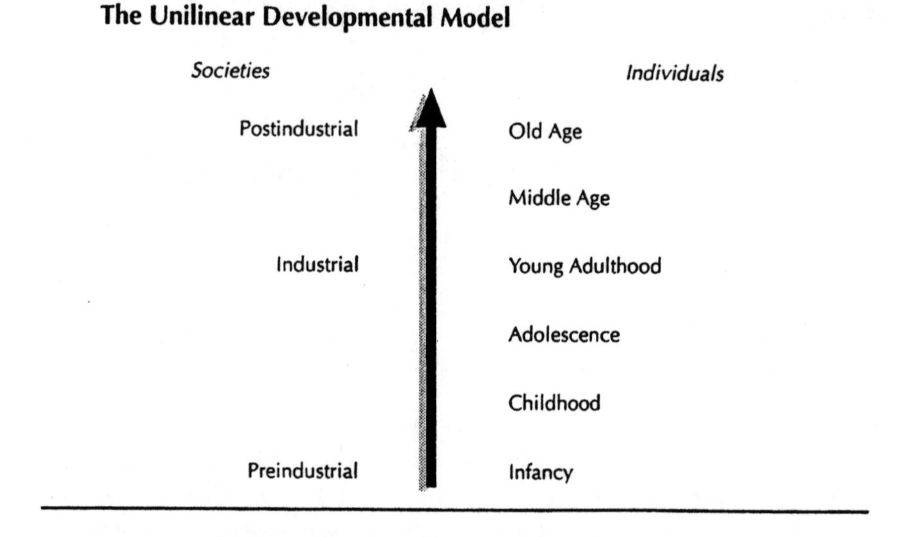

Many developmental theorists believe that as individuals develop through stages over time so do societies, which develop from preindustrial to industrial to postindustrial systems.

Twentieth-century unilinear developmental theorists also borrow this individualistic model and apply it to societies, which are seen as being in an ever-present process of gradual change to attain the societal equivalent of "old age." For societies, old age involves having highly developed levels of industrialization and urbanization.

These social theorists wrote that as individuals develop through stages over time, so do societies. Oswald Spengler (1926: 106), for instance, wrote that "every culture passes through the age-phases of the individual man. Each has its childhood, youth, manhood, and old age. . . ." The number of stages theorists created varied as did the names they applied to each stage. Some nineteenth-century social evolutionists (Steward, 1956) believed that all societies started at historically the same point, but some did not advance as far as others because of natural disasters (floods, famines, earthquakes) or because of specific historical events (such as the losing of a war). Sir E. B. Tylor (1871/1958) saw societies progressing from a stage of savagery to a stage he called barbarism and, finally, to a stage he labeled civilization.

In tracing the path by which Europeans attained civilization, social evolutionists looked with interest at less developed societies, believing that they represented the earlier stage of development through which European civilization must have gone at some time in the past. They believed that all societies went through the same stages in a singular developmental path, just as all individuals must go through the same stages to attain old age (Hofstadter, 1959). As individuals can only get older and can never reverse the process of aging, so it was believed that societies could never regress to a former, earlier stage of development. Change was believed to be *unidirec-*

tional. A society could never go backwards to become less highly developed, less industrialized, or less urbanized.

Just as an individual cannot skip any developmental stage in attaining old age, so it was believed that neither could society. According to this theory, all societies must go through the same stages in developing. The basic tenets of many nineteenth- and twentieth-century social evolutionary theorists can be summarized as follows:

1. Change is ever-present and gradual.
2. Change occurs in stages.
3. Change occurs because it is the essential nature of a society to change; society is always moving toward the realization of its inherent potential.
4. Change is unidirectional; change cannot be reversed.
5. No society can skip a stage of development.

Many sociologists used these tenets to create their unilinear theories of change (Reich, 1970). Marx (1885/1932) saw the economic development of societies as continuing from the stage of feudal mercantilism to capitalism to socialism to communism. He saw all societies moving along this continuum through a process called dialectical materialism, where there is a constant conflict of economic ideas and ideologies that create change.

Many nineteenth-century social evolutionary and developmental theorists were ethnocentric. **Ethnocentrism** is the belief that one's own culture is more advanced, better, and more important than other cultures that exist in the world. Western European theorists often believed that their civilization was more advanced, both technologically and morally, than others in the world (Spencer, 1852/1972a; 1857/1972b).

More recently, unilinear developmental theory was used by David Riesman et al. (1953) in tracing the source of norms people use to guide and construct their behavior. In preindustrial societies, where norms came out of historical custom, people were **tradition-directed**. In early industrializing societies, people were **inner-directed**: They internalized norms and became self-directed and self-motivated. In highly industrialized societies, people are **other-directed**—seeking cues on how to behave from others in their immediate environment. Other-directed persons seek approval and acceptance from others and try to understand the expectations of others, feeling that they can gain acceptance if they can meet those expectations. Riesman wrote his work in the 1950s, a decade of concern for overconformity, reflected in book titles like *A Nation of Sheep* (Lederer, 1961).

Unilinear developmental theory is also operating in the work of Toffler (1984), who describes three technological waves of social history, the first **agricultural**, the second **industrial**, and the third **postindustrial** or postmodern. In the first wave, societies have an economy based on agriculture and other occupations that harvest raw materials (lumbering, fishing, mining). In the second wave, societies convert raw materials to manufactured goods. In the third wave, the economy of a society is focused on providing human services, rather than on producing a product. Service occupations include teaching, social work, public relations, advertising, recreation and leisure management, and financial management services.

The Pace of Change

The proposition that change is ever-present and gradual is consistent with the pace of individual aging. Sometimes social change occurs so slowly that it is imperceptible unless it is observed over a long period of time. Today, however, one may well challenge the notion that social change occurs gradually. Toffler (1970) suggests that the rate of social change accelerates with increasing industrialization and urbanization.

Certainly, over the past 50 years, families have changed gradually but, more recently, with increased acceleration. People now marry later in their lives. They have fewer children. They divorce more and are more likely to remarry and create stepfamilies. Mothers with young children are more apt to be gainfully employed in the workforce, resulting in more young children spending more time in day care or preschool facilities than they did 50 years ago. There are more relationships involving gay and lesbian couples and those relationships are more public than they were 50 years ago. Women use contraceptive pills, condoms for women, and hormone therapy for menopause, which were not yet on the market 50 years ago.

Stages over Time

Change is described as occurring in stages, but there is usually no unanimity among theorists as to how many stages exist for any process of change that is described. The precise boundaries marking where one stage ends and another begins is difficult to ascertain. For instance, when does the **premarital stage** begin? When the prospective husband and wife are first born? When they are betrothed to one another? (In some societies, marriages are arranged by parents while husband and wife are still infants or children.) When they first meet? When they publicly announce their engagement? Getting married is a *process,* a stream of many events that occur over time. It is not easy to articulate the exact moment when the premarital stage begins.

The movement from one stage to another requires transitions (Falicov, 1988; Pittman, 1987), and these transitions are sometimes problematic and difficult for people engaged in them. The transitional experience has to be described as well as what happens within the various stages.

Just as individuals cannot skip childhood or adolescence, so it was thought by early unilinear social evolutionists that all societies took the same path toward urbanization and industrialization. When applied to families, however, this proposition is difficult to support. Some people never marry so never experience the stage of a childless married couple. Some couples have children without marrying and thus experience the **parenthood stage** but skip the earlier one. Some couples are voluntarily childless or are unable to have children, and thus skip the parenthood stage. Some couples, whose children live with them in perpetuity, never are left with an empty nest.

Despite the fact that the precepts of unilinear developmental theory may be flawed when applied to change in families, this approach has been used to study changes in families over the life course for the past 60 years. As we will come to see, because of the problems inherent in the theoretical framework, however, the theory is still undergoing revision to enhance its utility.

Family Development Theory

The family development approach to studying families traces the historical development of a family through stages over time. It is a unilinear model (see Figure 1.1, p. 10), which borrows from the prototype of the individual aging through stages, from infancy to old age, over time.

Since life does not conveniently organize itself into discrete stages, but progresses as a stream of behavior occurring over time, the division of a continuum into stages is an arbitrary and artificial enterprise. Developmental theorists have exhibited no consistency in the number of stages that they have used in creating a family life cycle. Evelyn Duvall (1957) created a system of 8 family stages, while Roy Rodgers (1962) had 24 stages in his.

Developmental theorists do not use the same words for stages. They may even use different analytic criteria for the labeling of stages (Aldous, 1990). For instance, Rowntree (1906) studied *poverty* in families living in York, England (cited in Hill & Rodgers, 1964: 173). He established a 3-stage process in which families were poor when their children were young and an economic liability rather than an asset capable of bringing in an income. Families experienced relative prosperity when the children grew up enough to become wage earners who contributed to the family's financial resources. Families again became poor when their children left the nest to start their own families. Income was again lost to the family unit. Rowntree's 3-stage process depicted family poverty over the family life cycle going from poverty to relative prosperity to poverty.

One can create a developmental scheme based on the fact that family size usually changes over the life span. Families either expand, contract, or are stable. Using these as concepts, a 5-stage model can be created (Hill & Rodgers, 1964: 189) in which the first stage features stability for a childless married couple, followed by an expansion stage that extends from the birth of the first child to the birth of the last child. Another stability period of childrearing follows, which extends until the first child leaves home. When this happens, a contracting stage begins, a period of launching children out into the world. This contraction extends until the last child has left home. There is then stability again in a postparental childless stage. The 5-stage progression is thus stability, expansion, stability, contraction, stability.

Duvall (cited by Hill & Rodgers, 1964: 174) created a 4-stage developmental scheme based on the idea that families expand and contract over the life cycle creating pressure on the family regarding their changing need for living space. In the early stage space is relatively plentiful because there are no children yet. As children are added, the family enters the crowded stage. When the children are adolescents, the family is in the peak stage, featuring a significant shortage of space. Not only are there adolescent family members occupying space but with these teens' concern for incorporation into a peer network, there are the adolescents' friends also using family space. The later-years stage features a gradual reduction of space urgency as children leave the nest.

Family development researchers tend to conduct interviews with individual family members, or they do participant observation. The researchers meet with whole families and discuss with them what happens in the family. The focus is on experiential data. Researchers try to capture what it is like to be in a family at this stage of development.

To illustrate how a developmental theorist might describe interactional processes and challenges in family development, we will examine what occurs in five arbitrary stages, which we call premarital, childless couple, parenthood, empty nest, and retirement/widowhood. Remember that one goal of any sociologist is to describe the dynamics of social interaction in groups. What the developmental perspective provides is a context, namely that the nature of interaction and the challenges people face may change depending on which stage of development the family is in.

Developmental Tasks in the Life Cycle

An important part of the life-cycle approach is the recognition that families usually perform certain **developmental tasks**. This concept is borrowed from developmental psychology, where it was posited that individuals must accomplish certain developmental tasks as they progress from infancy to children to adulthood. Havighurst (1953: 2) wrote that "a developmental task is a task which arises at or about a certain period in the life of an individual, successful achievement of which leads to his happiness and to success with later tasks, while failure leads to unhappiness in the individual, disapproval by the society, and difficulty with later tasks."

Duvall (1957: 517–522) wrote of seven family developmental tasks: reproduction, physical maintenance, protection, education and socialization, recreation, status-conferring, and affection-giving. At each stage of development, some of these tasks are primary and others are secondary. The successful or unsuccessful completion of a task at an earlier stage impacts upon the ability of the family to perform tasks at later stages of development. For example, if a couple cannot reproduce, they may have no children to educate and socialize unless they adopt children. Or, if children are not given affection and attention, they may turn to gangs for this, a circumstance that makes it very difficult for the family to protect them when they become adolescents. Both physical maintenance and education impact on the status families confer on their children. The way in which parents show love to each other and to their children influences how these children show love to others when they grow up. In later work, Duvall (1977: 179) expands on her list of developmental tasks.

Each stage of development carries with it certain challenges to the survival of a family. If a family system does not have the ability to meet the challenges of a particular stage of development, the family unit may not survive. We begin our analysis of developmental tasks in families by discussing the tasks of play and work. At different developmental stages these tasks become more or less important as critical dimensions of family interaction.

Play and Work throughout the Life Cycle

Families are initiated based on a couple's ability to play, but much of the time spent in families will ultimately call for the spouses to be able to work together to raise children (Ehrensaft, 1990) and maintain a nest. In the premarital stage, couples are challenged to play well together. The success of a dating relationship is partly dependent upon the parties' ability to enjoy each other, to have fun, and to feel good about themselves when in the presence of the other.

SOME WORK, SOME PLAY Play continues to be a challenge in the childless married couple stage. But now, in addition to play, the couple must work to build a nest. This work involves generating a level of financial security so that an apartment can be rented or a home purchased. The domicile must be furnished. Money must be saved for the arrival of a child if that is what the couple wants. There must be funds for baby furniture, clothes, and medical care for both the pregnant mother and the child. Role negotiation also occurs in this stage, with partners carving out a division of labor about who will perform the tasks necessary for family survival. The parties discuss and create agreements as to who will pay the bills, cook dinner, wash dishes, do the laundry, be responsible for keeping the car maintained, washed, waxed, and so forth.

ALL WORK, NO PLAY Work is the dominating challenge of the parenthood stage. The parents must work to raise their children to adulthood, sharing the responsibilities of physical care and emotional support. One important challenge of this phase is that even though the parents have been raised in different families with very different parenting role models, styles, and philosophies, they must work for consistency between themselves.

Because the focus of parenting is on work, it is all too easy for the spouses to forget to play together. They often fail to take time out to function as a couple apart from children, and to engage in fun activities as a twosome. Often in this stage, the family focuses so heavily on togetherness that parents never consider the importance of maintaining their relationship as a couple, which is critical to happiness in this stage and in making a successful transition to the time when children leave the home.

Table 1.1

Stage-Critical Family Developmental Tasks throughout the Family Life Cycle

Stage of the family life cycle	Positions in the family	Stage-critical family developmental tasks
1. Married couple	Wife Husband	Establishing a mutually satisfying marriage Adjusting to pregnancy and the promise of parenthood Fitting into the kin network
2. Childbearing	Wife-mother Husband-father Daughter-sister Son-brother	Having, adjusting to, and encouraging the development of infants Establishing a satisfying home for both parents and infant(s)
3. Preschool age	Wife-mother Husband-father Daughter-sister Son-brother	Adapting to the critical needs and interests of preschool children in stimulating, growth-promoting ways Coping with energy depletion and lack of privacy as parents
4. School age	Wife-mother Husband-father Daughter-sister Son-brother	Fitting into the community of school-age families in constructive ways Encouraging children's educational achievement
5. Teenage	Wife-mother Husband-father Daughter-sister Son-brother	Balancing freedom with responsibility as teenagers mature and emancipate themselves Establishing postparental interests and careers as growing parents
6. Launching center	Wife-mother-grandmother Husband-father-grandfather Daughter-sister-aunt Son-brother-uncle	Releasing young adults into work, military service, college, marriage, etc., with appropriate rituals and assistance Maintaining a supportive home base
7. Middle-aged parents	Wife-mother-grandmother Husband-father-grandfather	Rebuilding the marriage relationship Maintaining kin ties with older and younger generations
8. Aging family members	Widow/widower Wife-mother-grandmother Husband-father-grandfather	Coping with bereavement and living alone Closing the family home or adapting it to aging Adjusting to retirement

Source: Evelyn Millis Duvall and Brent C. Miller. "Stage-Critical Family Development Tasks," from *Marriage and Family Development,* 6th ed. Copyright © 1985 by Harper & Row, Publishers, Inc. Reprinted by permission of HarperCollins Publishers, Inc.

Duvall portrays an eight-stage process of family development. In each stage, the family must mobilize its resources to complete tasks that are unique to that developmental stage. The tasks can be seen as constituting challenges to the family at this stage of its development.

Both a **parental subsystem** and a **spousal subsystem** coexist in intact nuclear families—the couple as mother and father as well as husband and wife. These subsystems are different and both need to be nurtured and supported. Courting behavior should not be restricted to just the premarital stage, but should pervade the marital relationship. Social scientists often write of courtship and marriage as if courtship ends when marriage begins. If this happens, the spousal subsystem may well suffer. The married couple must continue to court and date and support each other as spouses throughout the family life cycle.

PLAYING AGAIN The challenges of the empty nest stage are multiple. The parties must successfully return to becoming a childless married couple, capable of interacting with each other in a meaningful, rewarding way. They must recapture the ability to play and have fun together. Retirement lies ahead and the parties should look forward to a relationship where play—together and with the grandchildren—becomes more of a focus than it has been for years. Often, they must overcome the challenges of a midlife crisis or of supporting and caring for dependent parents, or children, or both. They must also care for each other. The wife in this stage may have significant caretaking responsibilities of her husband who may be older and who may be showing more severe symptoms of aging. On average, women in this society outlive men by almost eight years. Women are statistically likely to face approximately ten years of widowhood. Women have an eight-year longer life expectancy than men, and husbands are often about two years older than their wives.

For the surviving widow, engaging in play may invoke feelings of guilt. Going to dances or social activities, where one interacts with members of the opposite sex, may result in feelings of disloyalty to the departed spouse. Or simply, the survivor may feel guilty for having fun while the spouse no longer can. Learning how to play without guilt is one of the developmental tasks, one of the challenges in the widowhood (or widowerhood) stage. For most widows, financial survival is another critical task. In an inflationary economy, economic survival on a fixed income becomes particularly challenging.

Having explored the role of work and play in various stages of family development, it is now appropriate to examine the challenges, the tasks, and the nature of interaction that occur in these stages. Particular focus will be given to the developmental tasks of each stage. We begin where a family begins, in the premarital stage.

The Premarital Stage

Courtship behavior occurs in the premarital stage. Courtship behavior requires first getting another person's attention, then, that the love object recognize your existence, and, finally, doing or saying things that will cause the love object to like or love you. This often involves doing something distinctive and unusual.

Another task in the premarital stage is to establish power relationships. **Power** is the ability to get others to do what you want them to do. Power relationships become established as each partner tests out strategies for getting his or her needs met. Each explores what it takes to get the partner to acquiesce to those desires, whether it is by crying or getting angry, by acting needy and dependent, or by being assertive and bold.

SEPARATION AND SELFHOOD A critical task, also, at this premarital stage is to create boundaries that allow the couple to become a distinct entity. Some family therapists believe that for a person to be ready for marriage, there has to be a separation between the individual and his or her family of origin (Bowen, 1974; Carter & McGoldrick, 1989). **Family of origin** means the family into which a person is born and in which he or she is raised, consisting of the person's mother, father, and siblings. These therapists believe that there has to be a differentiation of self from the family system before an individual is ready to enter into an intense premarital relationship as his or her own unique self. Selfhood can only fully develop when individuals have differentiated themselves out of their families of origin to gain their autonomy, and to become self-determining adults.

SPACE FOR FAMILY AND FRIENDS In addition, as deep emotional relationships develop, a separation from friends frequently occurs. There is only so much time for work, family, friends, and a lover, and when the lover seeks more time and attention, time has to be given up somewhere else. This results, sometimes, in less time spent with family, and, sometimes, in less time spent with friends. For working out boundary management of friends in the premarital stage, decisions must be made regarding how much friends will be allowed to intrude into a couple's relationship, in which social activities the friends will be included, and from which activities they will be excluded.

Sometimes a potential problem can be created when one of the partners will neither give up time spent with friends, nor share it. The significant other may feel that he or she is not a very high priority for the partner as the latter spends evenings away with friends. The problem that has to be resolved is how one individual can maintain connections with friends without causing the partner to feel abandoned, rejected, and powerless.

The reverse of this happens when a person wants to spend all of his or her time with the partner, expecting that partner to meet every personal need for companionship, intellectual stimulation, recreation, sex, security, and sense of well-being. Once there is a significant other, some people sever their relationships with friends. This places great pressure on one person to meet the partner's diverse needs. The relationship then has few external resources for assistance and support later, when it becomes difficult or impossible for all of those needs to be met within the marriage setting.

The transition from the premarital stage to the **childless married couple stage** may require significant adjustment if either or both parties have never experienced living with someone of the opposite sex who is approximately the same age. Here brothers and sisters may be helpful in setting expectations about what this is like. If a person has no such experience, the newness may require considerable adaptation. The couple must realize that living with a spouse is not the same as living with a roommate, which each may have experienced in the past. The difference is in the level of emotional involvement and commitment, the sexual intimacy, and the deep one-on-one conversation that marriage requires.

The Childless Married Couple Stage

Marriage is not just the linking of two people. It involves the merging of two families with different systems of interaction and with different cultural belief systems. Marriage can be described as a struggle between two people to see who will re-create his or her family of origin (Framo, 1981).

Each partner comes to the marriage with legacies from his or her own family of origin. Each family did things in its own way. The newly married partners each reflect those behavioral patterns and values. They each use their own family of origin as a reference point, either to replicate or to change it.

These partners must decide how they are going to celebrate holidays and with whom, how they will handle money, how they will distribute household chores, when and how to sleep, eat, and have sexual relations. They have to create norms or rules that will govern their interaction. They must decide how much emotional closeness or distance they will create in their relationship.

ISSUES OF CLOSENESS AND DISTANCE Salvador Minuchin (1974) sees that the effect of behavior in families is to regulate either emotional closeness or distance. Fights, extramarital affairs, and substance abuse all enable people to create emotional distance when relationships get "too close" for their emotional comfort. Many couples come to establish the roles of **pursuer** and **distancer** in the relationship, one trying to become emotionally close and the other trying to create emotional "space" or distance. Sometimes even the selection of furniture, the placement of that furniture in the home, and the utilization of space in the house can function as a metaphor for issues of privacy and emotional closeness or distance.

The couple has to feel out how much or how little involvement each will achieve in his or her partner's family of origin as well as in the partner's network of friends. They have to establish which friends will be joint friends of both partners and which will be friends of just one. The marriage may involve losing some friends, particularly when singleness was the bond that cemented that friendship. Of course, other friends may be gained through the marriage.

The couple needs to establish trust in the relationship. The level of trust is affected by the ability of each partner to convince the other that he or she is the number one priority in that partner's life. Marriage involves commitment

Boundaries

The family we are born into, which includes our parents and siblings, is called our family of origin. The family we create through our own marriage, including our spouse and children, is called our **family of procreation**. Creating **boundaries** between one's family of origin and one's family of procreation is a task, a challenge, often confronted in the initial stages of marriage. Minuchin (1974) distinguishes three kinds of boundaries that exist between people: clear boundaries, diffuse boundaries, and rigid boundaries.

Clear boundaries are ideal. A boundary exists, yet there is interaction between people on either side of it. The couple with a clear boundary between themselves and their families of origin can interact with members of the family of origin and permit family members to make suggestions and offer assistance and support. The couple also have the ability to say "no" to family members, to reject intrusions, and to turn down invitations sometimes.

Diffuse boundaries mean that there are really no boundaries at all, that a person has not individuated enough to be separate from another person or system. Diffuse boundaries often exist between a chemically dependent person and his or her protective spouse. When one acts out, the spouse feels guilty and embarrassed. Diffuse boundaries lead to people becoming **enmeshed** with one another. Enmeshment exists when one person becomes highly involved in the life of another. Two enmeshed people often act as one person through an absence of personal boundaries.

In-law problems exist for couples when the bonds between a married person and a parent are stronger than those between the spouses. One of the significant messages that comes from structural family therapists (Minuchin,

---

to the marital relationship, which was not present when both parties were single (Sternberg, 1988). People who have difficulty assuming this level of commitment may report feeling trapped or enslaved by marriage, having less freedom because of it. People who successfully cohabited with each other, sometimes for years prior to marriage, may find marital commitment difficult to handle. They report that, before marriage, they felt that they did things because they wanted to, but that, somehow, after marriage, they were doing things because they had to.

FEATHERING THE NEST One of the tasks of the childless couple stage is to establish a nest. This usually involves both parties working and saving for goals: to establish an independent residence apart from either set of parents; to buy furniture; to establish savings for buying a car or a house or to afford a child. In this regard they must establish rules about handling money. If a goal is to save, how much? Where will the money go and on what will it be spent? If one party is a spender and the other a saver, the management

1974) is that the strongest bonds in families should exist between members of the same generation. Most family problems arise when generational boundaries get crossed or broken, when a married person's bond to a parent is stronger than the bond to the spouse or when a parent's bond to one or more of the children is stronger than the bond is to the spouse. In-law problems in families often arise when there has been incomplete or insufficient separation by one or both spouses from the family of origin.

From this perspective, when there is conflict or a difference of opinion between one's parent and one's spouse, a person should always support the spouse. It is the spouse who represents one's future. Without a viable, supportive spousal relationship, the nuclear family becomes fragile.

Rigid boundaries exist as distancing phenomena. People who create rigid boundaries between themselves and others are **disengaged**. Disengaged people are emotionally or behaviorally unaffected by events or behavior going on around them. When a parent comes home and vegetates in front of the television set or plants his or her nose in a newspaper while the children are fighting and screaming for attention, that parent is disengaged, unaffected by the behavior or actions of others in the family. There is such a rigid boundary between this parent and others that family members cannot penetrate this boundary to interact.

When a person leaves the family of origin, cutting off all ties with that family, he or she creates a rigid boundary that means that this individual and his or her family of procreation cannot receive any emotional or physical support from members of the distanced family of origin.

---

of money can be a problem, because how it is spent reflects basic personal values about what is important in life.

ADJUSTING TO CHANGE Marriage affects change for both partners. All change involves loss (as well as opportunity). For the woman, marriage may involve a name change, which involves a change of identity. There is also a status change from single to married person. The familiar environment in which a person was living as a single person may change to a shared environment as a married person. Friends may be lost. The loss may include freedom, autonomy or independence, privacy, leisure time, and the availability of others as potential sexual partners. Coping with these losses and grieving over them is part of being newly married. Part of the process involves depression (Kübler-Ross, 1969), which some parties experience after marriage as part of their grieving process. They cannot understand this depressed state because they expected the early days of marriage to be one of the happiest times of their lives. Yet postmarital depression is a frequently occurring phenomenon.

Downwardly Mobile Parents

In the parenthood stage, issues arise related to sharing the responsibilities of child care and to maintaining the family's standard of living. Today, predictions run rampant that the generation of new parents now in their twenties will be downwardly mobile compared to their parents (Newman, 1988; Strobel, 1993). By downwardly mobile, we mean that they, as adults, will be in a lower social class than were their parents. They will not be able to attain the same standard of living that they enjoyed when they were living with their parents as children.

In an effort to resist this trend, both parents often work, frequently juggling their work schedules so that somebody is always "on" with the children. One may work a day schedule, the other a swing shift. This can result in a deterioration of the spousal relationship as husband and wife become "two ships that pass in the night," spending little time together as parents or spouses. If both work the same schedule, the child is usually placed in day care facilities, where the child will be raised partly by professionals, not solely by the parents.

There is considerable debate on the pros and cons of day care for preschoolers. Some argue that these children fail to receive the parental emotional support that is necessary for emotional attachment to develop (Belsky, 1988; Belsky & Rovine, 1988) or for developing positive self-esteem.

ALTERNATIVE STATES Some couples never experience the stage of the childless married couple. Rates of premarital pregnancy and illegitimacy are increasing (Adams & Adams, 1990; Chilman, 1980; Mott, 1986), particularly among teens. Some couples thus begin marriage with a child. Others have the child, and get married only when they feel that their marriage signifies a commitment to their relationship as a couple. These couples may go directly from the premarital stage into the parenthood stage, never having been a married couple without a child.

Voluntary childlessness for married couples is also an increasing phenomenon in the United States (Bureau of the Census, 1989). These couples are in the childless married couple stage for the duration of their marriage, never moving to the parenthood stage.

The Parenthood Stage

The transition between the childless married couple stage and the parenthood stage is for many couples the most challenging of all the transitions. As a childless married couple, the family was a **dyad**, a two-person system, in which each

The children sometimes feel that they are not valuable enough or important enough for mom and dad to stay and interact with them. The message that these children get from their parents is that there are many more important things in their parents' lives than themselves. They feel that they are a low priority for their parents in terms of how those parents choose to spend their time, or with whom they choose to spend it. Missing the positive reinforcement that encourages the development of the self, the development of the person's unique character, these children can become insecure and aggressive (Belsky, 1986).

Others argue that child care fosters independence and autonomy, skills that are needed for survival in the real world (Caldwell & Richmond, 1968; Clarke-Stewart & Fein, 1983; Clarke-Stewart & Gruber, 1984). These researchers argue that day care increases maturity and social competence and that children in day care generally thrive physically, socially, and intellectually. In a day care setting children may be freer to explore, discover, and experience their physical and social world than they would be if they are monitored by parents at home.

So new parents must decide whether or not both will work and whether both will work full- or part-time. They must negotiate and delegate child care responsibilities regarding who will do what and when.

---

party had the other's undivided attention, affection, time, and energy. When a baby appears, the dyad becomes a **triad**, a three-person system, and now scarce emotional resources must be shared with the new arrival. One spouse may feel great losses in this transition. "When I used to come home, my spouse had time and energy for me, we'd talk to each other; now there is nothing left for me at the end of the day." The partner thinks, "When he came home, he used to recognize my existence, spend time with me, talk to me, and now he makes a beeline for the baby and spends hours playing and cuddling with the baby, ignoring me as if I wasn't even there, as if I didn't exist!" Each may feel abandoned and neglected as time, energy, attention, and affection are turned to the new arrival.

Parenting in this country is an anxiety-provoking experience because the society provides little education or experience in becoming parents (Schvaneveldt & Young, 1992). Sometimes when two people realize they are about to become parents, they rush to take a crash Red Cross or Adult Education course to learn how to at least hold, feed, and bathe an infant because nobody has ever taught them these skills.

Parenthood is an unstructured experience in this society. When people are exposed to unstructured and anxiety-provoking experiences, they usually revert to the familiar, which is what they saw their parents doing. Parents are powerful role models because society does not provide us with alternative models that become part of our experience. Some parents are positive role models whom we seek to emulate; others act as negative role models, and we seek to treat our children differently from the way that we were treated.

If two young parents have had very different parental role models, and if the process of socializing children was very different in each of their families, the two new parents are apt to exhibit different parenting philosophies and styles, which need to become integrated. This may result in conflict and arguments over parenting issues. When parents disagree about how children should be treated and cared for, the couple becomes torn by conflict. Perhaps one parent accuses the other of being too hard on the child, too authoritarian and disciplinary; the other accuses the partner of being too soft, too indulgent, or too permissive. The two sabotage each other, undermining each other's power.

FURTHER DIVISION OF PARENTHOOD STAGES Some developmental theorists subdivide the parenthood stage into subphases that follow the career of children, usually the eldest child (Duvall, 1977), through schooling from preschool through elementary, junior high, and high schools to college. Others create separate stages for families with young children and families with adolescents.

With young children, the parents must integrate the children into the family system and find a way for grandparents and other extended kin to have access to the children and serve as a support network should they wish to. Parents must teach their children basic values in addition to transmitting knowledge and skills. They must create a system of rewards and punishments so that the children conform to norms and yet have the freedom to explore and develop their own personalities.

FAMILIES WITH ADOLESCENTS Families with adolescents are faced with some unique and difficult challenges that cause parents to report this as the stage of least marital satisfaction (Rollins & Cannon, 1974). During adolescence, teens are defying authority, acting rebellious, and searching for their own identity. Often, particularly in middle-class families, at just the time that teens are experiencing their adolescence, one or both of their parents are experiencing a midlife crisis of their own (McMorrow, 1974; Fried, 1967).

As part of their adolescence, teens seek autonomy, yet they are financially and emotionally dependent upon their parents. The financial dependence becomes more difficult for parents the older their children become, because the older they are, the more expensive children are to support. While the expenses of supporting adolescents escalate, the amount of contact between parents and adolescents diminishes, as teens increasingly value the time spent with peers. Parents may thus see themselves valued by their adolescent children for their money but not as people in their own right, as their children become increasingly inaccessible to them. Under these circumstances, the burdens of parenting seem to be disproportionately high relative to the rewards that the parents experience. Parent-adolescent conflict is a prevalent phenomenon in our society, and this will be explored further in chapter 3.

The departure of children when they are launched from the family nest may thus be met with significant relief by parents. And yet, the launching of children can engender feelings of loss, as if a part of each parent is gone as the children depart. Anger or depression, feelings of boredom or emptiness may result. Fear or doubt may accompany the last child's departure as the parents question how they will survive on their own, just the two of them, particularly if they do not have a rewarding, satisfying intimate marital relationship.

The Empty Nest Stage

When the last children have left home, in a sense the parents return to being a childless married couple again. This is called the **empty nest stage**. Particularly for economically advantaged couples, retirement, which is ahead of them, is a time for play. For years they have worked together to raise their children; now they must recapture the ability to play well together, for their remaining years will be largely devoted to recreation and leisure activity, doing things that they want to do rather than things that they have to do. Where the couple has spent years talking to each other either about the children or through the children, they must now re-create the ability to talk to each other directly about other things, about themselves, their thoughts and feelings in the present and their dreams and aspirations for the future. Divorce is becoming increasingly common at this developmental stage in part because of the significant transitions that must be made.

If the couple has not developed its ability to play together, to court each other, and to have fun through parenthood, the empty nest stage can prove a huge departure from their previous everyday life. Without practice or experience at dating, at functioning as a spousal couple, they often cannot recapture their ability to play and have fun, and eventually one party may leave to find somebody else with whom he or she can play in retirement. For less affluent couples, retirement may involve less severe transitions inasmuch as they are apt to work in their retirement years and perhaps parent their grandchildren. The failure of family development theorists to take into account class differences in the developmental process will be discussed in the critique section of this chapter.

Because people are living longer and longer, historically, this stage is increasing in length. More and more years exist between the time children leave the nest and the death of one of the spouses. During this time, parents must adjust to becoming somebody's in-laws as their children marry and, later, gracefully to becoming grandparents.

Sometimes at this stage, the wife, who previously devoted most of her time to childrearing and parenting, may decide to begin a career of her own. She either goes back to school or begins to work full-time, establishing herself in a profession that she expects will be rewarding and fulfilling. Meanwhile for years her husband has heard from his family that he should not work so hard or spend so much time away from home, and he decides to cut back on his workload. He is tired, perhaps bored, and finds his work less rewarding than it used to be. As he begins to cut back in order to spend time at home, his wife is spending less time there, busy launching her career. She is distressed, believing, "Why didn't you do this before when we all needed you," and he is distressed, bemoaning that "there's nobody home for me." This is a common scenario creating conflict and adaptation challenges, particularly for middle-class couples in their fifties.

This stage also provides challenges in caring for elderly parents, who may come to need help both financially and physically. It is usually males who help financially and females who are called upon to be chauffeurs and physical caretakers. This author often advises female students to take a good look at their future mothers-in-law because someday they may be called upon to take care of them. This caretaking can create stress in a marriage because couples often do not consider the caretaking of elderly parents as part of their responsibilities when they enter into marriage, so this responsibility comes as a shock. Frustrated by the fact that twenty-five years have been spent caring for children and suddenly they are back in the caretaking role, caring for parents, a couple might think, "When are energy and resources ever coming to us?" They seem to be constantly consumed by others. "When is it ever going to be our turn to enjoy what we have worked so hard to earn?" Stress is created in relationships when questions have to be answered about the care of elderly parents; that is, at what time does it become too much or too unreasonable to do it all yourself, and when do you enlist the services of others to care for parents? Considerable feelings of guilt and need for support come with these decisions.

Retirement and/or Widowhood Stage

In the **retirement stage** couples usually spend more time together. This requires considerable adaptation because they have to decide what they will do to fill that time. Will they spend it together or apart? If together, they need to develop shared interests and values. Increased time together can strain a relationship that is not solid to begin with, as the partners may be increasingly exposed to behavior that irritates them.

LOSSES AND OPPORTUNITIES All life experiences contain losses and opportunities. Retirement is no exception. Work provides people with a means of structuring time. If a person works an eight-hour day, not only are those eight hours structured but so are the hours spent in preparation for getting to work, lunch hour time, and the time spent getting from work to home. Retirement involves a loss of this structured time. Now one has to structure time oneself, rather than having it structured externally. Often people who have difficulty structuring their time, people who are unemployed, for instance, sleep a lot. Sleep can be an escape from boredom.

Work also provides people with an identity. It allows them to answer the questions "Who am I?" and "What do I do?" The fact that a person is gainfully employed in a profession is socially acceptable and at times brings with it prestige. Retirement involves a change of identity.

Work provides an arena for social interaction, for meeting people, and interacting with people who have shared interests and goals. Retirement removes a person from that arena. New arenas for interaction must be found if the retiree is to avoid social isolation.

Finally, work provides a source of income. Retirement usually results in a reduction of that income. Adjustments must be made in a person's standard of living to accommodate this reduced income, and both the adjustments and the existence of reduced income can strain a marital relationship.

Offsetting the losses experienced because of retirement, there are new opportunities. People can participate in activities and events that truly interest them. They have the opportunity to explore new interests and develop new competencies that they did not have the opportunity to explore when they were working. Part of this exploration may involve travel if there are sufficient funds. There is a certain freedom with regard to time that allows people to be their own playwrights, the scripters of their own existence, rather than having others telling them where they have to be and when, as used to occur at work. It takes a person who has relatively high self-esteem and who is self-motivated and energetic to make productive use of this new-found autonomy.

Part of life at this stage of family development involves experiencing the death of friends and colleagues, which is a reminder of our own mortality. People also face some physical deterioration, whether it involves muscle pulls, weight change, a pot belly, hair loss, new wrinkles, reduced energy, or actual illness. These physical changes may require some caretaking assistance from the younger generations, resulting in important family change—former caretakers now needing assistance.

DEATH OF A PARTNER It is usually the husband who dies first, leaving his wife a widow. This creates many questions that families must answer: What assistance or support does grandma need in surviving this loss? Does grandma continue living alone in a home she may find difficult to maintain or does she move? If she moves, where to? Her choices include moving in with her children, into a retirement community, into a smaller home by herself, or into some shared residence that she occupies with others.

In widowhood, there is the challenge of dealing with loss, of establishing autonomy to script an existence, to structure a life. There is the multiple challenge of overcoming loneliness and social isolation and designing a life that is rewarding and fulfilling.

A grandparent's death is often traumatic for everyone in a family. Parents are faced with their own mortality and children may come to grasp, for the first time, that they may well lose their own parents someday. This is often the first experience they have in realizing that death is a part of everyone's life. The family must experience separation and loss and cope with reorganizing itself as a function of this loss. As Froma Walsh (1989) suggests, how they do this creates a model for coping with separation and loss for succeeding generations.

Using Macroanalysis

In the preceding sections, the development of individual families was discussed. However, sociologists theorize at many different levels. They have, at one time or another, created theories about individuals, families, corporations, schools, cities, racial or ethnic groups, social classes, and whole societies, as well as interaction between societies in a global context. The distinction between microanalysis and macroanalysis relates to the number of people included in the research investigation or theory being used. When individuals or small groups are the focus of inquiry, sociologists are engaged in **microanalysis**. When very large numbers of people are the focus, such as whole societies, they are engaged in **macroanalysis**. Some theories that will be discussed in this book lend themselves more to the microanalysis of small groups (for example, symbolic interaction theory); others to the macroanalysis of whole societies (structural-functional theory).

The writings of William Goode (1963) illustrate how developmental theory can be used in the macroanalysis of families. Goode looked at global patterns and trends that are exhibited by families in all societies throughout the world. He maintained that all societies are in a process of evolving from preindustrial to more highly developed industrialized and urbanized structures. The structure of families within a society changes as that society develops technologically. For example, as societies move from preindustrial, agriculturally based societies to urbanized, industrialized societies, the place where adult married children live changes. In agriculturally based societies, adult married children often live with their parents. As societies urbanize and industrialize, however, adult married children tend to establish independent households, apart from either the bride's or groom's parents.

Residence Patterns

One way to look at families in societies is to explore their residence patterns in historical contexts. There are three major types of residence patterns in the world: patrilocal, matrilocal, and neolocal. **Patrilocal residence** exists when brides and grooms, after marriage, live in the household or village of the groom's family. This type of residence supports **patriarchal authority**—the groom has more power than his bride because she comes into the groom's family as the most recent arrival, with no relatives or friends who support her. Her husband, on the other hand, is surrounded by life-long friends and relatives. The bride is usually given the least pleasant tasks and tends to be dominated by her mother-in-law.

Matrilocal residence exists when the newly married couple is expected to live in the household or village of the bride's family. This pattern supports **matriarchal authority**. In this case, women would tend to have more power than men. (Contemporary anthropologists are hard pressed to find any contemporary society in which this happens.) However, even in societies where women own the property, their brothers or husbands manage and control the assets.

Neolocal residence exists when husband and wife, after marriage, establish their own independent residence apart from either spouse's parents or family. Neolocal residence is the pattern that generally exists in the United States. For couples who marry at a very young age, however, it is difficult financially to establish an independent residence. They often start out living with whichever set of parents is able to house and support them.

HISTORICAL EUROPEAN RESIDENCE PATTERNS When residence patterns are examined historically, it can be seen that throughout the Middle Ages in western Europe, patrilocal residence tended to exist in an agricultural environment. As sons married, they brought their wives with them to live on their parents' farm. When daughters married, the bride moved in with her husband and his family. Single children continued to live with their parents until they married. Eventually, with industrialization and urbanization, there was a steady erosion of this rural, agriculturally based economy. With money to be made and new occupations evolving in cities, men moved from farms. More and more men left their parents' home to make their fortune on their own, resulting in an erosion of patrilocal residence patterns and an increase of neolocal residence among young adults.

Goode generalized from this European experience. He hypothesized that, with increased urbanization and industrialization in any society, one can expect reduced incidence of patrilocal or matrilocal residence patterns and an increase of neolocal residence.

Changing Household Patterns

Goode saw every society of the world as being in an evolutionary process toward greater urbanization and industrialization. As a result of this, families in these societies were in the process of moving from joint family systems to stem families to nuclear or conjugal families. He saw this change as positive:

> I see in it and in the industrial system that accompanies it the hope of greater freedom: from the domination of elders, from caste and racial restrictions, from class rigidities. Freedom is for something as well: the unleashing of personal potentials, the right to love, to equality within the family, to the establishment of a new marriage when the old has failed. . . . For me, then, the major and sufficing justification for the newly emerging family patterns is that they offer people at least the potentialities of greater fulfillment, even if most do not seek it or achieve it. (Goode, 1963: 380)

JOINT FAMILY HOUSEHOLDS Patrilocal and matrilocal residence are most apt to be found in preindustrial societies. These residence patterns encourage the existence of households consisting of multiple and multigenerational nuclear family units. In these households grandparents live with their biological children and their spouses as well as their grandchildren. Such households are called **joint family households.**

Joint family households could prove difficult if the brothers disagreed over management issues or if they did not get along with each other. Such disagreements could result in the need to divide the farmland so that each son could use it and manage it as he saw fit. If these divisions occurred over many generations, the family land could be so subdivided that no one parcel would be very profitable.

PRIMOGENITURE AND STEM FAMILIES There were significant debates in most western European countries in the fifteenth through the nineteenth centuries over inheritance practices. The question was whether all children should receive inheritances from their parents in equal amounts, whether some children, particularly the firstborn, should receive more than children born subsequently, or whether firstborn children should be the only recipients of the family's assets (Thirsk, 1976). The latter option was called **primogeniture**, literally meaning "firstborn." Particularly in Great Britain, but also in parts of France and Germany, laws were passed that resulted in the firstborn son in each family inheriting all the family assets. These laws affected the structure of families; as younger, disinherited sons married, they no longer continued to live with their parents, since their labor would only enhance the profits of their eldest brother.

In those areas of western Europe where primogeniture laws existed, stem families were created (Berkner, 1976: 86–95). In **stem families**, a household consists of two couples, the parents and their eldest son and his wife. In a stem family, patrilocal residence existed only for the eldest son, who brought his bride to live with his parents. Neolocal residence existed for the younger sons, who had to leave the family to seek an independent existence upon marriage.

PRIMOGENITURE AND THE COLONIZATION OF AMERICA Where did these disinherited sons go? When these younger sons married, they moved with their wives to cities to look for work or they moved to developing colonies, such as Ireland or the United States, to create new lives for themselves. Many of the colonists who founded this country were disinherited younger children, victims of British primogeniture laws. Thomas Jefferson was a staunch opponent of existent primogeniture laws in Virginia because he saw primogeniture as a vehicle for creating the "accumulation and perpetuation of wealth in select families" (Cooper, 1976: 195). Arguments favoring primogeniture were that its opposite—partitioned inheritance—invited the division of family property and the destruction of family wealth that often occurred because of sibling conflict.

PRIMOGENITURE AND THE INDUSTRIAL REVOLUTION Primogeniture laws played a role in facilitating the Industrial Revolution in the mid-nineteenth century. Particularly in Great Britain, the cities were teeming with disinherited children and their families, creating a ready pool of labor for fueling the Industrial Revolution.

Primogeniture laws were more popular in western European countries than in other parts of the world and more popular in France, Germany, Spain, and Great Britain than in other western European countries. In the evolution from joint family households to conjugal family units, stem families were created through primogeniture in some countries and not in others.

NUCLEAR FAMILY HOUSEHOLDS As urbanization and industrialization intensified in western Europe, it became more and more tempting for the eldest son also to leave the family farm and move to the city, because big money was to be made in the city. There was more likelihood of upward mobility in industrial life than in farming. If the eldest son did move, he usually sold the family farm. As eldest sons did this in large numbers, toward the end of the nineteenth century, the structure of families changed from stem to nuclear family units, in which all children established neolocal residence. A **nuclear** or **conjugal family** is a household composed of a husband and a wife and their children. This structure significantly weakened the power of parents over their adult children.

Goode found that as societies urbanized and industrialized, families within those societies moved to accept romantic love as a basis for marriage. Youth gained greater independence from elders who, in preindustrial societies, often arranged the marriage of their children. Divorces became easier to obtain through institutionalized means. There came to be a greater stress on monogamy and legal marriage as opposed to polygamy and concubinage. Lower birth rates and smaller families were the result of a greater reliance on contraceptives and other birth control measures. Families also had fewer children because in urban settings children become economic liabilities rather than the economic assets they were on farms, where their free labor was valued. In cities, child labor laws prevent the young from gainful employment. The more children a family has in cities, the more space they need, and since space is expensive, many families are discouraged from having large families. Goode also found that there was greater acceptance of remarriage after divorce or widowhood, and greater acceptance of conjugal as opposed to joint or extended families.

Since one of the tenets of developmental theory is that change is ever-present, it is clear that no final stages are allowed. Just as, in economics, something will eventually arise to replace communism as an economic system (Karl Marx failed to realize that the dialectic process never ends), so, in sociology, something will arise to replace urbanization and industrialization. We know that such societies "advance" to become postindustrial societies.

Now that we have reviewed family development theory at both the micro- and macrolevels, let us apply the unilinear developmental model to the analysis of romantic love and divorce.

Applying Developmental Theory

Any unilinear developmental model, as has already been noted, will depict change as occurring through stages over time. Here two theories of love are explored in which it is possible to portray the development of romantic love as a multistage process.

Postindustrial Life Industrialization and urbanization are not final stages of development. As futurists assert (Toffler, 1970, 1984; Naisbitt, 1984), the industrial world will give way to a postindustrial world where the focus is not on converting raw materials to manufactured goods but rather where manufacturing gives way to an economy based on service-oriented industries and information storage and exchange, such as in computer-interactive networking (Bell, 1973, 1989). Such occupations require significant education. Many writers envision a postindustrial world with a reliance on science and technology development (engineering) and a highly educated populace (Fiala, 1992). There will also be noticeable social engineering with the creation of a greater welfare state and significant social planning. Greater education will pressure incomes to rise so that people will have more disposable funds to pay for the services they consume, including health care. Consumption of goods and services will occur at the expense of self-restraint, work, commitment, and a sense of historical connection with the past. In a postindustrial society, greater percentages of women will be gainfully employed. Issues of environment and quality of life will dominate political debate as corporations come under increasing pressure to do more that is socially constructive, rather than just maximizing profits (Ingelhart, 1977; Lipset, 1976). Futurist writers envision a more politicized and conflicted citizenry. As more of the population gains access to goods and information, traditional hierarchies will break down, leading to a rise of populist politics.

The basic structure of postindustrial society can be described as decentered. Huge corporations will become restructured as smaller, more adaptive companies filling specialized niches in the economy. Already we see great investment in restructuring companies to enhance their efficiency and flexibility. The population will organize themselves into relatively small special-interest groups, which are politically active, to promote specific goals. The population will be heterogeneous, reflecting diverse ethnic groups, religions, races, and lifestyles. These groups will become increasingly fragmented, with subgroups arising within them to advocate alternative agendas and concerns.

Divorce is also portrayed as a multistage process that occurs over time. The process is unidirectional, although it is possible to become fixated within a stage for a very long time.

Developmental Theories of Romantic Love

Developmental theories of romantic love must, of course, include a presentation of different sequential stages that evolve over time, such as the Wheel Theory

There will be an increase of competition and conflict between groups and the ideas and goals they advocate. Societies will be hard-pressed to achieve social integration at a national level. There will be a resultant decline in the power of the nation-state. Interaction will occur at a global level, where societies are interrelated and interdependent. There will be a world military order and an international division of labor (Giddens, 1990).

Families in this postindustrial world will change to reflect and be consistent with the decentered, diverse outside world, exhibiting greater diversity in form and structure. There will be an increasing emergence of gay and lesbian relationships, of people who remain voluntarily single, and people who have babies out of wedlock (with and without artificial insemination, or the use of surrogate birth mothers). There will be people who create families through increasing racial, religious, and class intermarriage or through cohabitation, and even people who create communities as "families." There will be persistently high divorce rates with resultant single-parent households and stepfamilies. Families in this postindustrial world (Kirkendall & Gravatt, 1984) will exhibit greater diversity as a function of the societies' more permissive attitudes toward diversity.

People in the postindustrial world will experience constantly **changing identities** as they move from job to job (Giddens, 1990). Job stability will not be high; it will be rare that a person stays employed in one company for most of his or her life. Identity is often linked with occupation, and that will change many times during a person's lifetime. Marital status will change as a function of family instability. A person could easily move from single to married to divorced single parent, to remarried in a stepfamily, to a divorced single parent, to remarried and in a stepfamily, to perhaps widowed or single. In this process a person may move from single without children to single with children, or from married with children to single without children, when those children grow up and leave the nest. Toffler (1970) questions how much change human beings can tolerate before they go crazy. Postindustrial existence will test that question.

---

of Love proposed by Ira Reiss (1960: 142–43). Reiss takes a unilinear straight line and curves it around to create a wheel or circle. In this wheel there are four stages of romantic love that occur consecutively as the wheel turns clockwise. The stages are rapport, self-revelation, mutual dependency, and personality need fulfillment.

In the first stage, **rapport**, cultural similarity of the partners is critical in attracting them to each other. People are attracted by shared social characteristics such as being of the same race, social class, ethnic group, or having similar family backgrounds. This gives them something in common on which to build an early interest in one another.

Figure 1.2

Reiss's Wheel Theory of Love

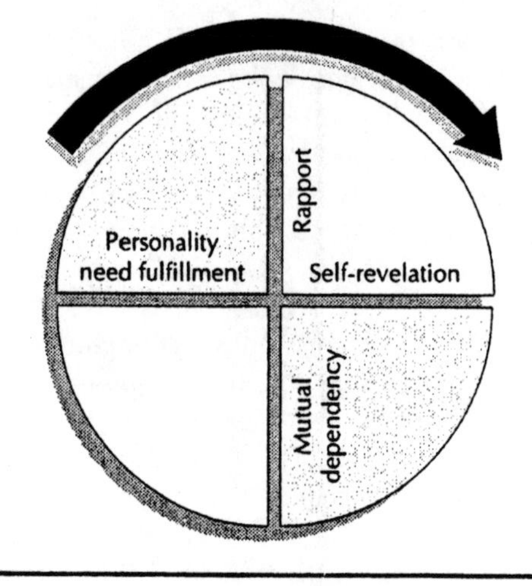

Source: Nijole V. Benokraitis, *Marriage and Families.* Copyright © 1993, p. 112. Reprinted by permission of Prentice Hall, Englewood Cliffs, New Jersey.

In Reiss's model, intimate relationships revolve around four processes: gaining rapport, self-revelation, mutual dependency, and personality need fulfillment. The concepts represent four spokes of a turning wheel. One feels rapport, at ease with another, when there are culturally similar values and socially similar characteristics. Feeling at ease leads to self-revelation and mutual dependency, thus fulfilling personality needs. Fulfilled needs further enhance rapport. The wheel revolves at various speeds based on the intensity of the relationship. The wheel and the relationship can unwind when an argument or competing interest reduces rapport, which decreases self-revelation and mutual dependency, reducing personality need fulfillment, which reduces rapport.

In the second stage, **self-revelation**, the parties communicate with frequency, sharing thoughts, feelings, hopes for the future, desires, and fears. This communication enables each to feel more at ease in the relationship, which, in this stage, leads to sexual intimacy.

In the third stage, **mutual dependency**, the parties become emotionally attached. They create a division of labor that makes them interdependent and they begin to make mutual plans for the future as they merge their hopes and desires.

In the fourth stage, **personality need fulfillment**, the partners confide in each other, make mutual decisions, reinforce each other in realizing their ambitions, and support each other, helping the partner to gain confidence in confronting the challenges of the outside world.

Each stage is like spokes on a wheel that is constantly turning. The wheel may turn for 50 years in a long-term relationship, where the partners resequence the stages in an endless progression. The wheel may spin only a few revolutions in a short-term relationship. The wheel may unwind in one evening through conflict or the failure of one partner to engage in self-disclosure or in the discovery of one

Table 1.2

Taxonomy of Kinds of Love

Kind of Love	Intimacy	Passion	Decision/ Commitment
Non-love	—	—	—
Liking	+	—	—
Infatuated love	—	+	—
Empty love	—	—	+
Romantic love	+	+	—
Companionate love	+	—	+
Fatuous love	—	+	+
Consummate love	+	+	+

Note: + = component present; — = component absent. These kinds of love represent idealized cases based on the triangular theory. Most loving relationships will fit between categories, because the components of love occur in varying degrees, rather than being simply present or absent.

Source: Robert J. Sternberg, "Taxonomy of Love," from *The Triangle of Love*. Copyright © 1988 by Basic Books, Inc. Reprinted by permission of Basic Books, division of HarperCollins Publishers, Inc.

Sternberg analyzes different kinds of love along three dimensions: passion, intimacy, and decision/commitment. These three dimensions are the three corners in his Triangle of Love. The kinds of love differ from each other in terms of whether they contain or lack these qualities.

partner's dishonesty. Note that the last three stages require considerable verbal interaction. These partners are constantly learning about each other.

Robert J. Sternberg (1988) created a typology of different kinds of love based on his belief that all kinds of love can be analyzed in terms of intimacy, passion, and decision/commitment. He pictures these three concepts as corners in a "triangle of love." **Intimacy** involves the sharing of thoughts and feelings, mutual self-disclosure in a relationship. **Passion** involves the energetic longing for a union with another, which can be sexual and/or emotional. **Decision/commitment** involves a short- and long-term component. There is a short-term decision to love a certain other and a long-term commitment to maintain that love. Romantic love, in his theory, involves the presence of intimacy and passion, but not decision/commitment. Sternberg's (1988: 51) typologies of love are represented above.

Although Sternberg's theory is not a developmental approach, it can be converted to one. Couples can be seen as moving from having none of the corners in the triangle of love as part of their relationship to having one, then two, then three. Of course some relationships become fixated, stuck, and never develop all three components. Other relationships have three components and then, over time, lose one or more. The Sternberg model could be used to trace the development of a relationship in terms of the presence or absence of intimacy, passion, or commitment over time.

In western European societies, romantic love usually precedes marriage. The first year of marriage has romantic elements, but then romance often wanes and, as Ernest Burgess et al. (1963) contended, the marriage moves from a **romantic stage** to a **companionship stage.** In the companionship stage, the

Romantic Love

Romantic love combines intimacy with passion. The intimacy involves a sharing of thoughts, feelings, a sharing of oneself, coupling an emotional and physical attraction. One way of facilitating this is through the asking of questions. We are born with two ears and only one mouth, which might be taken as meaning that we should be doing twice as much listening as talking. Marital communication is often enhanced by asking questions and then listening intently to the response. Two useful questions are "How are you doing?" and "What do you need from me?" The parties should understand that when the first question is asked, an automatic "fine" is not the expected response. The partner is genuinely asking "How are you doing in your life, how is your health, how are your spirits, how are you feeling, how was work for you?" The latter question is often helpful in avoiding recriminations that occur when the partner does not meet unexpressed needs. This is an invitation to express those needs, so that the partner does not have to be a mind reader and so that disappointments and frustrations do not build because one of the partners failed to meet the other's needs, which were never expressed. Spousal conversation involving mutual self-disclosure is an important ingredient in successful marriages.

---

passion is diminished or gone but the partners feel a deep sense of commitment and attachment. The partners are friends, and they tell each other anything and feel that they can count on each other for sympathy, advice, and encouragement (Yorburg, 1993: 107).

Harville Hendrix (1988) uses the five stages of grieving that were developed by Elizabeth Kübler-Ross (1969) to discuss the demise of romantic love in a relationship. Hendrix argues that romantic love involves a power struggle that ultimately destroys the illusion that romantic love ever existed. The demise of romantic love occurs in five stages. The first stage is **shock**, when a person exclaims, "This is not the person I thought I married!" This is when the person realizes that he or she has bought an illusion of who the partner is and that the illusion is different from the reality. Shock is replaced by **denial**, in which the person denies the negative traits or characteristics of the partner. Denial is replaced by **anger**, when the partner feels hurt and betrayed. This is a confused state of not knowing whether the partner changed drastically or whether one's own perceptions were actually fantasies. When the anger begins to dissipate, **bargaining** sets in. Here the parties offer *quid pro quo* deals: If we have more sex I'll participate in cleaning the house, or, If we go out more, I won't talk on the telephone as much. Finally there is **despair**, in which the parties seek either divorce or outside relationships while remaining married.

A MACROLEVEL VIEW When developmental theory was discussed at a macrolevel, the point was made that in preindustrial societies, marriages are

Figure 1.3

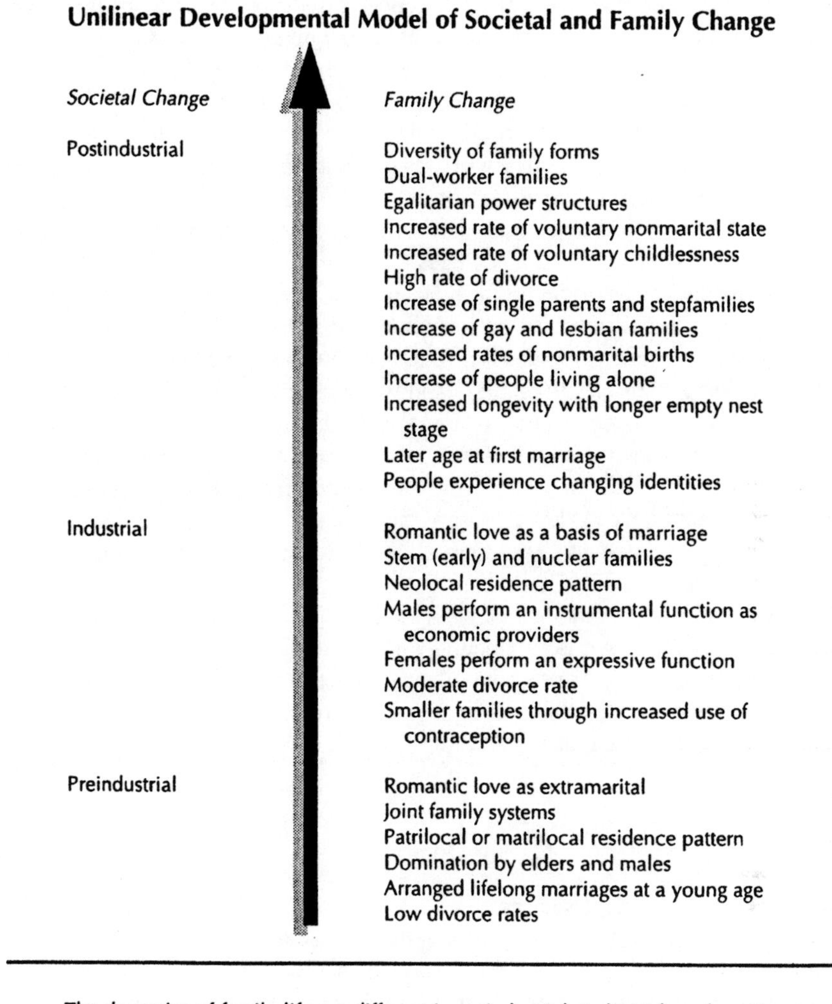

Unilinear Developmental Model of Societal and Family Change
Societal Change
Family Change
Postindustrial
Diversity of family forms
Dual-worker families
Egalitarian power structures
Increased rate of voluntary nonmarital state
Increased rate of voluntary childlessness
High rate of divorce
Increase of single parents and stepfamilies
Increase of gay and lesbian families
Increased rates of nonmarital births
Increase of people living alone
Increased longevity with longer empty nest stage
Later age at first marriage
People experience changing identities
Industrial
Romantic love as a basis of marriage
Stem (early) and nuclear families
Neolocal residence pattern
Males perform an instrumental function as economic providers
Females perform an expressive function
Moderate divorce rate
Smaller families through increased use of contraception
Preindustrial
Romantic love as extramarital
Joint family systems
Patrilocal or matrilocal residence pattern
Domination by elders and males
Arranged lifelong marriages at a young age
Low divorce rates

The dynamics of family life are different in preindustrial, industrial, and postindustrial societies. Family life changes as societies change economically, technologically, and politically. Changes in families can also affect changes in other social institutions.

usually arranged by parents. Romantic love has little to do with marriage. Marriage often results from an economic contract between families, in which dowries or bride wealth are central components of an economic exchange. A person marries the person that the parents select. A person is the best spouse it is possible to be to bring honor to parents and family. Each person is seen as a reflection of his or her parents and family. A dutiful spouse reflects on the competence of a person's parents to raise a productive and loyal adult. In preindustrial societies, romantic love exists, but rarely between spouses. Rather, it is usually in an extramarital relationship, and must be secret. Tragedy can occur if the lovers are discovered. They might be killed or they might, in disgrace, commit suicide. Sometimes there is a gender-based double standard that gives men, more than women, permission to have extramarital relationships.

Only with industrialization, with an increase of neolocal residence among younger children has parental control become weakened in families and romantic love become a basis for marriage. Romantic love as a basis for marriage is only about 150 years old in the history of western Europe. Since people now had to find their own mates, a process of courtship came into existence that was not needed previously. Marriage based on romantic love is largely a phenomenon of industrial and postindustrial societies.

In postindustrial societies, with increased diversity of family forms, romantic love is not necessarily heterosexual, but rather expands to include gay and lesbian relationships. Likewise, romantic love does not necessarily lead to marriage. People are wary of the stability of marriage. This leads to higher nonmarital rates among adults. It may also lead to higher rates of nonmarital births since pregnancy may not result in marriage. Also, because many adults were children of divorced parents, they are often afraid of marriage. They do not want to experience what they saw their parents experience in the divorce process, nor do they want to put their children through what they went through in that process.

Romantic love constitutes a shaky foundation upon which to construct a marriage. Romantic love is an emotion, and as such, it is subject to change over time. If the marriage is based primarily on the existence of romantic love then, when the love dissipates, the marriage ends in divorce. It is to a developmental exploration of divorce that we now turn.

Divorce

The developmental approach provides an interesting view of divorce. Divorce can be explained as the inability of a system to successfully meet the changing challenges confronting it at its given stage of development. From this perspective, divorce is nobody's fault. Rather, the family is seen as overcome by the challenges facing it at a particular stage of development or by the demands of making transitions between stages.

One of the most widely cited research studies on divorce is the work of Judith Wallerstein and her colleagues (1980, 1982, 1989). She divides the divorce process into three stages, which she calls the acute stage, followed by a transitional stage, and finally the restabilization or stabilization stage (1982).

The **acute stage** begins with the family rupture and often involves intense feelings of anger, abandonment, rejection, hostility, and the behavior that often accompanies these intense feelings. In her sample of largely middle- and upper-middle-class, white Marin County, California, families, 57 percent of the 131 children she interviewed said that they saw some physical violence exhibited by their parents as part of the divorce process.

The **transitional stage** involves experimenting with new forms of family living arrangements, new forms of relating and coping with the realities of life in now single-parent households. The transitional stage involves a search for stability, which may involve taking new jobs or careers, moving to new geographic areas, or taking on a number of sexual partners in a series of intense emotional relationships that may or may not lead to another marriage. The boundaries of the family at this stage often become permeable, with new members coming in and out of the family system—lovers, relatives, friends. On average, it took women in Wallerstein's study approximately three and a half years to get through the acute and transitional stages, and to achieve a sense of stabilization in their lives. It took men, on average, two to two and a half years to achieve this stabilization in their lives.

The **stabilization** of the divorced family system comes either with stability and predictability in the postdivorce family or with the remarriage of the divorced parent. If a child is seven years of age at the onset of the stabilization, he or she has probably spent half of his or her life in the chaotic turmoil that characterizes the acute and transitional stages. This can have traumatic, lasting effects on the children of divorce. Wallerstein's warning, coming from her research, is that divorce is generally more traumatic for children than is generally believed, and that these effects are long-lasting in the lives of these children. Whether the trauma is from the divorce or from what happened in the years leading up to it is difficult to determine.

There is no inevitable transition of people through these stages. Some people become fixated in a stage and cannot get out of it. Over 10 percent of families become fixated in the acute stage, where they wage constant war with one another, arguing and fighting incessantly and taking each other into court for round upon round of combat. Other families become fixated in the transitional stage and are subject to adaptive changes for much longer than the average time for stabilization.

Critique

The unilinear developmental model focuses on change that occurs through stages over time. Whether studying societies that industrialize and urbanize or couples that divorce, developmental theorists see all social systems as going through the same process of change, the same stages. By depicting change as occurring in stages, developmental theorists are able to describe the course of change over time and the processes of interpersonal interaction and developmental tasks at each stage. By organizing the description of change into stages, developmental theorists are able to show the uniqueness of each stage, as well as to compare and contrast stages, showing how they differ from each other. The theory also invites analysis of transitions between stages, which often involves dynamic processes of adjustment and adaptation.

Despite its many followers, developmental theory does have its flaws and its critics. The model tends to divide time into artificial segments or stages; sometimes the boundaries of the stages are fuzzy because the processes of life are not always so neatly and cleanly segmented.

The family development approach to studying families was originally created in the 1940s by sociologists such as Evelyn Duvall and Reuben Hill (1948). At the time, a much larger percentage of families in the United States were intact nuclear family units than exist today. A major critique, today, of the developmental approach is that it focuses on the development of an intact nuclear family unit and tends to neglect divorce and the development of families post-divorce. Now the developmental model would have to include stages of adjustment to divorce (Ahrons & Rodgers, 1987; Carter & McGoldrick, 1989; Wallerstein & Blakeslee, 1989) as well as the development of single-parent households (Weiss, 1981) and stepfamilies (Visher & Visher, 1989).

The family development approach often overlooks the effects of gender, ethnicity, and social class on family dynamics. Feminist theorists (Carter & McGoldrick, 1988; Faludi, 1991; England, 1993; Hochschild, 1989) remind us that gender influences one's experience of the life cycle. For instance, it is often easier for males than for females to separate from their family of origin, in part because autonomy and independence are more highly valued for males than for females in our culture. Females are sometimes viewed as more dependent, needing to be protected or sheltered by male family members. Marriage, rather than gainful employment, is still seen as the primary route for a woman to take out of her family of origin. Since marriage tends to occur later and later in peoples' lives, launching out of the family prior to marriage is generally harder for women than it is for men (Carter & McGoldrick, 1989).

Ethnicity also affects life cycle transitions (McGoldrick, Pearce, Giordano, 1982). In many cultures, people are not expected to gain autonomy and independence or launch out of their families of origin as adults. Rather, for Mexican Americans, Italians, Greeks, Native Americans, and many Asian cultures, one is forever part of the family system. Interdependence, affiliation, and familial cooperation are highly valued (Mindel & Habenstein, 1981). For people in these cultures, the belief is that since, as children, they were nurtured and supported, as adults they should expect to nurture and support parents and other kin in need. Differentiation of self from the family unit sometimes conflicts with ethnic cultural norms. To some extent, differentiation of self represents an Anglo-Saxon middle-class ideal, whereby the family launches an autonomous, independent, self-reliant adult into the outside world. This is not necessarily the ideal of other cultural groups.

There are also social class differences that affect the life cycle. In upper-class families, children are often sent to boarding school to be reared by professionals more than by parents (Davis, 1983). Upper-class children spend less time with their parents than do middle-class children. Moreover, poverty affects female-headed, father-absent families, particularly in states that forbid welfare payments to families where an adult male lives in the domicile. Since the divorce rate tends to be inversely related to social class, it is higher in low-income families. Lower-income families are less apt to experience an intact nuclear family structure, devoid of desertion, separation, divorce (Tumin, 1985). Family development theory seems overly simplistic because it overlooks how family development is affected by social class.

Multilinear Theory

Family development theory also seems overly simplistic when family development is viewed at a macrolevel. The changes in family structure and values that Goode depicted as societies moved from preindustrial to industrialized societies were seen as general tendencies. These phenomena did not exist in all societies of the world. Goode wrote that all societies were not moving along the same path toward the attainment of these structural patterns. He was extremely aware of the diversity in the patterns of change. Although there may have been a singular direction toward which societies were changing, the paths of change and modes of changing were quite different within the subcultures and strata of a society as well as between societies. Goode (1963: 25) thus attempted to use a multilinear model when he wrote:

> Even though the larger trend toward some type of conjugal family system is under way, family systems differ among themselves. Thus they will exhibit very different trends with respect to such matters as age at marriage, illegitimacy rates, or the ratio of divorce to marriage. Their systems began from very different points; even if they converge toward the conjugal family, their various characteristics might move in very different directions within different systems. Some family systems may change easily; others may resist strenuously. Certain traits persist while others weaken swiftly. The elements which change first in one family system may hold firm in another.

Goode may well have been influenced by a book written by Marshall Sahlins and Elman Service (1960), in which the authors distinguish between what they call "general evolution" and "specific evolution." **General evolution** referred to a general direction of change that societies seem to exhibit toward greater urbanization and industrialization. There is an implicit determinism in general evolution because the forces pushing toward greater urbanization and industrialization cannot be denied. They will inevitably exert their influence in affecting change. **Specific evolution** referred to the fact that not all societies follow the same path toward attaining urbanization and industrialization. There is some autonomy that exists in terms of how societies respond to the forces for change. Societies can affect change quickly or slowly, and they have alternatives available to them for implementing urbanization and industrialization. Although they take different paths, the flow of change is still in one general direction. This allows for a tree-like portrayal of change whereby different societies take different paths yet all paths lead generally "upward" (see Figure 1.4 on page 42). This is a multilinear approach.

The multilinear evolutionary theorist starts at the bottom of the tree and envisions change as occurring upward, through the branches. A familiar use of this theory lies in the research of Charles Darwin. Species reproduce until a mutation occurs that produces a new, structurally different kind of being. If that new being is more adaptable within its physical environment than are other kinds of beings with whom it is in competition for survival, it will survive to

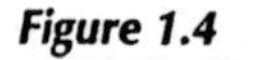

Figure 1.4

Model of the Multilinear Approach

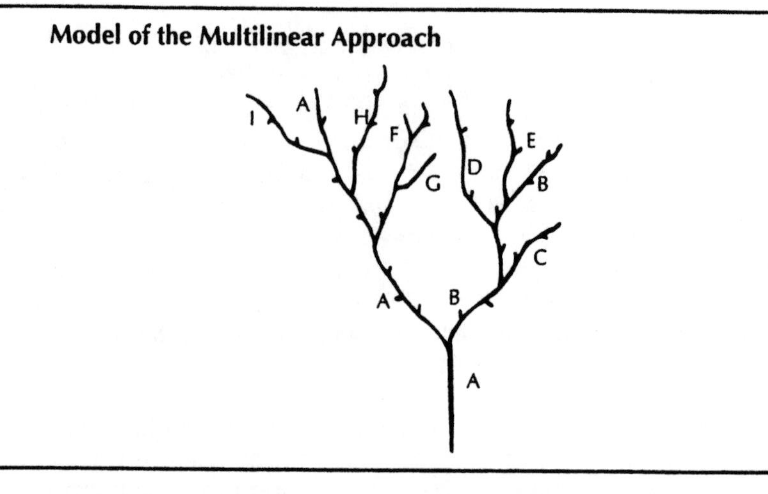

Charles Darwin's description of evolution as depicted in this drawing of a tree applies not only to the creation of new, different biological species but also to the creation of new, different kinds of societies and families. In this model, change occurs along many different paths, hence the title "multilinear."

reproduce itself. It occasionally produces mutations, most of which do not create beings that are adaptively advantageous and those beings do not survive to reproduce (the buds in Figure 1.4, above). When an adaptively advantageous mutation occurs, it again reproduces its own kind, and the new species survives. This multilinear approach can be applied not only to species but to societies and families.

Families or societies at various times reach forks in the road—points of choice that may alter the path. Using Figure 1.4 as a guide, you will be able to chart the following life courses.

For families within a society, A might be joint families, B is the existence of primogeniture and the creation of stem families and C is the creation of nuclear family units. Some societies or regions in societies follow path A and never adopt primogeniture laws. They stay joint family households over time. Others do adopt primogeniture and create stem families, while societies that follow path C create nuclear family households.

An individual within a family might be a single young adult who follows a status (A) path. Or he or she might take Path B, marriage without children. Voluntarily childless married people might also stay on path B. Path C, which might involve having children, is another possible choice.

There are many other multilinear possibilities. A single person on path A might enter into a gay or lesbian relationship, taking path B, which is without children. If this couple were to adopt a child or get pregnant via artificial insemination, they would be taking path C. The forks are choice points in their lives. The buds here are relationships that do not lead to marriage, that terminate in time. People within any society do not follow the same path in their lives—some marry, others don't; some have children, others don't. The multilinear perspective allows one to depict that diversity. The unilinear model portrays all people going through the same stages, which ignores diversity and portrays a uniformity that just does not exist in reality.

This multilinear perspective constitutes a critique of unilinear models. That critique is that the view of a singular path to change belies the reality that change exhibits significant diversity. Change does not occur in the same way in all societies. Even within a society, there are many variations in which change occurs. Families in the postindustrial United States exhibit great diversity in the 1990s. When family development theory focuses only on the intact nuclear family unit, alternative family lifestyles tend to be omitted or overlooked. What of gay and lesbian relationships and their developmental process? What of the family of mother and children with no husband and father around, perhaps because of desertion, perhaps because the mother preferred to rear her child alone, without marriage? What of the increase of voluntary childlessness—families that never experience the parenthood stage? Singleness used to be seen as a transitional stage, occurring either prior to marriage or between marriages. Increasingly, however, people are choosing to stay single, rather than marry, and they experience a very different life cycle process than do married people. The family development framework seems increasingly simplistic for describing the process of change over time in our diverse and complex contemporary world.

Summary

Unilinear developmental theories characterize change as occurring through stages over time. All systems change in a unidirectional path through the same stages. Family development theory illustrates a unilinear developmental model, but it often fails to take into account the diversity of development in families, based on historical circumstance (the effects of war or depression), cultural issues (ethnicity), and social factors (gender and class).

Multilinear evolutionary theories recognize that the patterns of change in social systems are not consistent. Not all systems take the same paths to change, although they do tend to change in the same general direction.

In conclusion we can say that the eyeglasses of the developmental theorist focus on the existence of change over time—change that is seen as being natural, normal, and inevitable. However, not all theories in sociology share this view, as we shall see in the next chapters.

Chapter Two

Structural-Functional Theory

The Focus

Structural-functional theory dominated sociology in the United States and western Europe from approximately 1940 to 1965. This framework is organized around four basic concepts: system, social structure, function, and equilibrium.

A person wearing these theoretical eyeglasses would see reality as being organized into interrelated and interdependent social systems. In this approach a person is a part of many different systems: a family of origin, a family of procreation, a work setting, a neighborhood system, a religious system, an educational system, and a political system. Structural-functional theorists never see the individual as an isolated entity, as some psychologists do, but rather focus on how people interact with one another in groups (Turner & Maryanski, 1979).

From a structural-functional perspective, the discipline of sociology can be defined as the study of human behavior in social groups, which involves studying social relationships. An individual's behavior always must be interpreted through interpersonal analysis. This theorist asks how a person's behavior is affected by the behavior of other people and by social institutions and how this behavior in turn affects the behavior of other people in a continuous process of action and reaction.

The Theory of Survival

One of the early creators of structural-functional theory was Talcott Parsons, a Harvard sociologist. Parsons analyzed systems at many different levels that ranged from the macroanalysis of whole societies to social institutions, such as families, religion, education, politics, and economics, within a society, to the microanalysis of small groups. The smallest social group is a two-person system.

Parsons believed that survival is the primary function of all societies. Societies, therefore, have to create constantly new populations to replace those who have died. They must also integrate into groups whose members shared common values and ideals, common perspectives of right and wrong, of good and bad. In this regard, families perform important functions through procreation and through socializing children to internalize the values that bind members of the society together into a cohesive whole.

Socialization for Survival

According to Parsons, the process of **socialization** involves learning the things that bind members of any society together, from their language to their values. In the United States we are bound together by the shared values of democracy, capitalism, individualism, and, yes, even television. Integration, a critical component that is needed for societal survival, is achieved by people sharing common definitions and values. Teaching these is done in the cultural system (probably the most important of Parson's four systems), which provides the cement that holds the diverse elements of a society together.

FUNCTIONAL REQUISITES FOR SURVIVAL The idea that survival is a key function for all societies led some structural-functional theorists to create lists of **functional requisites**, those things that would be needed or tasks that would have to be accomplished for any society to survive. Thus Robert Winch (1963) created the following list of functional requisites for survival that were to be performed primarily in families:

1. Replacements for dying members of the society must be provided.
2. Goods and services must be produced and distributed for the support of the members of the society.
3. Provision must be made for accommodating conflicts and maintaining order internally and externally.
4. Human replacements must be trained to become participating members of the society.
5. Procedures must be created for dealing with emotional crises, for harmonizing the goals of individuals with the values of the society, and for maintaining a sense of purpose.

CONFORMING TO NORMS Parsons believed that survival of societies also demanded conformity to **norms** or rules, which created an order or structure that would protect people from acts of violence, immorality, or unfairness. Deviance was seen as dysfunctional since it threatened the normative order.

Deviance was further considered to be dysfunctional because it sometimes led to rapid change that led to disorganization within a social system. So the survival of societies sometimes means personal sacrifice and loss of individual autonomy for those members who integrate harmoniously into group structures and who conform to norms that exist as part of those structures.

These norms are **sanctioned** inasmuch as behavior that conforms to the rules is rewarded while behavior that deviates from norms is punished. Structural-functional theorists tend to see the individual as a product of powerful external forces that impinge upon people, constraining them to act in normative ways. We are all affected by forces such as age, gender, religion, race, ethnicity, and marital status.

Not all social systems have the same norms for behavior. Some groups, for instance, practice attaining wealth through theft or drug dealing, and the dominant culture defines these as "deviant" groups, because they do not subscribe to the norms of the dominant, or majority, culture. These deviant groups subscribe to the same values as the dominant society. They both value money.

SHARING VALUES A **value** is any characteristic or object that is deemed to be desirable in a society. High grades in school are a value; money is a value; BMWs and Corvettes are values; honesty, capitalism, and democracy are values. Deviant subcultures often have the same values as the dominant culture, but the means they adopt to attain their values are not within the norms of the dominant social structure. As in the larger society, these groups have their own norms or rules, and they socialize their members to adhere to those norms. Members are rewarded for conforming to the norms and punished for deviating from them (Merton, 1968).

When a structural-functional theorist is asked why people behave as they do, the answer will be that all groups have learned and shared norms and values. People are constrained through rewards and punishments to conform to those norms and adhere to those values.

Both developmental theory and structural-functional theory have deterministic elements. In developmental theory, individuals are affected by the powerful forces for change within any social system. In structural-functional theory, individuals are seen as affected by the existing norms and values of social systems as well as by forces that are part of individuals, such as their age, gender, religion, and ethnicity.

With regard to these latter factors, researchers who use a structural-functional model tend to use **questionnaires** to determine what external forces exist in the lives of respondents and how these forces are affecting the behavior of the respondents. Questionnaires normally use forced choice questions to obtain data from large numbers of people. The data are analyzed quantitatively. The researchers believe that if they know a person's age, gender, occupation, level of education, religion, race, ethnicity, and marital status then they can predict with great accuracy how those people will behave; for instance, how they will vote in elections and what products they will purchase. These external factors, which are a part of our existence, influence how we think, which in turn will influence how we act. Using questionnaires in survey research is consistent with structural-functional theory. Through questionnaires, one can quickly and efficiently obtain information on the social forces impinging on an individual.

System—The First Basic Concept

The first central concept of structural-functional theory is **system**, which embodies many ideas that are essential to the theory. The concept focuses our attention on *interrelatedness*, the idea that no individual and no system functions independently but rather is affected by, and in turn affects, other people and other systems. The concept asks us to consider **levels of systems**—a global system of societies within which are individual societies within which are social institutions within which are small groups. We thus have many different levels of analysis that add to the complexity of this approach. The system concept also connotes the existence of *boundaries*, both within and between systems. This concept of boundaries can be both intriguing and controversial when analyzing family systems.

A system, then, is a boundary-maintained unit composed of interrelated and interdependent parts. Borrowed from the biological sciences, the concept was applied to social systems. The human body is a prototypical biological system that contains within it a skeletal system, a muscular system, a digestive system, a reproductive system, a circulatory system, and so forth. Within each of these systems are interrelated and interdependent organs. In the body's division of labor, for example, in the circulatory system the lungs oxygenate blood, the heart pumps it, and the kidneys clean and filter it. If any of these organs were to malfunction, each of the other organs in the body would be affected. If any of these organs were to fail to function, the entire system might die.

The body, then, is a biological system whose boundary is the skin. Other systems and other people are external to us. We may be affected by the actions of others in our environment. For instance, if we interact with others who have viruses or germs, we may catch colds or other illnesses. If our actions anger others, they might hit us or shoot us. Alternatively, if others compliment us, we might feel good in their presence. We, in turn, affect others in our environment by our behavior.

The smallest social system that can exist is two people. The United States is an example of a large societal system. Within it are many subsystems: political, educational, military, religious, economic, and so forth. And within the political subsystem are the national parties: Democratic, Republican, Peace and Freedom, American Independent Parties, and so forth; and within these national party systems are state, county, and precinct party subsystems. The military subsystem is composed of the Army, Navy, Air Force, Marines, Coast Guard, and National Guard subsystems. The educational subsystem is composed of public and private school subsystems; and within these are preschool, elementary school, junior high school, high school, vocational school, community college, four-year university, and graduate school subsystems. Within the religious subsystem are the Catholic, Protestant, Jewish, Islamic, Buddhist, and other religious subsystems. Within the Protestant subsystem are the Episcopalian, Methodist, Baptist, Congregationalist, and Presbyterian subsystems. Within the Jewish subsystem are the Orthodox, Conservative, and Reform subsystems.

When we say that systems are interrelated, we mean that a change in any one system effects changes in other systems. If the leaders of the political system decide to fight a war, the economic system is affected because money has to be poured into the war effort, and some companies will make sizable profits from making war materials. Students may be pulled out of the educational system to fight the war. The religious system becomes important as families grieve

Figure 2.1

The Four Systems in Parsonian Theory

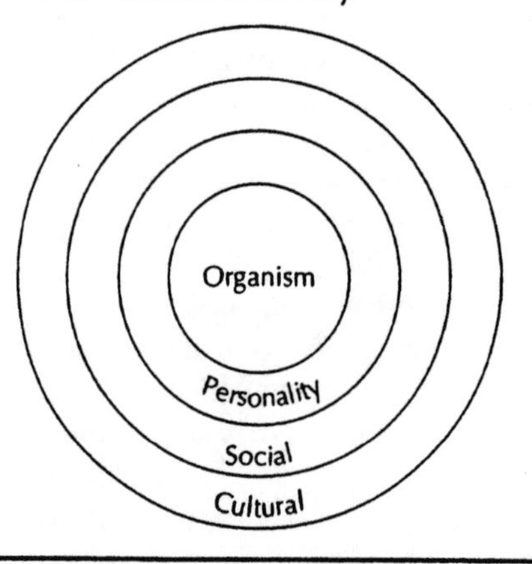

The cultural system (outer circle) contains goals that influence norms at the next, or social system, level. These norms may then affect the behavior of people at the personality system level. Cultural values define physiological characteristics at the organism system level as either desirable or undesirable.

over the loss of loved ones. The military system gets resources and attention. If the war goes poorly, it may reverberate to affect the political system because leaders responsible for the country being at war may be voted out of office.

The United States exists in an environment of other countries external to it: Israel, Syria, Jordan, Cuba, Somalia, Iraq, Germany, Great Britain, France, Japan, and so on. A change in any one country may effect changes for us and vice versa, as when one of these countries raises or lowers interest rates, decides to invade another country, or makes peace with a neighbor.

Families are social systems. Within a nuclear family there can be a spousal subsystem when the parties relate to each other in the roles of husband and wife, a parental subsystem when they relate to each other in the roles of mother and father, and a **sibling subsystem** composed of brothers and sisters. All exist within an environment of **extended kin**, including a subsystem of grandparents, aunts and uncles, cousins, nieces, and nephews. Also in the family's external environment are the neighbors, the parents' work cohorts, the staff of the children's school, members of their church or synagogue, and any clubs or organizations to which they might belong, such as Little League, political organizations, and parent groups.

Parsons believed that all social interaction can be interpreted in terms of four interrelated systems: the cultural system, the social system, the personality system, and the organism system (see Figure 2.1 above). We begin by analyzing the cultural system because it is here that social behavior can be said to begin. In the process of socialization, values are taught and learned. In Parsons's own words, "A value is a conception, explicit or implicit, distinctive of an individual or characteristic of a group, of the desirable which influences the selection from available modes, means, and ends of action" (Parsons & Shils, 1951: 395). People behave by making choices that are derived from their values, which exist in the cultural system.

The Cultural System

Shared beliefs that are collectively held by its members make up the cultural system of a group—what people are taught, what they think, and what goes on inside their heads. When a structural-functional theorist uses the term cultural system, he or she does not refer to ethnic groups.

The cultural system of a family may include beliefs that Debbie is a "brain" or Joe is a "clown"; that father is an incompetent cook; or that mother has a hot temper. It may include political beliefs such as that Democrats are good and Republicans bad (or vice versa), or that all politicians are crooks. It may include prejudices held by family members about "outsiders," whether toward religious or ethnic groups. These beliefs are transmitted from parents to children in a process of socialization. Socialization is the primary function of the cultural system.

Part of what exists at the cultural system level are values. In early childhood socialization, we teach young children values—the goals that are worth striving for in life. In later socialization, we teach them the skills and knowledge they will need to attain those values.

These shared values have a function of maintaining the basic patterns of the group despite adaptive changes that occur within the system or new inputs that impinge upon the system from outside. The cultural system helps the group distinguish itself from other groups; they are different by virtue of their distinctive values, what they hold to be desirable.

To summarize, what exists at the cultural system level are learned and shared thoughts and ideas that exist in peoples' heads. Within the cultural system, there are shared perceptions and definitions of objects and events in peoples' lives. It is these that will guide behavior. Behavior, or action, is what is analyzed at the social system level.

The Social System

At the social system level, patterns of interpersonal interaction are described. Here we are observing not an individual's actions in isolation, but rather *interpersonal interaction,* the *behavior* of two or more people or two or more groups toward each other. Thus, as mentioned earlier, a husband and wife constitute a spousal social system and a mother and father constitutes a parental system. The unit of husband, wife, and children constitutes a nuclear family system while aunts and uncles, nephews and nieces, grandparents, and cousins constitute **an extended family system.** In an educational institution, teachers and students

Figure 2.2

The Dining Room Table

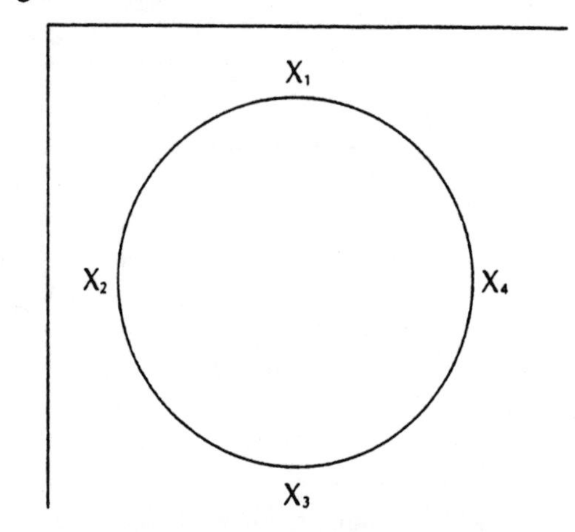

Seats X1 and X2 are where people with the most status are apt to sit. They allow people to see out into the room. What one sees, one can have some control over. If this were a table in a restaurant and two people came to sit at it in the corner of the room, they would most likely sit in seats X1 and X2, rather than sitting with their backs to the other people in the room. If this table were at home, people in seats X3 and X4 would be closest to the kitchen and thus are most likely to serve the food from the kitchen. People in X1 and X2 have to go around the table to retrieve items and thus are more likely to be served by the others. Try testing the norms in your family. Take someone else's seat at the dining room table, someone with a more powerful position than yours, and observe how your "deviant behavior" is sanctioned by others and how they seek to return to a state of equilibrium.

constitute one social system while faculty and administrators constitute a different social system; in a medical institution doctors and nurses constitute a social system as do doctors and hospital administrators and doctors and patients. At this social system level we examine how members of a system behave relative to one another.

Family life is often very normalized, with those routine patterns of behavior called **rituals.** Think of your own family: You can probably think of someone who usually gets up first in the morning, who puts the coffee on, brings in the newspaper, or turns on the heat in the house. Part of a family's rituals might include having dinner at the same time every night. Where one sits at the dining room table is part of the ritual (see Figure 2.2 above). Where people sit at the table usually reflects the status structure of a family system. People with higher status occupy seats farthest from the kitchen, while those with lower status usually occupy seats closest to the kitchen. The person closest to the kitchen tends to retrieve things that might be forgotten and to serve the others.

Part of a family's ritual includes the TV programs that are watched throughout the week. This also reflects stratification in a system. Who wields the authority in a family that watches football every Monday night? Who washes dishes, clears the table, locks the house at night, turns off the lights, turns down the heat, puts out the cat, or walks the dog are all part of the family's ritual. What family members call each other and how they address each other are also part of the ritual.

Rituals reflect and reinforce a family's system of stratification. Who is being served by these rituals and who is serving others? If you want to try changing the ritual pattern in your own family, try violating a family norm. For example, try not putting on the coffee or turning on the heat in the morning. Try calling someone by a name that is not usual (call Dad by his given name). Once norms are violated, observe how these violations are negatively sanctioned by others.

SOCIAL ROLES Social roles exist at the social system level. The concept of role was usually linked to the concept of status in structural-functional theory. A status is a position that exists in a social structure. Role refers to behavioral patterns that people exhibit within a status. Fatherhood is a status that exists in family systems. As an occupant of that status, fathers assume many different roles.

Fathers are expected to act in nurturing ways with their children, being loving and caring, affectionate but not sexual, tender and emotionally expressive. Fathers are also expected to be authoritarian and disciplinary, setting limits and establishing norms, and reacting negatively when those norms are violated. Fathers are thus expected to punish when appropriate, even to spank sometimes, without being physically abusive to the children. There are, thus, at least two roles relative to the status of fatherhood, **nurturing father** and **disciplinary father**. These two roles can sometimes appear to be contradictory, but they are *both* necessary components to being a complete parent.

Each parent has to create for themselves how dominant or repressed these roles will be. Thus some fathers act primarily as disciplinary fathers with very little nurturing behavior while other fathers are overwhelmingly nurturing and exhibit very little disciplinary behavior. With a historical increase in dual-worker households, both fathers and mothers are increasingly called upon to assume *both* nurturing and disciplinary roles.

FATHER ROLE SETS The totality of roles that exist for any given status is called a **role set** (Merton, 1968). Not only are fathers nurturing and disciplinary but they are also financial fathers or banker fathers who give their children loans, maintain trust funds for their children's college education, and give allowances, or money for special expenditures, each week. There is also a medical father who gives children medication when they are ill, puts band-aids on when needed, sees that the children take allergy medicine on time, and takes the children to the doctor or dentist. There is a recreational father who may play games with the children, take them fishing or camping, or take them to the movies or to the skating rink. The educational father helps children with their homework, takes them to museums or galleries, helps them with their science project or their special school report.

Open and Closed Boundaries

The boundaries between the nuclear family system and the outside world can be described as being primarily closed or open. **Open boundaries** allow people within a system to go outside it to get their needs met (O'Neill & O'Neill, 1972). A criticism of monogamy is that, all too often, people in monogamous relationships expect that their partners will meet their diverse needs for companionship, intellectual stimulation, intimacy, recreation, fun, and emotional support. By opening up the boundaries of the relationship, other people besides the partner can also be resources for meeting each partner's needs.

At the other extreme, some relationships feature **closed boundaries.** This is where family members cannot or do not transcend the boundaries of the family system to get their needs met and where the outside world is not allowed into the family—where the external environment cannot provide resources and support for family members.

A closed boundary is created for a couple when a husband tells his wife, "No, you cannot go to college to further your education because I just can't trust you. I mean, how do I know what you are really doing when you say you are at the library studying?" A closed boundary is created by a jealous

---

In these roles the father interacts with other people who are in turn playing out roles, such as the mother, who also has her role set, and the child, both of whom are within the boundaries of the nuclear family system. However, the father also interacts with other status occupants who are outside the nuclear family system and who are in turn playing out their roles—the doctor, the children's teacher, other children, the coach of the sports team, the person who administers the college trust fund, and the ticket taker at the movie theater or roller rink.

THE EXPRESSIVE MOTHER ROLE Parsons saw social institutions as arising from an integrated pattern of roles that exist to serve a particular social function. The institution of the family, for instance, performs the functions of procreation and socialization of children. Societies and the institutions within them slowly evolve toward greater differentiation and specialization in the functions they perform. Parsons saw differentiation in family systems as involving males performing an **instrumental role**, which means they are primarily responsible for meeting the family's physical needs of food, clothing, and shelter through their gainful employment. Through their employment they relate the family to the outside world. Parsons saw females as increasingly assuming an **expressive role** in families, where they meet family members' psychological needs, make sure everyone is relatively happy and that people get along well with one another.

partner who, when leaving the house to go to work, padlocks the front and back doors of the house, locking the spouse inside. On the way out the door, the jealous partner also unplugs the telephones and takes them along. The person does this on a daily basis out of fear that the spouse might meet and fall in love with someone else. Both cases cited here involve actual couples with whom this author has worked clinically.

When boundaries around a family are extremely closed, the home becomes a prison. There are only two ways to get out of a prison—be released by the "warden" or escape. Very often the runaway teenager or the runaway spouse is escaping from a system with such closed boundaries that he or she must flee to escape from its rigidity. An example of this reaction can be seen in the first scene of the movie, *Kramer vs. Kramer,* where Mrs. Kramer (Meryl Streep) flees from the confinement of her marriage.

Most marriages do not lie at either extreme of an open–closed boundary continuum. They are closed in many areas but open in others, or they are open in many areas but closed in others. (For instance, they might demand the partner's sexual fidelity.) The extent to which boundaries are open or closed affects the ability of a family system to interact with the "outside world" and to partake of resources available in that world (such as education, religion, friends, or therapists).

In this role, the female relates family members to each other. Parsons wrote of this role differentiation in 1955, before women started entering the labor force in massive numbers.

Norms and roles govern how people behave. Recurrent behavioral patterns or styles are reflected in an individual's personality. The roles and norms and the social structure that exist at the social system level can influence the personality of individuals. People who work in repetitive, unchallenging jobs do not get much stimulus to develop creative, commanding, self-confident personalities. It is to personality that we now turn to see how the cultural and social systems influence the personalities of individuals.

The Personality System

This system exists at the level of the individual and here is where Parsons explored the interaction between individuals and between the cultural and social systems. At the personality system level, Parsons struggled with the interaction between individual goals, cultural values, and social norms. Because deviance, as a force for social change, threatens the equilibrium of social systems and the orderly structure of society that is essential for its

Table 2.1

Merton's Modes of Adaptation to Anomie

Modes of Adaptation	Cultural Goals	Institutionalized Means
Conformity	+	+
Innovation	+	–
Ritualism	–	+
Retreatism	–	–
Rebellion	±	±

(+) symbolizes "acceptance"; (–) symbolizes "rejection"; and (±) symbolizes rejection of prevailing values and substitution of different values and rejection of institutionalized means of attaining goals and substitution of different means of attaining goals.

Modes of adaptation are exhibited by individuals and exist at the personality system level. Goals exist at the cultural system level. Institutionalized means exist at the social system level. This shows how systems are dynamically interactive.

survival, Parsons asked how, by internalizing cultural values and accepting social norms, the individual can be motivated to conform.

At the personality system level, Parsons looked at *motivation* of the individual as an important ingredient in supporting a normative social structure and reducing deviance. Parsons saw deviance as dysfunctional, particularly when it promotes social change. Individuals have needs that may be frustrated by norms at the social system level or values at the cultural system level. This can lead to deviant behavior (Merton, 1968).

THE MANY FACES OF DEVIANT BEHAVIOR If the cultural system values money and the individual properly internalizes this value in the socialization process, but the social structure does not allow the person access to money through legitimate means—honest gainful employment—that person may then opt to obtain money through non-legitimate means, such as robbing a bank or selling illegal drugs. Robert Merton labeled deviant behavior **innovation** when individuals accept cultural values but do not use institutional means (at the social system level) to obtain the valued commodity. When people use institutionalized means, such as working honestly, but do not accept cultural goals, Merton called this kind of deviance **ritualism**. In these situations, a person may work honestly, but may not seek promotion and success (cultural goals or values). A male nurse, for example, may say that he is happy at his job and that promotion would just mean more responsibility and headaches. If he made more money through the promotion, he would only have to pay more taxes. Therefore, he passes up the promotion to someone else.

Retreatism exists when individuals reject both culturally accepted goals and socially institutionalized means for attaining those goals. An example would be the street person, a "bag lady," perhaps, who does not seek success and does not want to be gainfully employed; she opts voluntarily to "hang out" and be with her friends. **Rebellion** is a form of deviant behavior where people replace cultural goals and institutionalized means with an alternative set of goals and means. Innovation, ritualism, retreatism, and rebellion, then, are all forms of deviant behavior. **Conformity** exists only when an individual accepts both the cultural goals and the institutionalized means that exist at the cultural and social system levels of achieving those goals.

Merton saw deviant behavior as an adaptation by people who are confronted by malintegrated systems in a state of disequilibrium, where there are inconsistencies and incongruities between ends and means within social systems. He called these inconsistencies **anomie**, the existence of ambiguous or inconsistent values and norms within a system.

Families today face anomie within the social structure of this country. This is apparent when one looks at current cultural values and compares them with the dynamics that must exist for family systems to be successful. There are clear discrepancies between the values in economic capitalist institutions and the values that must exist in order that families may survive and prosper. Capitalism stresses *individual ownership* while families stress *sharing*. Capitalism is based on *competitiveness* while families require *cooperation* among members, not competition. Competitiveness in the economic sphere results in corporations' need to cut expenses to maximize profits, but that means that large numbers of employees get laid off through restructuring, which threatens family stability and security. If any corporation is to be really "family friendly," it must give employees financial security. This does not happen in a capitalist economy.

Independence and autonomy exist as cultural values for people, yet families are based on interdependence, affiliation, and cooperation among members. Individualism as a cultural value conflicts with the values of the collective group that are essential to the survival of family systems. We value leisure, fun, enjoyment of life, yet family systems are based on self-sacrifice, particularly in the rearing of children. The economic system tends to value adults for their economic productivity, and the polity values adults for their ability to vote, yet families, if they are to raise children with positive self-esteem, must value children as important and worthy of time, attention, affection, and money.*

Individuals, faced with this anomic situation, must make choices. Adopting family values may be seen as deviant in, say, the economic system of society. To give one's children proper attention, affection, and time, parents may relinquish fame and success, and may opt to work part-time in order to spend more time in their families. This constitutes a pattern which Merton might label "ritualism," since these parents reject cultural goals of success but work honestly, if not full-time. One problem that confronts people in this society is that to value family life and spend time promoting family happiness often involves

*The author is indebted to his colleague, Dr. Azmy Ibrahim, for stimulating some of the ideas contained in these last two paragraphs.

economic sacrifice. Economic institutions are malintegrated with family institutions; they do not support one another, but rather compete so that to succeed in one sphere sometimes involves failing in the other. Individuals are left to adapt as best they can to this anomic social structure. For Merton, therefore, deviance is not necessarily the result of flawed socialization but of anomie.

The Organism System

At the individual level, the organism system is the human body, and the skin is its boundary. The body, with its great variability, affects a person's social interaction with others. Just for starters, it can be tall or short, fat or skinny, male or female; it can have light or dark skin, eyes and ears that work well or poorly, and sturdy or feeble legs. All these factors about the body affect a person's interactions with others; awareness of his or her individual liabilities or resources helps a person make choices in terms of defining and achieving goals.

In the cultural system, people are taught the shared values and beliefs of their society. People learn to value particular physical characteristics over others. They learn that some physiological characteristics are desirable or undesirable. In the United States, thin females are valued as more attractive than are hefty, stocky females (the opposite applies in Russia, for instance), yet hefty, stocky males are defined as more desirable than are too thin males. Tallness in males is desirable while shortness in females is valued, because for heterosexual couples, norms prescribe that males should be taller than their female partners. The closer a person's physique is to cultural ideals, the greater is the likelihood of getting higher paying jobs. Thus, in this country, tall men make more money than short men and thin women make more money than do heavy women (Bielicki & Waliszko, 1992; Kuh, Power, & Rodgers, 1991).

THE IMPORTANCE OF PHYSICAL CHARACTERISTICS Culture also defines some physiological characteristics as being more important than others. For instance, in the United States the color of eyes is generally seen as irrelevant in defining people, and often we do not even notice this characteristic. People have varying hair color, and although there are cultural myths about hair color (blondes have more fun; redheads are hot-tempered), it is seen as irrelevant in affecting the definition of a person. Color of skin, on the other hand, is seen as culturally important, and, throughout our history, has been something that is noticed in this country. A person with dark skin has, historically, often received different treatment in social interaction with others than does a person with light skin. People are socialized to see skin color as making more of a difference in affecting social interaction than hair or eye color. At the cultural system level, people are taught about physiology, giving value to height, weight, gender, and skin color.

For Parsons, all social interaction can be explained and discussed through the interaction of these four basic systems. For example, if a male in the United States is five feet tall, the cultural system defines him as "too short"—and he may have difficulty with his social life, having few, if any, dates (social system). He may become motivated (personality system) to compensate by trying out for the football team. He will try to show others that just because he is short, he is no less a man. He gets injured (organism system) playing ball and then establishes a personal goal (personality system) of devoting his energy to academics and withdraws, becoming introverted and studious. His intellect causes him great financial success (social system). He meets and marries a princess, and they live happily ever after. Thus, Parsons's four systems affect and interact with one another.

Social Structure—The Second Basic Concept

We turn, now, to the second basic concept of structural-functional theory. To describe social structure we need to do two things: describe the parts of the system and describe how the parts are organized. In describing the parts of the system, we are asking who is *in* the family? This question, simple to ask, can prove very complex to answer.

Who Is in the Family?

A nuclear family, when intact, consists of a husband, a wife, and their children, either by birth or adopted. So, the social structure of a family might be described by stating that there are a mother, a father, and children named.... However, nuclear families exist within an extended family network. Extended family consists of grandparents and great grandparents, if living, aunts and uncles, cousins, nieces and nephews, and in-laws; people linked to the family by blood or marriage. People who are connected by blood ties are linked by a **consanguineal bond** and are **kin** to one another (siblings, grandparents, aunts and uncles, nieces and nephews). People who are linked by marriage are connected through an **affineal bond** and are **affines** to one another (brothers- and sisters-in-law, mothers- and fathers-in-law). Sometimes members of an extended family can be very powerful in affecting what goes on within a nuclear family. Particularly within upper-class families, grandparents, who constitute a conduit through which the family fortune is passed, can prove very powerful in affecting whom their grandchildren do and do not marry. ("If you marry this person, so help me, I will disinherit you.") In-laws who are very close to their children can affect where family vacations and holidays are spent.

If the question "Who is *in* the family?" means who has a powerful effect on interpersonal dynamics that occur within a nuclear family system, then nonfamily members might be *in* the family. If one spouse has a lover, that lover is *in* the family system, since that person has an effect on interpersonal dynamics between the spouses. A person who has a boss at work who makes unrealistic demands for productivity on the job, or who is harassing and unpleasant, could think of this boss as *in* the family because he causes problems that then affect family interaction. A teacher who makes unrealistic demands on students and has students returning home exhausted, frustrated, and angry might be *in* the families of his or her students, since this teacher is affecting family dynamics. In families where there has been divorce, the noncustodial parent is often *in* the family unit because of what does or does not happen at times—for instance, custody transitions or support checks that do or do not arrive. That parent is *in* the family system, even though not living physically within the household.

Who is included when the structure of a family system is described depends to some extent upon the purpose of describing the parts of the system. We describe the structure of a family in a particular *context,* which may be of kinship or by household members. The context determines whom we include (or exclude) in our description.

While visiting mainland China, this author once asked a man, on visiting his home, how many children he had. He said three. Later he admitted to having five children, but he said he answered "three" because he thought I was asking how many children were living in his house at the present time. He had excluded the two eldest daughters because they had left the family household. His answer was linked to the context in which he thought the question was asked. What appeared to be a very simple question became quite complex. I was reminded of how difficult it might be to conduct a census where questions such as "How many children are in your family?" might have multiple or ambiguous meanings. Does this mean how many children do you have or how many children are living in this household at the present time?

Norms sometimes help people define boundaries (see the box on page 52 for a fuller description) between who is in and who is not in the family. The norm that applies to some people is that they should phone before visiting. For others, the norm that applies is that they are welcome at any time with no advance warning. Those who can come at any time are being treated like family. Those who must ask for permission are "outsiders." Through norms, people articulate boundaries.

FAMILY ORGANIZATION The next task in describing social structure is to describe how the parts of the system interrelate and interact with one another.

The structure of a system has consequences for the people within it. If the structure of a family permits only the father to make important decisions, the result may be apathy for other family members. They may feel that they are unimportant. This may contribute to low self-esteem for some family members or to rebelliousness and anger for others.

Structural-functional theorists do more than just describe the structure of systems or the behavior of people within systems; they also ask what the consequences of human behavior are. They ask what the consequences of its organization are for people living and working in a social structure. In considering the consequences of one person's behavior on other people or the consequences of structural organization on many people, these theorists use the third concept: function, which we turn to now.

Function—The Third Basic Concept

Some of the questions concerning function that the structural-functional theorists ask include: What is the function of this child's acting-out behavior for other family members? Or, what is the function of a parent's working all day in a job where he/she has no decision-making capability on his/her ability to come home and be in charge, to control everything from family assets to children? If a social structure exists, what is the effect of that structure on other structures and people?

A **function** is the consequence of a person's behavior or of a group's action. It is what happens after an action occurs that is the direct or indirect effect of that action. Consequences of action that are beneficial for a system are called **functional** or **eufunctional**. Consequences of action that are detrimental for a system are called **dysfunctional**. Sometimes an action can be functional for a system in some ways and dysfunctional in other ways. Structural-functional theorists do not just label actions as functional or dysfunctional but rather describe in what ways an action is one or the other. Fluorocarbons in refrigerators are functional in enabling us to keep food cold, thereby reducing poisoning and disease, but they are dysfunctional in depleting ozone in the atmosphere and increasing the likelihood of skin cancers in people. Automobiles are functional in giving us very private and not too expensive transportation, but they are dysfunctional in contributing to traffic congestion, with its attendant stress and fatigue, as well as to air pollution.

Manifest or Latent Function

Merton (1957) distinguished between manifest and latent functions. **Manifest functions** are consequences of action that are both recognized and intended by the actors. **Latent functions** are consequences of action that are neither recognized nor intended by the actors. If a parent says something nasty or derogatory to a child, the consequence may be that the child feels hurt. If the parent intended to hurt the child by the comment, the hurt feelings are then a manifest function of the parent's statement. In Chinese families, humility is valued, and often, to teach children humility, parents tell them of their shortcomings and failures. They are often compared unfavorably to other children so that they will not develop a fat head. If children are thus criticized and develop humility, the humility is a manifest function of the criticism.

Likewise, parents may be critical of their child, frequently referring to him or her as dumb or stupid, which can lead to very low self-esteem for the child. The low self-esteem might not have been intended nor recognized by the parents, making it a latent function of the criticism. The parents might exclaim incredulously, "Do you mean that this child's opinion of himself is affected by the way we talked to him?" This thought may never have entered the parents' minds.

A goal of some social scientists is to make latent functions manifest, to bring the real consequences of peoples' action to their awareness. Parents may not be aware that by hitting children as a way of releasing parental anger and frustration they are teaching those children that it is acceptable to take out anger and frustration on others. This is, of course, the message the children receive from what they have seen and experienced. If this function is outside the awareness of the parent, the lesson the child learns is a latent function of the punishment. By telling the parent that this is what is happening, the latent function becomes manifest.

For structural-functional theorists, a primary function of social systems, including families, is to maintain their basic structure, to keep things as they are. These theorists believe that a function of systems is to maintain structural equilibrium. We go now to a discussion of this fourth concept.

Equilibrium—The Fourth Basic Concept

As we have seen, developmental theorists wear eyeglasses with which they focus on social systems as being in a constant, gradual process of change. Structural-functional theorists' eyeglasses focus on systems that resist change. The real world contains both change and resistance to change. These two theoretical frameworks differ in that developmental theorists focus on change and how it occurs through stages, while structural-functional theorists focus on how systems resist change to maintain a structural equilibrium.

The concept of equilibrium is another idea that is adapted from the biological sciences, which see organisms as maintaining what they call **homeostasis**. Homeostasis is the ability of a system to maintain stability within necessary ranges, for instance, of body temperature or of salinity. Adaptive mechanisms maintain systems within these ranges so that the system can survive. Homeostasis tends to be a more dynamic concept than is equilibrium.

Equilibrium and the Status Quo

Structural-functional theorists in the 1960s and 1970s saw the primary function of a system as the maintenance of a structural equilibrium, the resistance to forces for change that exist both outside and within the system. Equilibrium could be maintained in family systems, Parsons believed, if the system could get members to share common values and norms. Equilibrium could be maintained if people adopted differentiated roles, the husband performing the instrumental and his wife the expressive role.

Parsons sounded like a conservative voice at a time when more and more women were leaving the boundaries of the family system to participate in the labor force. The decade of the 1960s also witnessed a surge in the divorce rate, which lent some credence to Parsons's contention that role differentiation was critical to the survival of the family system.

It could be argued, however, that the fact that divorce rates were rising did not necessarily mean that people were more unhappy in families than they used to be. What was happening was that through their gainful employment women became free to terminate an unsatisfying relationship that had existed for a long time. Women were no longer economically dependent upon their husbands for financial support. Previously, economic dependence had functioned to discourage divorce. Women sought therapy rather than the services of a divorce attorney as the answer to their depression and misery; or they suffered in silence. Higher divorce rates were caused by economic mechanisms that made it easier for women to extricate themselves from unrewarding marital relationships.

The idea that systems were equilibrium-maintaining entities became more and more problematic for structural-functional theorists as time went on. The 1960s in the United States were a decade of rapid social change and included the Vietnam War and its attendant protests, political assassinations, and urban unrest. The concept of equilibrium became increasingly difficult to defend, and thus the theory began to incorporate into its language more and more concepts of change, such as a "moving equilibrium." Equilibrium was maintained in a short-term context only. Over longer periods of time, states of equilibrium changed to create an evolution of structural states, much like a movie filmstrip in which each frame shows the social structure at one point in time, but over time, the social structures display change (Davis, 1949:634; Rex, 1961:133).

STRUCTURAL DIFFERENTIATION While evolutionary change was acknowledged by structural-functional theorists, the structural-functional theorist and the developmental theorist tended to analyze change rather differently. Both saw change as occurring slowly over time. Both saw societies creating different social structures in a process of evolution. Developmental theorists focused on change and described how change occurred in stages over time. They saw undeveloped societies moving toward greater urbanization and industrialization. Structural-functional theorists, on the other hand, described societies as evolving toward greater structural **differentiation.** Their language was different.

Structural differentiation involves institutions specializing in a narrowly defined function, resulting in increased interdependence between institutions. It requires highly developed integration of specialized subsystems. For example, family systems in the United States have become highly specialized in the functions they perform and have, as a result, become interdependent with other social institutions.

Because, in the early New England colonies of 300 years ago, many families had to teach their children how to read, write, and do mathematics; had to protect themselves and their property; and were an important element in the religious education and moral training of children, there developed over time schools (and indeed an entire educational institution within society) whose specialized function was to teach academics. Likewise, police and fire departments exist to protect people and property, and churches exist to give children and

(Continued on page 64)

How Alcoholics and Their Families Resist Change

Roles in families with a chemically dependent person are coordinated and interrelated. The literature on families of alcoholics (Brown, 1985; Stanton & Todd, 1982; Blum & Blum, 1993) describes the roles that people play in these families. The roles are unwittingly taught by parents to children (Starr, 1989). Thus when children establish their own families of procreation, they become either dependents or enablers in these families. They maintain the structure that existed in their family of origin. In this way, through a process of subtle socialization, alcoholism exists in some families generation after generation.

The person who abuses alcohol is called the **dependent**. This person becomes socially isolated in his or her family, and as the isolation deepens, becomes more egocentric and self-pitying, touchy and likely to take offense easily. Dependents become angry at everyone, including themselves. They accuse others of not understanding them, not leaving them alone, and always making demands. They have much fear: that they will be discovered as alcoholics, that they will lose their jobs, that their supplies will be cut off, and that they will not be able to stop drinking. They feel guilt, shame, worthlessness, and remorse. As they continue to drink, their physical appearance deteriorates as do their skills, sexual desire, health, and satisfaction with life.

People are rarely alcoholics by themselves. They have others in the family who help them maintain their drinking, and these people are called **enablers** or **codependents**. This person, usually the spouse, is generally very nice, sympathetic, and understanding—a super-responsible person, who does things to cover for the alcoholic's deficiencies. The enabler usually feels constantly tired because he or she is doing the work of two. He or she is also often socially isolated for fear of being embarrassed by the dependent. As the spouse continues to drink, the codependent feels like a powerless failure, who has no control over the behavior. The boundaries between the alcoholic and the enabler are diffuse: When one drinks, the other is embarrassed; when one is incapacitated, the other does the work. Codependency exists when one person blocks the other from experiencing the full negative consequences of his or her alcoholism. Codependent behavior maintains the symptom because there is no reason for the symptom-bearer to change. Thus, by covering for their spouses, enablers unwittingly contribute to the maintenance of the drinking. Parents act as enablers for their children sometimes. When a child has procrastinated, not completing an assignment or not preparing to take a test, and the parent calls the school and reports the child ill, the parent's action is codependent behavior preventing the child from realizing negative consequences of his or her behavior. Chances are that the child will do this again since there was no price to pay for procrastination.

In a family with an alcoholic the oldest child often plays the role of **hero**. This person, often a superior student, a responsible person with a compulsion to be perfect in every way, demonstrates the lie to the outside world that everything is fine within the family. This person is often called a "little enabler" because he or she feeds into the dependent's denial system, which says that there is no problem, that everything is fine. If there were a problem, how could the family produce such a super-achieving child? Heroes often become enablers in their families of procreation, repeating the pattern by marrying an alcoholic and becoming the caretaker.

The child next to the hero often becomes a **rebel** or **scapegoat**. This child gets poor grades in school, has trouble with the law, and often gets involved in sexual activity at a young age. This sibling often distracts attention away from the alcoholic, calling negative attention to him- or herself. Although the alcoholic may bemoan the behavior of the rebel, there is often an underlying alliance between these kindred souls. The rebel may go on to become an alcoholic in his or her own family of procreation.

The next child may play the role of **lost child**. This child withdraws, becomes a loner, concentrates on just staying out of the way, spending much time alone in his or her room, sometimes even withdrawing into a fantasy world. This child is socially isolated with few if any friends.

The youngest child often plays the role of **mascot** or **clown**. These kids are cute, funny, always on stage playing out a theatrical performance. They often seem immature or hyperactive, dressing flamboyantly. Mascots perform a similar function to rebels, calling attention to themselves and drawing attention away from the alcoholic. Stuck in this rigid role, mascots rarely have the opportunity to discover who they really are beneath their theatrics. They have few opportunities to be serious, so they are rarely taken seriously by others.

Although these roles are linked to families of alcoholics, these families do not have exclusive rights to them. These roles can also exist in families where there is no alcoholism. The problem with playing a role is that the role carries with it expectations for behavior that do not permit the player to go outside those narrow ranges of behavior that are consistent with the role. Thus there is no place for the hero to be a failure or for the rebel to succeed. The roles narrow the possible range of human experience like straitjackets.

Once a person adopts a role, it tends to become rigidified, making it difficult for that person to change and break out of the role. Expectations of others help to maintain a continuation of the behavior. This resistance to change is consistent with equilibrium maintenance in structural-functional theory.

Furthermore, many of these roles function to maintain the chemical abuse. The enabler blocks the dependent from realizing the consequences of his or her behavior through cover-up activity. The hero supports the family denial process that there isn't any problem. The rebel and the clown deflect attention away from the dependent. These all function to maintain an equilibrium of abuse, to prevent change. The participants neither want to do this, nor are they aware that they are doing this. The maintenance of chemical abuse is thus a latent function of their role behavior.

adults religious and moral education. Families now spend much less time carrying out these functions than they did 300 years ago. As these functions are relinquished to other social institutions, the family itself has become more specialized in its function of providing an emotionally safe refuge, a haven of peace and protection from the rigors and stresses, the competitiveness and hostility of the outside world. At any rate, that is the ideal. In reality, this refuge does not exist in physically and emotionally abusive families or in violent neighborhoods that intrude on family households.

The family is one of the few venues where emotion can be expressed—where feelings, rather than just ideas, can be discussed. It is one of the few places where love can be expressed, where sadness can be disclosed, where frustration and anger can be shared with others. It is also one of the few places where people can be seen in their totality, as whole individuals, rather than as just role occupants. Ordinarily seen as just a worker in the work setting, a student in school, or a customer in a store, an individual in his or her own family is seen in all his or her complexity by family members.

The contemporary family performs some specialized functions that most institutions in society do not perform. However, this specialization in families—such as the giving and receiving of affection—cannot be generalized too liberally. Although hospitals exist to care for the sick, many families cannot afford that medical treatment, and the family must still care for their ill. Although schools exist, they often fail to educate, and families are left to educate their own children. Where public social institutions fail, families have to pick up the pieces with very little external support. The specialization of function is far from a complete process in this country.

Applying the Theory

In this section, we will continue to apply structural-functional theory to the dynamics of family life by exploring two concepts that are important parts of Parsons's writings: the five pattern variables and the four functional requisites of a system. For each of these concepts, significant additions have been made by this author to Parsons's original work to facilitate the application of his concepts to an analysis of family systems. The five pattern variables are seen as constituting value-orientations at the cultural system level, and are also used as norms regulating social interaction at the social system level.

The Five Pattern Variables

Parsons presented a system of **value-orientations** that influences the nature of social interaction between people. These value-orientations existed in Parsons's scheme at the cultural system level. At a macrolevel Parsons asked how social

Table 2.2

Parson's Dominant Pattern Variables Governing Social Interaction in Preindustrial and Industrial Societies

Preindustrial societies	Industrial societies
Diffuseness	Specificity
Affectivity	Affective neutrality
Collectivity	Self
Particularism	Universalism
Ascription	Achievement

Data source: Adapted from Paul Johnson, *Sociological Theory: Classical Founders and Contemporary Perspectives.* Copyright © 1981 by Macmillan College Publishing Company, Inc. Reprinted with the permission of Macmillan College Publishing Company.

Norms that govern social interaction are different in preindustrial and industrialized societies. How these norms differ can be described using the five pattern variables.

interaction differs in undeveloped, preindustrial societies and in highly industrialized, urbanized societies. He used five variables to discuss this distinction.

Each set of variables constitutes two opposite value alternatives. Every social system makes a choice between the two alternatives that they could adopt. There are five dimensions with two opposite alternatives in each dimension. These pattern variables were functional for macroanalysis when doing comparative analyses of whole societies. However, when doing microanalysis of families, there is an alternative way to use the five pattern variables.

Rather than using the five pattern variables as just value-orientations that exist at the cultural system level, these variables can be used also at other system levels to analyze interpersonal interaction (Johnson, 1981: 403). Consistent with Parsons's belief that there is an interaction that exists at the various system levels, cultural values influence norms that exist at the social system level, thus making it possible to use the five pattern variables as norms at the social system level. These norms constitute ground rules governing interaction between people in groups.

In the following analysis of the five pattern variables, each of the variables will be presented first as Parsons articulated them, as value-orientations existing in the cultural system. They will then be presented as norms existing in the social system and will be applied as interactional ground rules in families.

SPECIFICITY–DIFFUSENESS The first value-orientation, **specificity–diffuseness,** asks whether mutual obligations between actors exist in a narrow context, encompassing only a small segment of the peoples' lives, or whether they are broad-ranged, covering diverse contexts and encompassing the totality of these lives. Do people relate to each other in the specific roles that they mutually occupy, or multidimensionally, using many different contexts? In industrialized societies, when people know each other in a work setting they usually limit their interaction to the narrow context of work, and help each other out only at work (specificity). In families people are expected to help each other out in any context, covering the totality of their lives (diffuseness)—wherever and whenever help is needed.

Using this variable as a norm, specificity-diffuseness deals with the fact that there are usually interactional ground rules related to the question: What can and can't we talk about? The more formal and public the setting, the more this question is answered with specificity.

If you are in Macy's department store and approach a sales clerk and ask, "How was your weekend? Did you go out on a date? What did you think of your date? How is your life going in general? Are you basically happy or bored?" the likelihood is that, should these questions go on for very long, the clerk would soon reach for the security button. You might find this scenario humorous because you know it violates rules of behavior that govern public places. These rules prescribe that one cannot talk about just anything (diffuseness); conversation must be specific to the merchandise being sold.

Likewise, when a student visits a professor's office, there are rules prescribing that they should discuss material relevant to the classroom or to the student's major or minor or to career possibilities. They should not be discussing their personal lives outside the academic setting. Rules of specificity govern the situation. The same rules also apply to a patient visiting a doctor.

One might expect that in a family there would be great freedom to discuss any and all aspects of family members' lives. Parents sometimes say to their children, "You should feel free to talk to me about anything," which verbally encourages rules of *diffuseness*. Yet, despite this ideal, many families have rules forbidding the discussion of key topics, which usually are problem areas for that family. There may be a rule that tells everyone not to mention Lucy's boyfriend, because everyone knows that this will cause a volcanic emotional explosion from father with which nobody wants to deal. Probably there was never an overt, explicit verbal discussion between family members at which they established their consensus. Rather, this rule was established nonverbally; everyone just knew not to raise this subject.

The concept **conspiratorial avoidance** refers to a norm, generally agreed to by group members, whereby discussion of a controversial or emotion-laden topic is avoided. The function of this avoidance is that the problem is just hidden under the rug. The refusal to discuss it leaves the problem unresolved in the system, where it continues to exist because nobody is doing anything to alter it.

In some families the avoided problem may be Johnny's grades in school, Jennifer's abortion, Dad's drinking, or Mom's depression; or it may involve sex, money, religion, or politics. When families cannot talk about everything, they establish rules of specificity. There are some things that members can talk about and others that they cannot discuss.

AFFECTIVITY–AFFECTIVE NEUTRALITY The value-orientation **affectivity–affective neutrality** asks whether actors can seek or expect emotional gratification from a relationship. Family members usually expect emotional involvement and gratification from one another. Relations between doctors and patients, professors and students, employers and employees usually do not involve emotional involvement; they have an expectation of affective neutrality.

As a norm, affectivity–affective neutrality relates to the question "How much emotion can one demonstrate?" Is a person free to act wildly and crazily when feeling ecstatic and happy? Or free to cry if feeling sad? Rules that permit the free show of emotion prescribe *affectivity*. In a family it might be expected that there would be rules that permit members to show emotion.

In many families, however, there are rules that prescribe that only happiness can be shown, not sadness. There may be implicit rules that sadness can be shown to mom but not to dad, because everybody knows that he cannot cope with tears. There may be implicit rules that sadness can be shown, but not anger. The rules are not necessarily overt. They may be implicit rules the family does not verbally discuss or acknowledge, yet that everyone knows and is governed by.

Affective neutrality means that people are expected to act as if they have no feelings. The more formal and public the setting, the more affective neutrality is prescribed.

SELF–COLLECTIVITY The value-orientation **self–collectivity** features a dilemma over whose interests shall have priority in a relationship. Do people function out of self-interest or do they subvert their self-interest to value the collectivity or group? In a business context, people usually function out of self-interest. In relations between family members and close friends, people are expected sometimes to make personal sacrifices for the sake of the collectivity.

As a norm, self–collectivity relates to the question "Whose interests should predominate?" Can a person function out of self-interest or must they put the welfare of the whole, the collectivity, first? This is an issue that often arises when there are teenagers in the house. The teens want to function through self-interest while their parents expect them, at times, to work toward the welfare of the group.

A teen, for example, is expected to mow the lawn each weekend as a contribution to the family welfare (collectivity). On Sunday evening, the grass is thick and high, clearly not yet mown. Parents ask why the grass has not been mowed. The teen gives a lengthy excuse, which is countered by the parents, argued by the teen, and on and on. The parents, of course, continue to insist that there are some jobs that just need to be done for the family to function and that everyone has to pull his or her own weight in contributing to the family welfare if the family is to survive. The teen's job is to mow the lawn each week, and that must be his contribution to the collective whole (collectivity). This is a discussion over the rules of self versus collectivity that everyone has experienced at one time or another. Families expect people to make sacrifices for the general welfare.

Some people even make the sacrifice of staying in unrewarding, unfulfilling marriages for the sake of the group. They sacrifice their personal happiness for the stability and security others get from an intact family.

Feminists may argue that women in families are called upon to make many more personal sacrifices for the collectivity than men are. As Hochschild

(1989) shows, women usually put in a second shift of work after they return home from their place of employment. Feminists may well argue that there is a gender-linked variance in normative expectations in families, where men expect their wives to operate under norms of the collectivity while they act out of self-interest ("I've worked hard all day; I deserve time off to watch TV and relax.")—a privilege they do not afford their wives. The outcome of this perceived imbalance can be divorce, for the wife may come to see an unfair division of labor in the relationship; unless the husband is willing to participate in a flexible division of labor, her frustration and anger may build.

UNIVERSALISM–PARTICULARISM The value-orientation **universalism–particularism** features a dilemma over whether normative standards shall be applied to all persons equally (universalism) or only upon particular dynamics of relationships. The value in the United States that "all people are created equal" and that people in educational or work settings should not be discriminated against because of race, ethnicity, religion, or gender is a universalistic standard. When people are treated differently because of these factors, particularism is operative.

Norms concerning universalism–particularism relate to the question "Do we relate to each other as one in a category of persons, or do we relate on the basis of a special relationship that one person has with another that nobody else has?" A wife may expect to be treated specially by her husband as the only wife he has. She may be disappointed that she is treated like just any other woman in the world. The expectation of particularism may be met with behavior from another that is universalistic. The failure to meet, or at the least discuss, expectations results in relationship problems.

Universalism–particularism arises as a problem for parents raising children. An older child may expect that, by virtue of being the oldest, he or she should be entitled to special privileges, such as going to bed later than the younger siblings (particularism). This child may resent the fact that the parents treat all the siblings alike (universalism). Alternatively, a girl may resent what appears to her to be a double standard, since her brothers get to go more places unsupervised and stay out later than she does. She may seek equal treatment of all siblings, feeling that as the only girl, she is excessively protected by her parents. Here she seeks universalism—all children to be treated alike—rather than the particularism she feels exists to her disadvantage.

ASCRIPTION–ACHIEVEMENT The value orientation **ascription–achievement** deals with the question "Which is valued more, who people are or what they do?" Is it status that affects relations between people or performance and behavior? An employer who chooses to hire relatives over others or to promote relatives within a company over nonrelatives applies standards based on *ascription.* Another example is a merchant who charges less for goods and services to relatives than to nonrelatives. Special treatment is given to some by virtue of their status as family members. In a meritocracy, promotion and salary is based on performance or achievement—a person's competence rather than membership in any group.

The value-orientations of families as systems are akin to those held in gemeinschaft-oriented societies. Both are communal-type systems based upon familiarity of members, in which social control is based on intimate knowledge of people. Social control is exercised in both families and gemeinschaft societies through instilling guilt and shame among members when they deviate from accepted values. Control is exercised through a shared **collective consciousness** held by the group, a concept that means a shared, collective sense of morality. This collective consciousness is important in the writings of the pioneering nineteenth-century French sociologist, Émile Durkheim. People are somewhat more easily controlled if their membership in the group, the respect they get from members, and their status in the group, is important to them. Under these conditions, they tend not to do things that would bring disrespect or disappointment from others. They are not likely to do things that would bring dishonor to the group in the eyes of people in external systems.

Norms concerning ascription–achievement also deal with the question "How should we relate to each other?" However, this patterned variable asks "Does a person relate to another on the basis of status (ascription) or based on what he or she thinks of another's behavior (achievement)?" A person may have a parent who is boorish, rude, incompetent, and demeaning, but that person is still the parent. Does the teen or adult child show deference by virtue of the parent's status or disdain based on what he or she thinks of the parent's behavior? Is the relationship going to be based on ascription or achievement?

There is a commandment, "Honor thy mother and thy father" that is based on ascription. Parents are honored because they are parents, because of their status. Children today are rewriting that commandment to read "Honor thy mother and thy father, if they deserve it." The honor only comes if the children perceive the parents as deserving it, based on the child's perception of the parents' behavior and achievement.

The five pattern variables were originally presented as value-orientations. However, they can also exist as norms or rules that govern interaction in groups such as families. These are not the only norms that might govern interaction in families, but they constitute five areas in which norms often exist. Norms governing social interaction exist in the social system.

The Four Functional Requisites

Talcott Parsons (1937) believed that if social systems were to survive, they had to perform four basic functions, which he called the four functional requisites of a system. Parsons believed that systems could collapse if they had too little of these functional requisites. This author changes Parsons's theory by adding that systems can collapse by having either too little *or too much* of these functional requisites—to survive, social systems must create a balance. The four functional requisites of a system are latent pattern maintenance, adaptation, integration, and goal attainment.

LATENT PATTERN MAINTENANCE **Latent pattern maintenance** refers to the fact that for a system to survive, it must get loyalty from its members, even if those members are not physically present. Underlying this concept is the assumption that members of any group will not be together all the time. They have interests and commitments in other social systems, such as schools, work settings, clubs and special interest groups, athletic groups, or religious groups. All groups must provide periods when the members disband and go their separate ways. During this time, members' commitment to the system must remain intact so that, appropriately, their roles can be reactivated and the system interaction can be resumed.

Parents take the presence of adult children at family functions (Thanksgiving dinner, Christmas, birthdays, or anniversaries) as a symbolic indication that loyalty to the family exceeds loyalty to anyone or anything else outside the family system. That is why they get upset if children are not present at these functions. The parents may come to define a once-weekly phone call as a symbolic gesture of loyalty and thus expect their children to call them every Sunday evening. Sexual fidelity can be seen as a symbol of loyalty, and it is usually expected that spouses will maintain that loyalty even though they are not physically present, as when away on a business trip or conference.

Extremely jealous people sometimes make great demands of their partners to demonstrate loyalty. They may make accusations of infidelity, ask questions incessantly to be assured of their partners' fidelity, ask the partners to check in periodically when away, or ask them to stay at home where they can be monitored. Jealousy can be a normal feeling, but it can also function to drive the partner away, when what is hoped for is to keep the partner close. (The driving away is a latent function of the jealous behavior.) Parents who demand excessive signs of loyalty from children may also drive their children away. Family systems can thus collapse from these excessive demands. They can be destroyed by both too little loyalty or demands for too much loyalty.

ADAPTATION **Adaptation** refers to the ability of a system to adjust to change, leaving its basic structure intact. In biology, the analogy is the sweat glands, which, as an adaptive mechanism, turn on or off to maintain a homeostasis of internal body temperature, for the body must be maintained within a range of temperatures. If the body gets either too cold or too hot, it will die. The sweat glands prevent the internal body temperatures from getting too hot.

In marriages, people are growing and changing, but they often grow in spurts, slowly some times and rapidly at others. Family members must be able to adapt to the growth spurts of individuals if the system is to maintain balance. A wife may be engrossed in an activity that stimulates her intellectually and emotionally, and that becomes the focal point of her energy, enthusiasm, and interest. The ability of the rest of the family to cope with these changes demands adaptation. If the family cannot adapt and absorb these changes, divorce could ensue. Often the family members will put the blame for such disintegration on the individual who has changed and fail to realize their own responsibility in the dissolution. They have not been able to be flexible enough to adapt to the mother's changes, her new interests. Mother may leave not because she does not love her family anymore, but because it is too inflexible to give her freedom to change and grow intellectually and emotionally. This is lack of adaptation in the family structure.

In ethnic families who have recently emigrated to this country, one spouse may well adapt and accommodate to western values and behavioral styles more than his or her partner, who maintains traditional ideas and customs. The inability of the partners to adapt synchronically may place the marriage in jeopardy as arguments increasingly arise in which one partner espouses western values and customs and the other is the spokesperson for traditional ones. The culture conflict manifests itself in interpersonal conflict within the family system.

Great changes are occurring in the economic system of this country. Corporations are restructuring, resulting in the laying off of thousands of employees. Families have significant challenges adapting when a member becomes unemployed. They must adapt not only to the reduced income but also to having the laid-off member constantly present in the household. They must also adapt to the unemployed person's probable mood changes.

Some schools today are reducing the length of the school day because of budget cutbacks. This also requires adaptation by the family, who must now provide after-school day care for longer periods of time, as well as deal with children who may be bored or unhappy at losing activities such as physical education, music appreciation, or art class that were formerly fun, creative, and therapeutic.

Not only must the family adapt to changes in its external environment, but social institutions external to family systems must adapt to changes that occur within families. Since there are more single-parent households due to high divorce rates, corporations are challenged to provide employees with on-site day care for employees. Schools, too, are challenged to provide more after-school day care for students.

Charles Darwin stressed that for species to survive, they must be adaptable within their physical environment. In a competitive struggle for resources, the most adaptable species will survive at the expense of the less adaptable species. Just as adaptability is essential to species, so it is crucial for families and other social systems. Adaptation is a dynamic function because the source of the adaptation does not usually come from the same person all the time. A husband may provide the adaptability on some issues, his wife on others.

Adaptability is a characteristic of the system; it does not have to be present in each system part. Thus in a family, one person may be very adaptable, flexible, and accommodating, and the other members may be very rigid and unyielding, manifesting remarkably little adaptation. The adapting partner provides the adaptation to the system and thus the family may survive, as long as the adaptive person continues to "give in" or accommodate. However, should this person withdraw his or her adaptive function from the system and become firm and unyielding also, then, unless some other system part lends adaptability, the system would be in danger of collapse—everyone functioning exclusively out of self-interest and nobody doing anything for the others.

Systems can collapse from too little adaptation, or they can suffer from too much adaptation, leading to an absence of structure and order, which makes for stress and anxiety among group members. An employee, adaptable to the demands of employment, may be willing to go into work whenever called to trouble-shoot a problem. He or she may do this out of fear of being fired. This can be very stressful for family members, who never know when this individual will or will not be present. Family members may receive a subtle message that work is more important to this person than they are, so his or her unscheduled work is experienced as rejection for them. This employee's adaptability results from the absence of boundaries that exist between work and home—boundaries best established by saying no.

Men are especially likely to accept being more adaptable in their work settings than in their families. They often expect their wives to provide the adaptation at home. As Carter and McGoldrick (1989: 33) state:

> Developmentally women have been expected from the point of early adulthood to "stand behind their men," to support and nurture their children, and paradoxically, to be able to live without affirmation and support themselves. Adaptability has probably been the major skill required of women. They were expected to accept being uprooted every time their husbands said it was necessary to move for a better job, to accept their husbands' lack of communication and unavailability, and to handle all human relationships themselves. It is ironic that women, who are seen as "dependent" and less competent than men, have had to function without support in their marriages, to be, indeed, almost totally self-sufficient emotionally. Women have typically had to bolster their husbands' sense of self-esteem, but have been seen as "nags" when they sought emotional support for themselves.

Weiss (1985) and Tannen (1990) suggest that in marital-couples therapy, the husband is likely to complain about his wife's emotional demands for him to spend time interacting with her; while the wife complains about her husband's emotional detachment, his inaccessibility and unavailability for meaningful intimate interaction. Each accuses the other of failing to adapt to his or her very different needs.

INTEGRATION **Integration** refers to the ability of a system to incorporate all members into a well-meshed, coordinated whole. A family must be able to integrate the activities of its members into a coherent system of interrelated parts. This can be seen in a division of labor where members each have certain duties that must be performed. Everyone's role, whether it is bringing home a paycheck or cleaning his or her bedroom, contributes to the whole in an integrated system. The family must be integrated as a unit, not only physically, in terms of work, but also psychologically and emotionally. This psychic unity provides members with a sense of identity and security. Harmony and stability prevail because roles, rules, and authority are balanced and perceived as just.

Some families and communes have a "do your own thing" value system that does not impose structure or rules on members. There is no assigned delegation of tasks so that the dishes are done when someone needs a dish and finds that no clean ones are left. Grocery shopping is done when somebody wants to eat and finds no food in the house. Nobody is assigned to do the grocery shopping, clean the toilets, pay the bills. This leads to anxiety about when things will be done and by whom. Anxiety can lead to system collapse as people seek to leave, not wanting to cope with such anxieties. Mental health is partly dependent upon our being able to take some things for granted, rather than having to worry about them. When there is structured delegation of tasks in a system, members only have to worry about the tasks assigned to them. They are theoretically free to take for granted that others will do what they are supposed to do.

Integration can be a problem in families with teenagers. Getting them to participate reliably in a division of labor or to participate in family functions, celebrations, or outings, can prove problematic. Likewise, the integration of workaholics into family systems can be difficult, because their loyalty to the job usually exceeds their loyalty to and participation in the family system.

Systems can suffer from too much integration, when boundaries become too rigid, family togetherness too overwhelming, and members cannot get outside the family to get their needs met. The runaway teenager or the runaway spouse may be a symptom of an over-integrated system, in which the family functions as a prison.

In addition, the family that has too much integration creates such rigid boundaries that its members are isolated from community resources. There is little interaction between family members and people in social systems outside of the family.

GOAL ATTAINMENT **Goal attainment** refers to the ability of a system to mobilize resources and energy to attain goals that have been set. In a family these goals might be to purchase a new home or car, to go on a vacation, or to establish a savings plan. The family defines and sets goals and specifies ways to reach them. The family must organize and mobilize resources to reach its goals.

Amatai Etzioni (1964) took issue with this functional requisite, writing that almost no organization mobilizes any more than 10 percent of its resources toward the attainment of goals. This is because once organizational goals are attained, everyone in the organization can pack up his or her tent and go home; there is no longer a reason to exist. This was certainly true of the March of Dimes, which for years sought funds for the eradication of polio. When that goal was attained, the March of Dimes either had to stop functioning or had to seek a new goal.

In response to Etzioni's critique, Parsons made a distinction between long-range and short-range goals. Systems must be capable of attaining short-term goals that they set. Some families have such poor communication that they cannot even define or set goals, and thus they never go on vacation or coordinate to acquire new things. Life in such family systems often does not provide members with much personal satisfaction or fun.

Some families are too goal oriented, as when everything is designed to achieve a pre-established goal; activities are rationally calculated and structured.

In this system, there is no room for spontaneity and fun. Members are not permitted to let their hair down and do whatever they feel like doing whenever they want to. Life is too controlled and contrived.

The four functional requisites of a system can readily be applied to families as social systems. In making that application, a concept of the framework was chosen and applied to families. In the next section, a phenomenon in the real world—romantic love—is chosen, and we explore how it can be analyzed using the structural-functional framework.

Romantic Love

The structural-functional theorist does not see romantic love as a random phenomenon that just happens accidentally. Rather, romantic love is seen as being carefully controlled and monitored so that it conforms to cultural values and social norms and maintains the structural equilibrium of a society. William Goode (1959) articulated a structural-functional perspective on romantic love in his classic article "The Theoretical Importance of Love." The vast majority of marriages in most societies of the world are **homogamous**, between people of the same social class. How can we account for this phenomenon? This does not just happen accidentally!

There are cultural values currently operative in the United States that prescribe that marriages ideally should be between people of the same race, religion, and social class. Court-mandated busing aside, residential segregation patterns tend to promote the interaction of people of the same race and social class and their going to school together. This maximizes the likelihood that people of the same race and social class will fall in love with each other. If white middle-class people marry other white middle-class people, then they will produce white middle-class children; and if black middle-class people marry other black middle-class people, they will produce black middle-class children. Thus, the structural ordering of the society will be maintained.

Social pressures are placed on people encouraging them to date socially appropriate partners. These pressures come from family members and peers. Relationships are encouraged that conform to social norms and discouraged if they violate those norms. Romantic love, thus, does not occur in a vacuum. It is, rather, affected by the appraisals of significant others in our environment. The function of these pressures, Goode argued, is to support the structural equilibrium of the society, a structural-functional perspective.

Since marriage is based on romantic love, there is considerable investment by social groups in having members fall in love with and marry members of their own group. The smaller a minority group is in a society, the more important this is, because in-group marriage is critical for the survival of the group as a distinct entity. Too many intermarriages threaten the viability of the group. Furthermore, if a group has significant intermarriage, it can adversely affect the availability of mates for other members of the group who wish to but cannot find partners within the group. This is a problem for Asian males in the United States because of the high intermarriage rates of Asian females, who are seen

Love and the Pattern Variables

As romantic love develops between two people, the nature of their relationship changes. The changes can be described in terms of the five patterned variables. Their relationship may have been characterized by specificity because their interaction had a specific context; they knew each other through work or as soccer parents or as neighbors. As love flourishes, their relationship becomes more diffuse, and they share and discuss issues that are relevant to multiple roles they play in their lives. They come to know each others' views on religion, work, education, sex, politics, family, and themselves. As romantic love develops, the relationship moves from a value-orientation based on specificity to a value-orientation based on diffuseness.

When they barely knew each other, their relationship had norms of affective neutrality. As romantic love develops, the norms shift to include affect. Demonstrations of love come to be expected.

As love develops, each is expected to become less self-oriented and more concerned for the collectivity, the relationship. Sacrifices may be expected to be made when conflicts arise between self-interest and coupling to demonstrate that commitment to the collectivity exceeds self-interest.

Initially, each related to the other as just another person or worker or neighbor. Bonded by love, however, the parties create a relationship based on particularism, where they have a relationship with each other unlike any they have with anybody else.

The parties at first knew each other based on what each did, for instance, at work or in the neighborhood. Now they love each other because of who they are as people, not for any role that they may play. The relationship moves from a value-orientation based on ascription to one based on achievement. Thus, we see how love changes the nature of a relationship in structural-functional terms in a society that bases marriage on the existence of romantic love.

---

as highly desirable partners by non-Asians because of their stereotyped image as being passive and submissive (Sue & Kitano, 1973). Furthermore, third-generation Asian women often prefer non-Asian males because, with the women's acculturation, the traditional Asian male's limited attitude toward women is not very appealing (Kikumura & Kitano, 1973; Staples & Mirande, 1980; Braun & Chao, 1978). It is thus sometimes difficult for Asian men to find Asian women to marry; with intermarriages among the women, there are not enough women for the available Asian men.

Love and Divorce

High rates of divorce are a latent dysfunction of a society that has romantic love as a basis for marriage. Romantic love is an emotion. As such, it is very subject to change over time. One can fall in love and out of love. Romantic feelings are changeable, and as such, love is a fragile, shaky foundation on which to base marriage.

We learn about love and how to behave lovingly toward someone in a process of courtship, which is often linked to adolescence. For instance, in the 1950s and early 1960s the courtship process started perhaps in the seventh grade, when people first "went steady." This first deep emotional relationship lasted for at most one week. However, it began a series of emotional encounters in which people learned how to enter into and extricate themselves from relationships. They learned how to survive when others initiated the termination of the relationship and they also learned how to initiate the termination, it is hoped with some compassion.

This courtship process was a training ground for divorce. Each romantically oriented relationship in the process was either changed to a nonromantic base or was terminated. The courtship process gave people much practice in entering into and terminating deep emotional relationships. Was it at all surprising, then, that marriage was an extension of that process? Marriage simply involved maintaining the equilibrium of the pattern that had preceded it. And just as all previous relationships were terminated, often the marriage relationship was also. One function of the courtship process as it existed in the 1950s was divorce. The courtship process was not the exclusive contributing factor to the surge of divorces that occurred in the decade of the 1960s, nor was it necessarily a primary factor, but it could have made some contribution to the high divorce rates.

Dating today is very different. Rather than stressing heterosexual coupling, dating today tends to be done in groups. Group activities afford potential partners time to learn about one another in a group context before they ever date as a couple. An invitation to a date is thus not just based on physical attraction, but rather on a mutual appreciation of each other as multidimensional individuals. Often prior to the first date, the couple knows a great deal not only about each other but also about their families. A function of this process should be fewer coupling relationships prior to marriage than existed in the system of the 1950s and less practice in terminating relationships. This may somewhat influence reduced rates of divorce.

Divorce: A Functional Analysis

How does a structural-functional theorist perceive divorce? Since it constitutes a change, it is seen as dysfunctional because the structural equilibrium of the family is not maintained. The theorist might account for this in terms of one or more of the four functional requisites of a system not being met. The system can collapse from too little or too much latent-pattern maintenance, adaptation, integration, or goal attainment.

This theorist would describe in what ways divorce is functional and in what ways it is dysfunctional. Structural-functional theorists analyze the ways

The Dual-Worker Household

In the contemporary intact nuclear family both parents are apt to be gainfully employed in an effort to maintain what they seek as an acceptable standard of living. In the contemporary single-parent household, the single parent must be gainfully employed, usually full-time, in order to maintain a single family residence. Because parents must spend so much time working, the contemporary family has created a network of **interdependent roles**, in which family members become linked to a variety of service personnel who perform the needed tasks that the parents do not have the time to do. Non-consanguineally related people become extended members of the family to help the family do the work that needs to get done. The middle-class family may link up with gardeners, maids, pool cleaners, handymen, day-care workers, accountants, caterers, car washers, seamstresses, launderers, and other service workers. The workers need the family for their income, and the family needs the workers. Families draw on non-kin resources from the community, and these people become integrated into the family system as part of its division of labor.

However, kin also become family resources. Grandparents are increasingly being called upon to function as caretakers for their grandchildren. Extended kin such as aunts and uncles or cousins, can also be called upon for the care of children, who in turn, are often called upon to perform adult tasks. The children become integrated into the family's division of labor by doing laundry or cooking dinner, particularly in single-parent households where their labor is essential. As these children work more and play less, one can talk of the loss of a carefree, labor-free, childhood that is occurring as a function of the breakdown of parental specialized roles. Both parents perform the instrumental function, leaving grandparents to adapt by performing expressive functions. Likewise, older siblings are called on to adapt by caring for their younger siblings.

---

in which divorce is functional for society, families, corporations, governments, and other social groups, as well as ways in which it is dysfunctional for these systems. These theorists would distinguish between manifest functions, consequences of divorce that were intended and recognized, and latent functions, consequences of divorce that were neither intended nor recognized by people.

Divorce is functional for a society economically because it creates business and moves products for many sectors of the economy. When two people maintain a household, for instance, they only need one refrigerator, one oven, one telephone, one set of carpets, one bed. When they split and establish two households, they need two of everything. The furniture business, the phone company, the carpet business all benefit economically. Attorneys benefit from

No-Fault Divorce

No federal legislation regulates family life. Laws regulating families are state and local. Most states in the United States grant divorces today based on the principles of **no-fault divorce**. This means that divorces are granted without assigning responsibility to either party for the marital dissolution. No-fault divorce is often granted on grounds of irreconcilable differences that existed between the partners and that have led to the irremediable breakdown of the marriage. Although it takes two people to marry—both have to verbally acknowledge that they take each other as husband and wife—it only takes one person to divorce. In no-fault divorce the decree is granted when only one party states that irreconcilable differences exist.

Prior to the existence of no-fault divorce, marital terminations were based on the guilt of one spouse and the innocence of the other. A plaintiff filed suit against a defendant alleging that the defendant was guilty of one of several grounds for divorce. The plaintiff had to prove the defendant guilty by presenting convincing evidence to a judge. A plaintiff alleged, for example, that his or her spouse was an adulterer, was guilty of extreme mental or physical cruelty, or was guilty of habitual intemperance (alcoholism), or willful neglect or desertion. He or she had to establish that the partner was an incompetent or abusive or immoral spouse. With no-fault divorce, the courts do not want to hear of abuse or immorality. The evidence of irreconcilable differences is somebody stating that there are irreconcilable differences. Nobody asks what they are.

However, there is still anger, disappointment, and frustration between the spouses. Those feelings have to go someplace. Partners can no longer vent them as they could with divorce based on fault. The anger gets vented in a way that most directly affects the children. Instead of arguing that their partner was a poor spouse, they argue that their partner is a poor parent and thus should not get custody or visitation rights to the children. A latent function

divorce; so do therapists. Realtors benefit because they often sell the family home so that the partners can realize their financial interest. They might also sell each partner a condominium. And on and on it goes, the cycle repeating itself. If the realtor follows both parties in a divorce through their life-cycle transitions, five or six properties could be bought or sold as the parties remarry and perhaps divorce again. Divorce can be functional and lucrative for realtors.

Divorce is also economically functional for capitalist employers who can hire divorced women at minimal wages because the women have interrupted their work careers to raise children. They may not have worked full-time for years. Now they are expected by the courts to work and be self-supporting and

of no-fault divorce is that there are more custody disputes over the children. Here is the arena in which the anger is evidenced. Before no-fault divorce, if the defendant was found guilty, the defendant would not get primary custody of the children; custody was much less an issue than it is today.

As Lenore Weitzman (1985) writes, no-fault divorce is economically functional for men and dysfunctional for women and children, because in California (from which Weitzman derives her data), one year post-divorce, the standard of living of men increased, on average 42 percent, while the standard of living for women and children decreased on average 73 percent. Although Weitzman's statistics have been criticized and challenged, the direction of her data has been replicated in other research (Hoffman & Duncan, 1988).

Where divorce was based on fault, the winning plaintiff received no less than 51 percent of the property and the vast majority of plaintiffs were women. Under community property law, community property is evenly divided by the spouses. No-fault divorce was particularly hard on women in long-term marriages, for their career prospects were not good, given their advanced age. They usually received no child support because the children were adults. They were often awarded minimal, if any, spousal support.

If no-fault divorce is dysfunctional for women and children, it is also dysfunctional for taxpayers who often have to support these divorce victims through welfare. As a function of their financial plight, the teenage children particularly might resort to crime as a source of survival, which would also be dysfunctional for society. The financial hardship leads to low self-esteem for the women and children. This is apt to make them less productive, less contributing members of the society.

The dysfunctional economic effects of no-fault divorce have led some to suggest, not that we return to divorce based on fault, but rather that fault should be considered when financial settlements in divorce are determined. The automatic 50–50 split of community property in community property states may not be in society's best interests in the long run.

---

self-sufficient even if they are primary custodial parents. They have little time to upgrade their skills or return to school or look for well-paying jobs. They provide a pool of inexpensive labor for employers, even if they have skills and are reliable. When they work, they must either find child care for their children, which is costly, or leave their children unattended at home, which is dysfunctional for the children.

While divorce may be functional for employers in the hiring of women, it may be dysfunctional for employers in relation to divorced men, who may experience divorce as their liberation. These male employees may seek to be footloose and fancy-free, becoming less motivated, dependable employees. They may also be less motivated and productive because they may not have to support wives and children as heavily as when they were married.

The research of Judith Wallerstein and Sandra Blakeslee (1989) demonstrates that divorce, in general, is *dysfunctional* for children. They may learn how to be independent and self-sufficient at an earlier age, but they are expected to assume many more adult responsibilities at much earlier ages than are children in intact nuclear families.

Although her findings are somewhat suspect because of the nature of her sample, Wallerstein claims that trauma from divorce is long-lasting and detrimental for the children. Inevitably they experience divorce as a blow to their self-esteem. They feel rejected. They feel not worthy enough for Mom or Dad to remain at home. These children often fear marriage themselves, because they don't want to experience what they saw their parents experience (a majority of these children saw physical violence as part of their parents' divorce) and they wouldn't want to put their children through what they went through. This fear partially explains why people are waiting to marry later in their lives and are opting, in greater numbers, not to marry at all.

Wallerstein believes that divorce is dysfunctional for children inasmuch as children of divorce often have difficulty entering into intimate relationships as adults. The women tend to fear abandonment and rejection and thus distance themselves in relationships. The men tend to fear that if partners really knew them, they would not like them, so the men tend to put up barriers preventing partners from really knowing them. Intimacy involves sharing thoughts, feelings, and self with a partner. It involves allowing the partner into one's life to share that life in all of its diverse dimensions. The fears that adult children of divorce have adversely affect the development of intimacy in their interpersonal relationships.

Although divorce may be economically and emotionally dysfunctional for women, it appears to be particularly emotionally dysfunctional for men. A structural-functional theorist would discuss divorce as dysfunctional for society since it seems to cause deviant behavior, particularly among men. Families function as agents of social control. When people are incorporated into family systems, they tend to conform to social norms more because there are people around to reinforce those norms and monitor the family members, knowing where they are and what they are doing. This discourages deviant behavior. Following divorce, men are more apt than women to commit suicide, to be arrested for drunk driving, to be involved in automobile accidents, or to be delinquent in paying bills (Gilder, 1973).

It may be that, when single, men are more willing to engage in high risk behavior. Men exhibit deviant behavior more than women perhaps because they have lost more in the marital separation than have women. Women have lost economic viability, but men have lost an emotional and physical support system upon which they had become dependent. Perhaps marriage serves men more than women. Furthermore, children, who are more often in the primary physical custody of their mothers, may be in a better position to socially control the behavior of their mothers than of their fathers. This is particularly true of **parentified children**. Their job it is to parent their own parent. This ranges from caretaking to negatively sanctioning parental deviance. If families are agents of social control, the breakup of families in massive numbers in a society will lead to increases in deviant behavior of all sorts.

Divorce creates emotional pain, which is sometimes creatively expressed in new poetry (Hemp, 1979), often literature, music, and art. Divorce is functional when it provides an impetus for this kind of creativity—a latent function of divorce.

A manifest function of divorce is that it sometimes provides relief from the physical or emotional abuse that had existed for a spouse or children. It is a manifest function because the abuse stopped as was intended and the cessation of abuse is recognized by the parties. Sometimes, however, the abuse continues into divorce, and then the abuse is a latent function of the divorce because, although the divorce was intended to stop it, the abusive behavior continued as an unintended consequence.

Critique

Much of structural-functional theory was created after World War II. This was, historically, a politically conservative time. This theory reflects the ideologies that existed in society when it was being constructed. The theory values order and structure, stability and conformity, integration and unity. The theory focuses on the processes that promote these qualities.

Families are important to the survival of societies because within families children are socialized. Families are functional because they teach children the cultural values that create integration in any society. Within families, children are taught norms that govern behavior. Conformity to those norms is assured when parents reward children for conforming behavior and discipline them for deviating from those norms. When parents fail to do this, people from social institutions external to families must intrude to assure stability and order: police, juvenile probation officers, social workers, and school officials. Deviant behavior is seen as dysfunctional to a system, because it promotes change.

The concept of equilibrium is sometimes applicable to families. The concept fits reality when a spouse is seen to leave an alcoholic or abusive partner only to enter into a new relationship with another alcoholic or abusive person. The concept fits reality when a troublesome child is removed from a family only to have a sibling suddenly assume the same behavioral traits as the child who left. The concept fits when people in their families of procreation are seen re-creating their family of origin. Equilibrium states in families are sometimes maintained with great tenacity.

Structural-functional theory, however, has many critics. Homans (1964) criticized the theory for not clearly defining some of its most basic concepts, such as equilibrium. How does one determine empirically whether or not any system is in equilibrium? This concept was generally embarrassing for many theorists, because if systems strive to maintain a structural equilibrium, how can one then account for the rapidity of change that exists, particularly in highly industrialized, urbanized societies (Toffler, 1970)? The forces resisting change must have been overcome by external forces more powerful than the adaptive mechanisms that attempted to create a structural equilibrium. Cancian (1960) discussed the difficulty of distinguishing between adaptive changes, which still maintain a structural stability, and basic structural change in a system. This distinction was made necessary by previous ambiguity over the difference between adaptive changes and basic structural changes in a system. With the rapidity of social change that was so prevalent in the decade of the 1960s, the theory seemed to contain little relevance to the real world, and the popularity of this theoretical framework declined significantly.

These theorists specified not only how phenomena were functional or dysfunctional, but they also specified "functional requisites" that must be fulfilled if systems were to survive. It was extremely difficult empirically to support the assertions that certain functions were more or less critical to survival, in part because it was difficult to assess at what exact point in time a social system no longer survived, let alone to attribute its demise to any particular dysfunction. What plagued these theorists significantly was a **functional teleology** whereby a phenomenon was assumed to exist in order to fulfill its function. In doing this, the theorists confused the concepts of "function" and "cause" (Dore, 1961). Whereas function is a *consequence* of action, cause brings it about, contributes to its existence; cause *precedes* action while function *follows from* action. Structural-functional theorists have been criticized widely for confusing function and cause (Hempel, 1959; Nagel, 1956; Sztompka, 1969, 1974; Isajiw, 1968). The French sociologist Émile Durkheim warned not to confuse these concepts, yet many structural-functional theorists did.

Just because families perform basic functions necessary for the survival of societies does not supply a causal explanation for why families exist in societies. Nor does functional analysis explain the historical process of how particular family forms came to exist in any given society. In a similar way, both Parsons (1954: 115) and Levy (1949: 21) tried to explain the existence of incest taboos in societies by articulating the function of these taboos, such as reducing rivalry between family members. These taboos may be functional, but the fact that they serve a given function does not explain how these taboos came to exist in the first place.

Durkheim tried to legitimize sociology as a unique scientific discipline in the social sciences. He warned that "social phenomena do not generally exist for the useful results they produce." Durkheim (1895/1964: 96) wrote:

> When, then, the explanation of a social phenomenon is undertaken, we must seek separately the efficient cause which produces it and the function it fulfills. We use the word "function" in preference to "end" or "purpose" precisely because social phenomena do not generally exist for the useful results they produce.

Structural-functional theory, moreover, has been criticized for being a politically conservative theory. Conservatives tend to support the status quo; they are generally resistant to change. Structural-functional theorists point out the functions of phenomena and then sometimes assume that the functions justify the existence of the phenomena, and that because something is functional it should be maintained and preserved. Conservatives, further, are supportive of "free market economies" where there is a competitive struggle for wealth. They believe that some people become rich through their initiative, creativity, and intelligence, while others become poor allegedly because of a lack of these traits. They believe that people with high status deserve to be there.

They would tend to justify the high status of a family member on the grounds that that person performed more important functions for the family more than did other members. Males usually had higher status in families than females because the instrumental function of providing for the family's physical needs through gainful employment was often seen in the culture as being more important than the expressive function of raising children, maintaining a household, and seeing that members were happy.

The argument that those who have higher status deserve it is particularly abhorrent to feminists, who argue that patriarchy (males having more power than females in a system) is maintained by the distribution of resources within a system. Patriarchal structures prevent women from gaining equal access to wealth, power, and prestige, which is dysfunctional for the system and for women. It is dysfunctional for the system because that system cannot benefit from the creativity, skill, and talent that women could contribute if they were given the opportunity. Since structural-functional theory often supports the status quo, it is antithetical to the goals of feminists, who seek to change the patriarchy that pervades most societies.

Feminists are particularly critical of Parsons's idea that families should exhibit role differentiation based on an instrumental–expressive dichotomy, because they see this as undermining the status of women in families. If women are gainfully employed, it legitimizes their participation in decision making over how money is to be spent in families. Income is the most important source of domestic power in families (Blumstein & Schwartz, 1983: 53–67). When women are not gainfully employed, it makes them economically dependent upon their working husbands, undermining their status in the spousal subsystem. Parsons's dichotomy is seen by feminists as antithetical to the best interests of women.

Analyses by structural-functional theorists tend to be comparative but not historical. They compare the social structure of family units, for instance, at two different points in time, and often in two different systems, which allows them to describe structural changes that have occurred. However, they do not describe the process of change over time. Because of this, they cannot really answer the question of why change occurs at a particular time and place instead of some other time or place and they cannot answer why change takes the form that it does rather than some other form (Bock, 1963). To answer such questions requires a historical analysis of process over the time and in the place in which the change occurs. When structural-functional theorists tried to incorporate change into their framework by seeing it as gradual and evolutionary, they asserted that societies always changed for the better (toward greater differentiation and specialization that was functional), a dubious assumption.

Structural-functional theorists tended to reify society, treating it as a real thing. By writing about its needs and its requirements for survival, these theorists often failed to recognize society as a mental abstraction that only existed in the mind of the theorist. They further dehumanized the people within societies, seeing them as status-occupants or role-occupants rather than with any humanistic appreciation of their uniqueness or of their feelings. The individual was socialized to conform to cultural values and social norms so that society could survive, so that society could avoid the stresses and strains that accompanied rapid social change. People were seen as constrained by forces at the cultural- and social-system levels. There was greater concern for society and the social institutions within it than there was for the people who occupied those social structures.

Contemporary structural-functional theorists have made some changes to the theory's earlier basic tenets. Because the concept of equilibrium was so problematic for these theorists, the concept was abandoned by some in the 1990s. Structures are sometimes seen as being in a state of dynamic equilibrium (Sewell, 1992), giving a much less static perspective to the concept of social structure. Social structure is seen as a changeable arrangement of interpersonal behaviors supported by changing rules and resources. These resources form a basis for power in a system, but they are not constant over time, as middle-class families who have experienced layoffs and declining spending power are well aware.

A further change, Giddens notes (1984), is that more contemporary structural-functional theorists are generally emphasizing the capacity of people to affect the social structure of a system. **Agency** is used as a concept to denote the ability of people to mold and construct social structure, not just be passive agents of it. Increasingly social structure is being perceived as a creation of human endeavor, rather than an impersonal system that determines and creates human behavior. People are seen as having the ability to define and socially construct behavior in life span statuses such as childhood, adolescence, or old age, and the interaction of spouses as either hierarchically structured or egalitarian. People are seen as having the ability to define families structurally. Must they be headed by a heterosexual couple? Can they be headed by gay or lesbian couples? Is a family a family if it is headed by a mother who never married? Current theorists give people more power to create the structure of systems in which they interact than did structural-functional theorists of the past.

Summary

With the eyeglasses from this framework, theorists see systems within systems within systems. They describe the social structure of systems, showing how they are interrelated and interdependent. They describe ways in which behavior is functional for systems in some ways and dysfunctional in others. They see systems as resisting change as they try to maintain their structure. In order to survive, systems must be able to generate loyalty from members. They must be able to adapt to change. They must be able to integrate members into the whole. They must be able to mobilize resources to meet at least short-term goals.

Integration is achieved through shared cultural values. The values are taught from generation to generation in a process of socialization. Norms or rules exist to reduce deviance, which is dysfunctional because it can lead to change. Sanctions exist to reward conformity to norms and punish deviance from norms. People are seen as having very little autonomy to construct their own behavior. Their behavior is dictated by the social structure, which makes this framework deterministic.

Chapter Three

Conflict Theory

The Focus

Conflict theorists wear the same eyeglass frames—use many of the same concepts—as the structural-functional theorists but end up seeing and, therefore, discussing system, structure, function, and equilibrium quite differently. They discuss conflict between systems or conflict within a system. They talk of the **structure of conflict**, describing who sides with whom against whom. They enumerate the functional consequences of conflict; and, finally, they describe an **equilibrium of conflict**, explaining how conflict is maintained over time. The structural-functional theorist tends to focus "rose-colored" glasses on harmony, cooperation, and integration in systems, while the conflict theorist focuses high-intensity lenses on the existence of competition, conflict, and disequilibrium within and between systems.

In reality social systems have both conflict and cooperation, competitiveness and harmonious interaction. Conflict theorists focus on the conflict and competition, which they see as natural, normal, and inevitable in social systems. Conflict for them is not only functional but necessary to the very survival of social systems.

The Theory

Twentieth-century conflict theory has its historical roots in the nineteenth-century conflict theory of Friedrich Hegel and Karl Marx. Hegel (1770–1831) created a conflict theory of ideas. Whatever "truths" are accepted at one point in time will eventually be challenged by an opposing, contrary idea. Hegel (1821/1972, and 1974) called the accepted truth a **thesis** and its opposing, contrary idea an **antithesis**. The conflict between them results in the development of a **synthesis**, which combines elements of both positions. The synthesis becomes a new thesis, which will, in time, be challenged by a new antithesis; and the process will perpetuate itself infinitely through time. The conflict of ideas is natural, normal, and inevitable.

Marx, using Hegelian theory, interpreted history as a perpetual struggle between those who own the businesses that produce goods and services, the **bourgeoisie**, and the workers, the **proletariat**—a struggle for power and other scarce resources of society. He also saw history as a struggle of ideas or consciousness, because from a person's economic status comes an ideology, a way of interpreting and defining the world. Owners of the means of production will have very different interpretations of the world than will the workers. All capitalist societies exhibit social inequality. If economic status influences the ways in which people interpret and analyze life, conflicts of ideology and perception are unavoidable in any capitalist system.

While the conflict that Marx analyzed emanates solely from the economic realm and is then reflected in other arenas, contemporary conflict theorists see it as arising from a wider range of sources. The first of these sources for conflict is that all social systems have **scarce resources** over which there will be conflict. A second source from which conflict derives is inequality of power. All social systems exhibit **social stratification**, in which some people are more powerful and have higher status than others. This will result in conflict as those who have less power will seek more, while those who are powerful will seek to keep the power that they have. The existence of inequality within all social structures will inevitably result in struggles over power.

Power is a concept that structural-functional theorists do not generally address. They write of status differentials—some people having higher status than others—in the structure of a system. Conflict theorists write much more of power, a dynamic concept that is considered a scarce resource in systems, something to be struggled over, something that may be fleeting over time in the ebb and flow of human activity. Power is based on **resources**, characteristics or qualities, skills or knowledge, objects of value that people have that enable them to generate power over others.

Conflict Over Scarce Resources

In all social systems, there are scarce resources over which there is competition and conflict. In families, scarce resources can include attention, affection, money, time, or space.

Children in families often compete for attention and affection from their parents. Birth order sometimes affects a child's ability to compete with siblings in this struggle. Sometimes the oldest child can use success in school and intellectual and social competence to gain advantage over younger siblings. Sometimes the youngest child, as the "baby of the family" uses immaturity to gain this advantage.

Each of the spouses may compete for attention from their partner with people who are external to the spousal subsystem. Where a spouse is a workaholic, the partner competes with the work setting for time and attention. Where one partner is integrated into a network of close friends, the other must compete against these friends for time and attention. The "football widow" competes against sports programs on TV, and some spouses compete against home computers. Automobiles, golf courses, tennis courts, or bars can all be antagonists in this struggle for attention.

In most families there are limited financial resources. This places family members in a competitive struggle for money. Who gets money this month to buy new clothes? If one person wants to buy new clothes and another person needs to repair a car or a TV set, with not enough money to do both, how does the family decide how to allocate the money? Often, with a shortage of money, spouses argue over it. One accuses the other of spending too much, or a partner accuses the spouse of being lazy and not making overtime pay or not taking on extra jobs.

Families also compete over space or territory. Does the garage get used to park a car or as dad's workshop? Does a bedroom get used for one of the children or for mom's crafts area? If the latter, then the children must share a bedroom. And when this happens there is often conflict over control of that territory. Who gets which side of the closet, since not all sides of the closet are perceived as equal? Who gets which drawers in the bureau, when all the drawers are not equally desirable? Who gets to put which posters on the walls of the room? Conflict over space is particularly acute when there is a remarriage and a stepparent, with children, moves into a house formerly occupied by a single-parent family.

COUPLES—CONFLICT OR CONSENSUS? Couple relationships are often focused on how the partners are either the same as or different from one another. There tends to be more conflict in the relationship when it is based on the complementarity of individuals. Such couples will often argue about who is right or wrong or whose way of doing things is better or worse. They often attribute value to their individual ways of doing things, rather than treating differentness as simply different. The challenge of this kind of relationship, then, is for each party to accept the differentness of the other as an asset to the relationship. The relationship focused on complementarity works when each accepts the other's uniqueness and individuality. This kind of relationship becomes problematic when one partner comes to be defined as someone who is wrong or who has to be changed. When this happens, that spouse does not feel validated for being who he or she is and suffers a loss of self-esteem. Nonacceptance eventually escalates to increasing anger, defensiveness, disappointment, frustration, and hurtful conflict.

Couple relationships that focus on how alike each partner is often manifest themselves as two people who function as one. They like the same music, the same food, the same movies. The norms in this relationship state that there can be no disagreements. Such relationships leave no room for individuation, for each to become his or her own person with unique ideas and likes. The couple may take pride in the fact that they never quarrel, never disagree; but the relationship may be stifling the development of two unique individuals, as they mutually, unwittingly, struggle to achieve sameness.

Inequality and Conflict

Ralf Dahrendorf (1958b) said that conflict was natural, normal, and inevitable within all social systems because all social systems featured **superordinate** people, those with more power, and **subordinate** people, those with less power. The subordinate people will always seek more power and the superordinate people will try to maintain the power that they have.

In any social system, whether it is two lovers, a family, or a society, power will be differentially held by people within the system; some will be powerful and dominant, others will be followers. Some theorists, like Jay Haley (1986), believe that all higher animal species, including *Homo sapiens*, arrange themselves hierarchically in a stratification system based on power and that interpersonal relationships can be understood and interpreted as a struggle for hierarchy and control, as a struggle to see who will be dominant and who will not.

This struggle comes not so much from a desire or need to dominate others, but rather from a desire or need *not* to be dominated by others. The struggle becomes one of preserving self-determination and individual autonomy. The aim is for people to be free to script their own lives, rather than having their lives scripted for them.

Teenagers are often in conflict with their parents. This conflict is the vehicle through which children turn into adults. It is through the conflict that teens wrest their own autonomy away from the parental control that formerly dominated and controlled them. Through this conflict also married partners seek to control their own lives, so that they are not dominated and controlled by their spouses.

THE STRUGGLE FOR POWER Who has the most power in a system is often difficult to ascertain because those who, in fact, wield the most power often appear to have relatively little. Power is the ability to get other people to do what you want them to do. It may appear that weak, sickly grandma, who hasn't the strength to swat a fly, has very little power, yet she can lie in bed all day telling everyone what to do and they will do it. Thus she may have much more power than is at first apparent (Haley, 1986). Through feigned weakness may come considerable power, such that indeed "the meek shall inherit the earth."

It has long been an issue in the feminist movement as to how power should be acquired by women. Traditionalists argue that women, feigning to be "the weaker sex," wielded more power than when they confronted men as equal adversaries. They were taken care of (Safilios-Rothschild, 1977: 50–51; Komarovsky, 1962: 231–234). More contemporary feminists (Flax, 1987; Luepnitz, 1988: 163; Goodrich et al., 1988: 16) argue that role-playing is not genuine and that the apparently weak woman is too dependent upon what the male is willing to give her, that she needs to become more assertive to get more than what he is perhaps willing to give.

In both Asian (Kikumura & Kitano, 1973; Staples & Mirande, 1980; Braun & Chao, 1978) and Mexican American (Zinn, 1982) families, women often publicly show deference to men in their families. Yet behind the public ritual, they may wield significantly more power than is apparent to outsiders (Hawkes & Taylor, 1975; Cromwell & Cromwell, 1978; Ybarra, 1982). Women may have power to influence as well as significant implementation, if not orchestration, power. Orchestration power deals with decisions over what will be done (We will go to the park this weekend). Implementation power deals with decisions over how it will get done (what we will take and what we will eat).

POWER—ON OR BEHIND THE THRONE? There is a difference between the **formal social structure**, what is shown to the outside world, and an **informal social structure**, what really goes on in the system. Often the formal social structure constitutes a **front**, which must be penetrated to know what really goes on within the system. The job of social scientists who study families is to break through family fronts and discover what really goes on in the family. The distinction between formal and informal social structure exists for studying both families and other social systems. For instance, corporations and the military often portray images of what they want outsiders to think happens in the system, when that is a fiction. It may be that it is not the vice president or general who makes critical decisions but a subordinate, who is *really* the power behind the throne. Families often portray to outsiders that parents are in charge, when in fact a teenager or child may have more power in the family than do the parents. Children are more powerful than parents when parents cannot get children to do what they want the children to do—getting good grades in school or being home by a curfew time.

Conflict theorists sometimes describe the social structure of a system by elaborating upon the power hierarchy existing within that system; at other times they articulate the division of labor in that system. They analyze who does what and who serves whom, which is often a reflection of the power structure. There are some jobs that are less desirable than others, such as cleaning toilets, perhaps, or ironing clothes. Who does those less desirable jobs? There are some jobs that have more power connected to them, such as bill paying and money management. Who does those jobs? Cultural values within society influence which jobs within a family are perceived as being more or less important than others.

COALITIONS IN CONFLICT Conflict theorists may also describe the social structure of a system through an analysis of dominant coalition patterns within that system. A **coalition** is two or more people who support each other against a third. Although coalitions may change as topics of conversation change, most families organize themselves around dominant coalition patterns. Normally you can think of someone in your own family on whom you could count to be on your side 90 percent of the time. Probably, you can also think of someone on whom you could count to oppose your opinion 90 percent of the time. Some dominant coalition patterns in a family might be: all the males against all the females; the parents against the children; a husband and his children against a second wife and hers; or all members against one.

The Functions of Conflict

The conflict theorist maintains not only that conflict is natural, normal, and inevitable in social systems, but that it is also functional for social systems. We like to believe popularly that a happy family is one that never fights, which is a misconception that William Lederer and Don D. Jackson (1968) have called a "mirage of marriage." The family that never fights can be more pathological than the family that does, for the family that never fights sweeps its problems under the rug.

These problems are never resolved but linger as sources of tension and anxiety, taking their psychological toll on all family members. All families have problems; people just cannot live with one another over extended periods of time without developing problems with which they must deal (Witt, 1987). In small groups, such as families, where there are close emotional ties between people, conflicts tend to be more intense than in large impersonal groups. Interpersonal problems in small groups often involve elements of personal criticism, ego involvement, ego protection, and defensiveness. Conflict often becomes highly charged with emotion that is both to be expected and healthy (Lauer & Lauer, 1991; Markman, 1989). Antagonism is a central part of intimate social relations; it is a by-product of cooperation.

ANALYZING POWER STRUGGLES The German sociologist, Georg Simmel (1858–1918), laid the theoretical framework for analyzing power struggles in small groups. Power struggles in dyads can be intense because there is no mediator or arbitrator, nor is there a third party to swing a balance of power. Within a dyad each member wields tremendous power because both are necessary for the maintenance of the group. Usually, in triads, a coalition of two against one will win; the twosome will be powerful. This gives us some indication of why only children have the reputation of being spoiled. In a power struggle, mother and father are courting the third party, the child. Whoever wins the child's support gains power through the child. However, children are smart, and usually they will not consistently show allegiance to one parent against the other, but will play this power game for all it is worth, shifting alliances from one parent to the other, protracting the competition for an alliance as long as it is possible. This gives only children power over their parents, since they have something that the parents need and want—support. Children are thus appeased, coddled, and spoiled in this parental attempt to form and be a part of a coalition of two against one.

CONFLICT AS A SAFETY VALVE Lewis Coser's book (1956), *The Functions of Social Conflict,* elaborates on the work of Simmel (Wolff, 1950) and gives Simmel's theoretical work a contemporary reworking. Coser stresses that conflict in families, or in any social system, can serve many positive functions for that system. It can provide a safety valve, providing the system with a mechanism for "letting off steam." Without small conflicts, pressures and tensions within the system may build and, at some point, the system blows apart with a major confrontation. Small periodic conflicts that diffuse tension and pressure allow the system to survive.

Conflict serves to foster communication and interaction within a system, and this is seen by both Simmel and Coser as good. Through their fighting, people come to learn things about one another, to exchange feelings, perceptions, and ideas that they might never have exchanged without the conflict. Conflict often encourages the parties to seek alliances and coalitions that foster their interaction with others, both within and outside of the system. In family quarrels these alliances may be sought with other family members, children or extended kin living outside the immediate household, or with friends, neighbors, clergy, or counselors who are outside the family network.

DISPLACED CONFLICT Coser distinguishes between what he calls "realistic" and "nonrealistic" conflict. Realistic conflict is when one person is genuinely angry at another and demonstrates this anger directly toward the other. Nonrealistic conflict, or what psychoanalytic theorists might call "displaced conflict," is when a person is angry at someone but cannot reveal the anger to that person. For example, a person, fearful of losing his or her job as a result, might not be able to show anger directly to the boss, and might, instead, displace that anger toward his or her spouse or child. The person will sense this as the safer way. In another instance, someone angry at his or her spouse might feel that showing that anger directly would raise the specter of divorce or separation. The anger is, therefore, vented onto a child instead. The child is thus the victim of an attempt to save the marital system.

Coser states that conflict with external enemies can create internal cohesion within a system. Without the external threat, internal divisions and fractures may come to exist. As long as an external threat exists, these internal divisions become latent, hidden. Thus, conflict with an external enemy can be manipulated as a way to create internal cohesion in a system. External enemies might be sought out in order to create internal solidarity. For example, families may coalesce against a teacher who is thought to be unfair, or against a probation officer who is unreasonable. Families may coalesce against a social worker or a therapist. This may not be done at a conscious level but the function exists nevertheless. However, it also slows down the work of finding solutions to internal problems.

THE INEVITABILITY OF CONFLICT The conflict theorist focuses on the inevitability of conflict within families. As George Bach and Herb Goldberg (1974: 324) state, "Conflict within the authentic family is constant and inevitable. . . . Clashes are automatically built in." In *Pairing* (1970: 248), George Bach and Ronald Deutsch write, "From the simplest cell to the most elegant meshing of organisms—the pairing of modern men and women—one rule is unvarying; where there is life, there is conflict." Families can become stronger through successfully completing constructive conflict. According to Bach and Deutsch (1970: 204–205), "In realistic pairing both the initial apparently trivial and extrinsic conflicts as well as the later and more obviously significant intrinsic conflicts deepen intimacy." Simmel (Wolff, 1950: 13–15) agreed that "conflict is designed to resolve divergent dualisms; it is a way of achieving some kind of unity."

Simmel and Bach both imply that the relationship of spouses who never fight should be suspect. Bach and Goldberg (1974: 283) write that "Spouses or any couples who rarely clash are probably relating to each other defensively and superficially. They are either afraid of or unable to reveal their real needs." Thus both theorists agree that the absence of conflict does not enable one to predict the stability of a relationship.

However, not all marital systems have the adaptability required to engage successfully in conflict. As Simmel (Coser, 1956: 157) writes, "Conflict tends to be dysfunctional for a social structure in which there is no or insufficient toleration and institutionalization of conflict." However, according to Bach, people can learn how to fight fairly and constructively and his major contribution lies in his outlining of fair fighting techniques. For him, the content of a fair fight is secondary to its process. The process must permit conflict resolution (Bach & Goldberg, 1974: 379–383).

The writings of Simmel preceded Bach's work by six decades. Bach never acknowledges Simmel's work, but their thoughts are very similar. Both focus on conflict and see within it the potential for rejuvenating a relationship. Conflict can be a positive, constructive experience (Bach & Wyden, 1968).

Applying the Theory

Having explored some of the basic principles of conflict theory, we will now apply that theory to a variety of issues related to interaction in families. We will explore the relevance of conflict theory to romantic love. Intimate romantic relationships involve exchanges of information. When there is an imbalance of resources and power in a relationship, the person who has the most resources will reveal less information than will the person who has fewer resources (Collins, 1975). Once information is received about another, however, it can become a resource through which a relationship can become more nearly equal than it was when it started.

We will examine how conflict can become a resource through which power can be generated. If a person threatens another with intense conflict, the threat can generate fear and result in submissiveness as a way of avoiding the conflict.

Conflict theory can be used to describe and account for intergenerational conflict in families. This conflict exists between parents and adolescents as well as between elderly grandparents and their adult children. Intergenerational conflict exists in many immigrant families as a result of culture conflict. How different generations do or do not acculturate and assimilate into their new culture influences the extent and intensity of intergenerational conflict in immigrant families.

Conflict theory is also used to describe the dynamics of domestic violence. Lastly, it is used to describe and account for the existence of divorce. Divorce can be seen as arising from insufficient conflict in families. Spouses who never quarrel are seen by conflict theorists as having a potentially fragile relationship. There is, however, no direct relationship between the amount of conflict in a marriage and the stability or instability of that marriage (Coser, 1956).

Romantic Love

Randall Collins (1975) maintains that social systems are stratified because people within them have differential resources from which status and power are derived. Resources can be diverse, from money to the occupancy of a powerful or influential position; it can be beauty and it can be sex.

Collins maintains that people who have similar resources are more apt to live near each other and thus are more likely to interact with one another. Social interaction can be engaged in when people are encountered by passing them on the sidewalk, seeing them in a neighborhood market or a local restaurant, or at a neighborhood playground.

Likewise, initial social interactions of people who are of the same social class, ethnicity, race, or religion are apt to proceed smoothly and comfortably as they are bound by the familiarity of common values, life experiences, interests, and information. Collins supports Winch's Theory of Complementary Needs (1958), which postulates that, socially, like is apt to be attracted to like, although in personality characteristics, opposites attract. Collins also reflects the findings of Alan C. Kerckhoff and Keith E. Davis (1962) who maintain that early in a relationship shared values attract people to each other, but, later in the relationship, need complementarity becomes more important to the stability of the relationship.

Collins claims that people with high resources are less apt to disclose intimate details about themselves. The quality of their interaction is apt to be superficial, while people with low resources tend to be more revealing about themselves. People with high resources tend to know many people and thus their interaction with each person is apt to be infrequent and superficial. People with low resources tend to know fewer people but have more intense interaction with those that they do have as family members and friends.

Feminist theorists bemoan the fact that for centuries men have had greater access to society's most valued resources than have women. Men make more money than women when they occupy the same positions in a company. Men have greater access to positions of high wealth, power, and prestige than do women. So, often, in interpersonal relationships the male is apt to have greater financial and status resources than the female (Rubin, 1984). The female has as her potential resources, perhaps, beauty, companionship, support services, and access to sex (Scanzoni, 1972).

Collins's notion that people with high resources are less disclosing also translates to imply that men early on in their relationships with women are apt to be less disclosing of themselves. This is consistent with the research of White (1989) and Tannen (1990) who both state that women exhibit a greater need for affiliation, joining with others.

In meeting this need, women, more than men, are apt to reveal information about themselves as a vehicle for joining with others. Women are apt also to facilitate the process of relating with others much more as equals. Men exhibit a greater need to create hierarchy and to create a competitive one-up or one-down relationship with others.

In our society, little boys are encouraged at a very early age to interact competitively. They are given sports equipment and put on athletic teams as early competitive training. Guns and video games encourage them to annihilate the enemy in a competitive struggle. In that annihilation there is no room for compassion for the vanquished. By contrast, girls are given dolls and doll houses, playthings that encourage them to play cooperatively rather than competitively, to show compassion, and to develop nurturing behavior. From very early ages, boys develop competitive behavior and create hierarchical structures (Who will be team captain? Who will be chosen for a team first, second, third?) while girls develop cooperative behavior and create egalitarian structures. The result of these differences is further explored in the box on p. 96, called Egalitarian Romantic Love.

Conflict as a Resource

The quality of a relationship is one thing; its stability is something else. Relationships may be unsatisfying to the parties yet may manifest a stability because each of the parties refrains from terminating the relationship. Indeed, people who divorce may often have better relationships than those who opt to stay married. The stability or instability of relationships may have no correlation with their quality.

Sometimes stability in relationships is achieved because one or both of the parties fear the conflict that will result in termination. That conflict thus becomes a resource for a person who wants the relationship to continue, since a dissatisfied partner will stay in the relationship through fear or a distaste for entering into conflict. An illustrative case history follows.

PREMARITAL CONFLICT: A CASE HISTORY A young Samoan (some details have been altered to protect the anonymity of the parties) couple came for premarital counseling.

The prospective bride did not seem very enthusiastic about the forthcoming wedding and was, therefore, seen separately from her prospective husband. When asked whether or not she wanted to get married, she responded that she had said that she would marry her partner in a weak moment. Once she had said "yes," wedding plans progressed outside of her control. His parents bought her a ring and a wedding dress and sent out invitations. At the same time, her prospective husband became increasingly jealous of her, asking her for accountings of where she had spent her day, with whom, doing what? Accusations were increasingly made about her infidelity. Her life had become hell; she felt like a prisoner. Did she want to get married? No.

Egalitarian Romantic Love

According to Randall Collins (1975), the more we know someone the more personal our communication with them becomes. Intimate conversations disclose information to the other about ourselves. We share information with intimate others that has the potential of discrediting us should these personal details become widely known. These might include our fears, our insecurities, our failures, experiences that we or members of our families have had—perhaps an arrest, an abortion, the revelation of an alcoholic parent, or our own previous experimentation with illegal drugs. We also learn through intimacy of the other's dreams, aspirations, concerns, goals, prejudices, values, and beliefs.

This sharing of intimate information tends to create an equalitarian relationship when people are bound by romantic love, because the intimate information that is exchanged becomes a resource to the partner. The information becomes a shared secret that further binds the partners to each other. Each is dependent upon the partner's keeping those secrets, keeping that private information that is not meant for the general public.

How egalitarian the relationship becomes is affected partly by the evenness of the exchange of this self-disclosing information by the partners. Wallerstein and Blakeslee (1989) state, for example, that some men who are children of divorced parents will be reluctant to disclose information about themselves because they fear that "if you really know me, you won't love me." They, therefore, often have difficulty developing truly intimate relationships. Likewise, some women who were children of divorce fear abandonment by partners, and thus they tend to be distrustful and cautious, which adversely affects intimacy in their relationships.

Collins's work suggests that intimate, romantic relationships have an egalitarian quality by virtue of the information that is exchanged. This suggests that romantic relationships may disintegrate when the resources of one partner significantly exceed the resources of the other, when the equality of the relationship begins to break down.

However, she felt that she could do nothing about this, because the invitations had been sent and the wedding was to be in two weeks. If she backed out, she would bring disgrace to herself and her family in the Samoan community. She could not bear to endure the conflict that would ensue between herself and her fiancé and between the two families. She was, therefore, enduring and was, indeed, willing to proceed with the wedding. The conflict she envisioned was the groom's resource, keeping her in the premarital relationship. Eventually, a judge, convinced that the decision to marry was not a free decision of both partners, denied the couple access to a marriage license. The bride was rescued by the legal system.

An example of the threat of conflict being used as a resource occurs when partners make threats like "If you leave me, I promise you will be left with nothing" or "If you leave me, I promise it will be without the children" or "You may eventually get the children, but it sure won't be without one hell of a fight." These threats, which promise ensuing intense conflict, are intended as resources by which one person can frighten the other into remaining in a relationship out of the fear that to do otherwise would entail too great a price.

Intergenerational Conflict

The conflict theorist sees intergenerational conflict as normal in families. This conflict, which can exist between grandparents and their adult children, may lead to physical violence called "granny battering." The conflict, when it exists between parents and children, can also lead to physical violence.

Kingsley Davis (1940) wrote that conflict between parents and their adolescent children is understandable because in many ways these members of different generations are opposites and in very different places in their life cycles. Biologically, teenagers' hormones are flowing, giving them more energy and sexual interest at just the time that their parents' hormonal flow is waning, giving them less energy and sexual interest. Socially, too, teens are just starting their lives with youthful enthusiasm and idealism as their parents are seeing their lives peak. Adolescents tend to hold idealistic perspectives by virtue of their naiveté and inexperience in the world, as their parents have tended to become realists by virtue of the disappointments and frustrations, the unfulfilled dreams and promises that clutter the landscape of their lives.

While teens may feel adventurous, their parents are calling for responsibility and predictability. While teens may be seeking autonomy and independence, their parents are struggling to maintain control over them. It is this author's observation that conflict between adolescents and their parents often accelerates when the adolescents are about seventeen years old. This increased conflict, though difficult for all, permits the parent to let go just at the moment when the child is ready to leave home to go away to college or to begin life as an autonomous adult. It also permits the adolescent to leave home with less guilt or ambivalence. Because of the conflict, the adolescent is ready and eager to leave. The conflict thus facilitates the launching process.

Conflict in Ethnic Families

Intergenerational conflict often manifests itself through culture conflict in ethnically diverse immigrant families. When adults come to this country from elsewhere, they are considered to be **first generation immigrants**. They tend to speak the language, hold the values, and practice the customs of the country from which they came. Their cultural identity is with the country from which they came. They often yearn to visit that country, to visit family and friends they know there. Their children, who are usually born and raised in the United States, are considered to be **second generation immigrants**. They are interested in integrating into a network of peers. They do not want to stand out as different. Since they want to see themselves as "100 percent American," they have no interest in the language or culture of their parents.

CULTURE CONFLICT BETWEEN PARENTS AND CHILDREN Often their differences result in conflict between parents and children. This conflict though experienced as personal, between two people, is really *culture conflict* manifesting itself as intergenerational conflict within the family system. The parent becomes a spokesperson for their home culture, its values and ethical standards.

The child becomes a spokesperson for American values and customs. Whenever these two cultures conflict, the parent and child will disagree and argue. The parent may expect the adolescent to attend a family function because that parent values affiliation, integration within the family network, cooperation, and interdependence. The adolescent may refuse, expressing values of autonomy, independence, individuality, and freedom. Their positions reflect the values of the culture each is advocating.

The children of second generation immigrants are **third generation immigrants**. They often feel that to be 100 percent American, to fully assimilate into the social structure of society in the United States does not give a person much of a distinctive identity. The United States does not have a very long history nor a very distinctive cultural heritage. To get a distinctive sense of identity, third generation immigrants may look to their ethnic roots. They may have an interest in learning the language of their grandparents, of learning the cultural traditions, of celebrating the cultural holidays in traditional ways, of learning how to cook ethnic foods, of visiting the country from which their grandparents originally came. Such endeavors might help to give them an answer to the question "Who am I?"

GRANDPARENTS AND GRANDCHILDREN AGREE Family therapists sometimes ask a joking question: "Why do grandchildren and their grandparents often have such close, warm relationships with each other? Because they share a common enemy (the generation in between)!" Indeed this is often the case in families from diverse ethnic origins. Among some ethnic groups, first, second, and third generation immigrants are named: for instance, first generation Japanese immigrants are **issei**; second generation Japanese immigrants are **nisei**, and third generation Japanese immigrants are called **sensei**.

ASSIMILATION CONFLICT IN MARRIAGE Young married couples who are first generation immigrants to the United States may not assimilate to European, Western, or Anglo values and ideas at the same rate. Often one will assimilate much faster than the other. When this happens, their arguments and quarrels appear to be personal. It appears to them that they are quarreling as individuals when in reality each is taking on the values and ideas of a different culture. Whenever these two cultures conflict they will quarrel. So the wife, who assimilated faster, wants to work or wants to be able to go out in the evenings with friends—reflecting the values of autonomy and independence—while the husband, who maintains traditional ethnic values and customs, resists, believing that a woman's place is at home caring for husband and children. This is a culturally based argument, with each spouse's position reflecting a different cultural tradition.

Domestic Violence

One of the problems that conflict theorists face is that they cannot maintain that conflict is always functional. Clearly there are situations where conflict creates great pain and suffering and has even led to massive destruction. It has the potential of destroying all of humanity.

In the decades of the 1980s and 1990s, sociologists have increasingly found the existence of domestic violence in families (Gelles, 1987; Straus & Gelles, 1988). Families are not invariably safe havens. It is not necessarily the fact, however, that family violence has dramatically increased in these decades. Rather, social scientists only recently came to discover it and to report it. Furthermore, violence in families exists in all social classes, and in all ethnic, racial, and religious groups. There is spousal violence, child abuse, and elder abuse (Finkelhor & Yllo, 1983).

THE MARITAL "ABUSE" OF POWER The conflict theorist views violence in the context of power. Once violence starts in a relationship, it usually escalates. It rarely diminishes. Violence can be addictive, like drugs, because it gives the abusive person a high, an adrenaline rush. It is exciting; a person does not know where it will lead, what will happen. Violence is usually a vehicle to power. In the absence of authority—legitimized power—people can get others to do what they want them to do through coercion or force. Likewise, through violence or the threat of violence a person can gain dominance in a relationship.

What resources are available to the victim for gaining some power in an abusive situation? One way is by sharing knowledge about the abuse with the victim's family of origin. Unfortunately, this is often an unsuccessful search for help, because the family of origin usually encourages the spouse to stay in the family system, to stay with the abusive partner. Sometimes this is because family members believe that the spouse must have done something to warrant the abuse or that the spouse somehow contributed to the abusive episodes. Sometimes the spouse is encouraged to "tough it out" to save the family from allegations that they did not raise a dutiful, loyal adult, or to save the family from the disgrace or pain of divorce or marital separation. The victim may reveal the abuse in an attempt to gain support and increased power, but other family members often are not willing to get involved in what they see as a "domestic dispute." They are simply not willing to take sides.

Sharing knowledge of the abuse with friends or neighbors often is also unsuccessful in generating power, for friends may feel powerless to intervene. If they did intervene, they would be met with an injunction to "mind your own business." They are reluctant to become involved because they fear the consequences for themselves; for, if the abusive spouse is willing to do violence to a partner, what would such a person be willing to do to them or their property? Out of this fear, friends and neighbors are often reluctant to make any report to the police.

The abused spouse is also reluctant to make a report to the police for fear that, should the police do nothing, punishment for making the report will follow. If the police arrest the spouse, job loss and jail will probably follow, and the victim will be left alone, financially destitute and unsupported, to parent whatever children exist. Then, when the spouse is released from jail, what retribution will have to be incurred for filing the charges? Only when the criminal justice system intervenes forcefully, however, does the abused spouse get the allies and the assistance that will generate the power necessary to escape this vulnerable situation.

CHILD ABUSE—PHYSICAL OR SEXUAL A similar predicament exists for physically or sexually abused children in families. The resource that generates power for them is sharing knowledge of the abuse with others who will take action to defend and protect them. Teachers, counselors, and physicians are often legally mandated reporters of abuse—people who are required by law to report all suspected physical or sexual abuse of children to the police or Child Protective Services, a national social service agency that investigates allegations of child abuse and neglect. It is only with the force of the legal system that children receive significant power to confront their victimhood. However, they are reluctant to report the abuse to others for fear that those others will be ineffectual in protecting them, and that then they will be further beaten or abused for making the report. They fear that their parent will be imprisoned. They fear losing a parent and being disloyal to that parent. They fear the loss that will be incurred by other family members when the parent is removed from the family. Older children fear the conflict that will result if the parent denies the abuse. They worry, too, about how the conflict will be resolved.

There are forces at work in families that support those with power. These forces prevent abused family members from using resources from outside the family to bolster themselves in dealing with their abuse.

The criminal justice system tends to prosecute physical violence in families because this kind of violence leaves physical evidence—cuts, bruises, broken bones—which can be photographed or x-rayed. However, physical violence is not the only kind of violence that occurs.

VERBAL VIOLENCE There is also verbal violence, where spouses, children, or elders are verbally assaulted and where the damage is not to the body but rather to the spirit, to the psyche. Verbal assaults result in low self-esteem in people who are habitually subjected to it. Verbal abuse can include calling a person dumb or stupid, a fat pig, a pejorative word for someone who is homosexual, or any number of the popular swear words used in verbal interchange.

Resources to counter this verbal abuse are not readily available to the victim because the criminal justice system tends to ignore such allegations. These victims are apt to be without allies who will come to their defense, and the damage that is done to them can be every bit as severe as that which occurs with physical abuse.

Divorce

For the conflict theorist, divorce can be interpreted as resulting from an absence of conflict in a relationship. Not only is conflict inevitable in a family system, but it also can be functional in allowing that system to survive. The myth that fighting in families is a sign of instability in the system—that it is bad to fight—takes its psychological toll on family members, particularly in middle-class families, which buy this myth the most. The family that avoids conflict, that never fights, is in greater danger of being split asunder than is the family that can fight and then recover as a stronger unit than it was before.

It was previously stated that a deep emotional relationship cannot exist without some disappointments, frustrations, and anger. If these are never articulated, they can build over time until, over something that is apparently innocuous, there can be a huge volcanic emotional response that results in marital dissolution. Although it appears on the surface that the reaction is to the immediate incident, it is actually a response to the sequence, the pattern of disappointments and resentments that creates an inner hostility. This hostility often manifests itself as "emotional divorce," a withdrawal from, a pulling away from the relationship, both affectively and sexually.

IS DIVORCE PREDICTABLE? At one extreme, the couple that never argues, disagrees, or fights may come to develop a relationship that is just boring. In this "devitalized marriage," (Cuber & Harroff, 1968) the parties are cohabiting in a lifeless relationship that has lost its zest, its passion. This relationship, devoid of energy, may be sufficiently draining for one party to seek a termination of the marriage.

At the other extreme lies conflict-habituated marriages, which are in constant turmoil. Here, the only way that people know that the other exists, the only way that they do not take each other for granted, is when they are quarreling. Such a relationship is illustrated in the play *Who's Afraid of Virginia Woolf?* (Albee, 1978). When one person eventually tires of the endless conflict, he or she may seek to terminate the marriage.

People also seek termination from verbally and physically abusive relationships, and they seek termination from marriages that have rigid, un-

A Feminist Perspective

Many adherents of feminist theory embrace the themes of the conflict approach, particularly those of power and inequality. However, the context of gender offers feminist theorists an opportunity to exhibit a passion and a camaraderie that conflict theory was never able to generate. As a result, many feminist authors identify themselves as feminists rather than as conflict theorists. Despite this, many are using the concepts and analytic style of the conflict framework. The conflict framework is vital and contemporary when a feminist overlay is applied.

Feminists (Aulette, 1994; Flax, 1982) tend to see families as political institutions. They are political since power, a scarce resource, may or may not be equally distributed. As a consequence of industrialization, work that provided the family with money to meet their physical needs was performed outside of the home. Men did that work, leaving their families for many hours each day. Women were left at home to bear and care for children and to maintain the family domicile. Families exhibited a rigid division of labor where men performed the instrumental function by working outside the home and earning an income. Women performed the expressive function by working inside the home. Men's work came to be culturally defined as worth more than women's work. This enhanced the power of men in families.

Also, in a capitalist system, money is a critical source of power. Men had access to it; women did not. Thus women became dependent upon their husbands for their physical survival. The fact that married women only had

---

yielding role structures where one partner is consistently dominant and the other is consistently dominated. In these latter relationships, there is usually a third party, such as a friend, relative, or counselor, who is an ally of the dominated party, giving that person the strength and support to leave the marriage.

Some couples who have physically violent relationships have very durable, if miserable, marriages. Other couples under these same circumstances seek to divorce. The existence of the violence does not allow one to predict the durability of a relationship. Some couples who have unequal power in their relationships manifest great marital stability while others divorce. Nor does the existence of inequality in the marital system allow one to predict which couples that exhibit significant inequality will remain steadfast and which will divorce. In other words, the quality of a relationship does not, in and of itself, permit social scientists to predict which marriage will be durable and which will terminate in divorce. The worst-looking marriages sometimes endure, while fairly average-looking marriages sometimes end in divorce.

access to money through their husbands prior to the decade of the 1960s often trapped these women in unsatisfying, unrewarding marriages from which they could not extricate themselves. They had neither freedom nor autonomy in this system of institutionalized dependency.

One of the political agendas of most feminists is to promote equality and individualism. Since political conservatives usually focus on hierarchy as leading to stability, and liberals focus on equality and individualism, the political agenda of feminists is usually seen as being liberal (Aulette, 1994: 25). This is a theory that makes no claim to value neutrality (Mies, 1983). It values equality in social systems and individual autonomy. Feminists seek to change the status quo. They have an investment in promoting social change to enhance the status and the political power of women in all social systems so that they can achieve equality and autonomy. Whereas structural-functional theorists held that the male-dominated nuclear family, with a male breadwinner and a female homemaker, was an ideal family structure, feminists decry this structure as patriarchal domination by men over women. Where structural-functional theory had a politically conservative agenda (resist change, promote hierarchy to ensure stability), feminists have a basically liberal agenda (promote change, equality, and individual autonomy).

Feminists tend to focus on the gendered nature of all social relations. They focus on gender as being a basis of social inequality and contradiction within social systems. They argue that gender is a phenomenon that is socially and culturally defined. The interpretations and definitions of men and women

---

OUTSIDE RESOURCES AND INFLUENCES Conflict theorists see divorce as one possible outcome of conflict, which is facilitated or hindered by social structures such as the law, the church, or families. Mexican Americans, for instance, exhibit very low divorce rates. A conflict theorist may look at Catholicism as an institution that provides resources to Mexican American families to mediate conflict and discourage divorce. There is also apt to be an extended family network that provides the couple with frequent contact with relatives who will help to mediate conflict and discourage divorce. The couple, thus, has access to outside resources that will support the relationship.

The mere existence of outside resources, however, does not automatically reduce levels of conflict. The attorneys hired by the couple may escalate the conflict and encourage divorce, depending on the style in which they practice family law. Neighbors and friends may also escalate domestic conflict and encourage divorce. The conflict theorist explores the influences of people outside the marital dyad in influencing the stability of the relationship.

Methodologically, adherents of conflict theory use direct observation as one tool. They also use historical and comparative analysis to seek the conditions

are artificial historical and social creations that are often derived from myths, stereotypes, and fictions (Bem, 1983). These definitions are created and can be re-created by human agency (Chafetz, 1988: 5). Feminists thus object to the structural-functional concept of "sex roles" on the grounds that this connotes a determinist link between biology and behavior. Any link between biology and behavior is culturally created, they believe. Furthermore, they see roles as restricting and confining, denying females the ability to realize their potential as creative individuals.

The definition of woman's place as being in the home has been drastically revised over the past three decades. The increased participation of women in the labor force has given them greater power in their families, because bringing money into the family legitimizes women's power to determine how money is to be spent. Gainful employment has freed women to initiate the termination of unsatisfying marriages because they are no longer economically dependent upon their husbands for survival.

Feminist theorists are generally interested in researching the world from a perspective of those at the structural "bottom," from the perspective of formerly ignored respondents of limited power, from the perspective of working and low-income people, racial and ethnic minorities, children and women (Mies, 1983). Such perspectives conflict with the views held by those at the structural top.

One topic that has been of concern to feminist theorists is the victimization of women in domestic violence (Goldner et al., 1990; Pizzey, 1974).

under which conflict is escalated or reduced. In this regard, small-group laboratory experiments are sometimes used to understand the conditions under which conflict is escalated or reduced.

Critique

Conflict theory arose as a reaction against some of the basic tenets of structural-functional theory. Conflict theorists believe that social systems do not just exhibit consensus, harmony, and integration; they also exhibit conflict and competition. They do not see conflict as dysfunctional, as structural-functionalists do, but rather conflict theorists see conflict as functional, as important in implementing social change.

At the present time, the conflict perspective is important both to social theorists and family therapists. Part of its strength is that it accurately portrays the real world in which we live. Daily we hear news of shootings, racial and ethnic wars,

Feminists have been in the forefront of establishing shelters for battered women and seeking funds for the maintenance of these shelters (Loseke, 1992; Wharton, 1987; Walker, 1979). Often part of the fees paid to obtain marriage licenses goes toward the maintenance of shelters for these women. Feminists have concerned themselves with criminal laws that victimize women when they kill or injure their physically abusive partners. Such laws send these abused women to prison, creating what some may see as double victimization—victimization by the abusive partner and by the criminal justice system.

Another topic that is of concern to feminists is the victimization of women in the welfare system and the ways in which the welfare system creates dependency among its "clients" (Zimmerman, 1992; Piven, 1990; Hill & Ponza, 1983; Tillmon, 1976). Job training and job placement programs, as well as day care for the children of women who enter these programs, are needed to assist women in becoming economically independent and autonomous. Advocacy of such programs conflicts with fiscal conservatives who define them as too expensive as well as too expansive for government to undertake.

Other feminist concerns include a woman's freedom of choice in reproductive issues. Maintaining her freedom of choice concerning abortion is part of enhancing a woman's individual autonomy. Feminists are also invested in ensuring that women receive equal pay for equal work relative to men. Women still earn approximately 60 cents to a man's dollar. Since money is a vehicle to power, this inequality of pay translates to the maintenance of patriarchy in our society (Lengermann & Niebrugge-Brantley, 1992; Gresham,

---

political parties in conflict, branches of government in conflict, and countries in conflict. The approach fits the realities of our contemporary world. The approach is important in reminding us that conflict can be functional, enabling us to overcome despair involving what, at times, appears to be a surplus of conflict.

Yet conflict theory also has its critics. Adherents to conflict theory never established a consistent, clearly articulated framework that contained sharply defined and interrelated concepts. Conflict theorists could not exactly articulate how conflict should be defined, what it is, and what it is not. How does anyone know exactly what constitutes conflict when it is encountered? How does conflict differ from disagreement? Do two differing perceptions of a situation constitute a conflict relative to those perceptions? How does conflict relate to the issue of complementarity? Under what conditions does differentness lead to conflict and under what conditions does it not? There is no clear consensus among theorists as to what exactly causes conflict. There is no consensus about the consequences of conflict for members of a group or for the group itself.

The theory suffers because its adherents have gone off in different directions with different ideas. Is conflict caused by scarce resources or by power

1989; Freedman & Thorne, 1984; Lerner, 1986). Feminists have promoted family-leave policies (Kamerman, 1991) and flextime in the workplace. They have, generally, also promoted universal health care policies. Active protest against the portrayal of women as sexual objects in the media has also been on the feminist agenda.

Pioneers (Friedan, 1963; Greer, 1970; Steinem, 1992, 1986) of the feminist movement tended to be white, middle-class, highly educated women. The movement has historically had some difficulty integrating working and low-income women of color into its ranks. The agenda's emphasis on seeking greater status, power, and autonomy for women was sometimes seen as assuming that women's means of survival were assured. This was not the case for many low-income women, who saw their need to survive as paramount before they could worry about the things that middle-class feminists sought. Furthermore, political activism involves a concern for the future. Only those who have present survival assured can worry about and work toward improving the future. Low-income people are in a daily struggle for survival. They can only be concerned with today, and thus they are usually not politically active. Class and income differences thus fragmented the feminist movement, sometimes creating conflicts of perspective and interest.

Women are further divided and fragmented by political persuasions. The feminist perspective is a politically liberal approach. Politically conservative women often have difficulty supporting the feminist agenda. Since one of the functions of conflict within any group is to reduce the power of the group,

---

inequalities? There has never been the integration that is required for a theoretical framework to be widely accepted within a scientific community. Some theorists focused on racial conflict, others on ethnic conflict, some on class conflict, others on economic conflict. Others focused on conflict between capitalists and environmentalists or on generational conflict within our society. The fragmented interests generated more enthusiasm than did an umbrella framework; therefore propositions were never developed that could integrate these diverse areas into general theoretical principles of conflict that would apply in any setting.

The political perspective of conflict theory stands in stark contrast to that of structural-functional theory. Structural-functional theory is a politically conservative framework. Structure and order are valued; hierarchy is important in creating that structure and order. Parents must have control of their children. Parents must socialize their children, teaching them the cultural values that promote integration, honesty, obedience, an appreciation for education, and morality. The crime and deviance of our times is seen as a symptom of the inability of families to instill in children the cultural values that would create order and

the conflict between these political camps serves to reduce women's power. Power tends to be accelerated when a group is unified. Indeed, as Coser wrote, conflict with an external "enemy" usually enhances the internal unity of a group. But women are not unified in defining themselves or their roles in families and societies. This should not be surprising since they constitute such a heterogeneous group, consisting of different social classes, religions, races, ethnicities, and ages. It is in the best interest of feminists to integrate as many women into their movement as they can, because the more they can do this, the greater will be their power. To do this, goals must be broadly articulated. The problem is that broadly articulated goals are likely to generate less passion than narrowly defined ones.

If political power is enhanced through unity, postmodern structuralists would not give feminists a very cheerful prediction. Postmodernists (Lemert, 1992; Foucault, 1980) see social structures in postindustrial societies as becoming decentered, losing unity by splintering into special interest groups that compete with one another for power. Power cannot be achieved by any single group, but rather is gained by the ability of any group to gain alliances and support from other groups to further its cause. If the postmodern view is accurate, the feminist movement may come to subdivide into caucuses (for example, African American, Mexican American, Asian), each promoting its own special concerns and agendas. As a developmental theorist might say, this may be the challenge facing the feminist movement at this stage in its development—to maintain its agenda in the face of fragmenting interests.

---

harmony. Structural-functional theory is politically conservative because it sees conflict as dysfunctional since as it often leads to social change.

Conflict theory tends to be a politically liberal perspective. The hierarchy that exists in industrialized societies is a patriarchy, and thus women are dominated by men, and children are dominated by their parents. Conflict is seen as functional in part because it leads to change, change that would promote equality in families and other social institutions. This would liberate women and children, and racial and ethnic minorities from the dominance and injustices of a largely white, male-dominated social structure. Greater individual autonomy, rather than hierarchical control, would free all people to realize their potential and become who they want to be. The society would be seen as enriched by the increasing diversity of lifestyles that accompanies individual autonomy.

Structural-functional theorists would critique feminist theory on several grounds. In focusing on the gender-based experience of reality and power/resource dynamics between men and women, it constitutes a special interest theory, promoting only the interests of women. As such, it promotes gender-based divisiveness within social structures, undermining the integration of those structures.

In promoting conflict that challenges the hierarchical structure in all social institutions—economic, political, military, religious, and family—feminist theory promotes social change. Such changes prove dysfunctional, inasmuch as there is a lag where social systems cannot adapt and adjust to those changes. Examples of dysfunctional adaptation might include increasing numbers of unemployed or underemployed men as well as unsupervised youth.

Structural-functionalists might also argue that hierarchy is critical to the stability of social systems and that egalitarian social structures are inherently unstable over time (Look at the political instability of troikas, for instance). Valuing equilibrium and stability, they would argue that hierarchy is necessary for stability.

In structural-functional theory and in conflict theory, political ideologies are reflected in their discrepant orientations toward social change, hierarchy versus equality, consensus versus conflict, and social control versus individual autonomy.

Summary

Conflict theorists see conflict as natural, normal, and inevitable in all social systems. Conflict arises, in part, because all social systems have scarce resources over which conflict will arise. In families these scarce resources include time, money, space, attention, affection, and love.

All social systems exhibit social stratification in which some people have more power than others and in which there will be an inevitable struggle over power that will create conflict. People have resources that they use in relationships as vehicles for generating power. Resources can include money, sex, information, labor, submission, or physical presence.

Conflict is functional; it is essential to the survival of systems. Without mechanisms for "letting off steam," resentments, disappointments, and frustrations can build up to create a colossal emotional explosion at some point in time, which has the potential of destroying relationships. Through conflict with "outsiders," internal cohesion is created within a system, which can be functional for the integration of that system.

Part Two

Bringing People Back In

The two frameworks that we will now explore emphasize the power of people to create their own behavior through their ability to think, to interpret, and to give meaning to their external world. In both social exchange theory and symbolic interaction theory there is an interaction between the individual and the external environment. Individuals have the ability to carve out behavior based upon their own thoughts and feelings.

Both theories have in common the attempt to understand human behavior and to answer the question of why people behave as they do. That understanding involves probing the definitions and interpretations made by actors. It is the individual's ability to give meaning to objects and events that enables people to construct their own behavior.

Chapter 4

Social Exchange Theory

Chapter 5

Symbolic Interaction Theory

Chapter Four

Social Exchange Theory

The Focus

George Homans is generally acknowledged as the person who brought social exchange theory into the discipline of sociology. Homans (1958; 1961) believed that, despite cultural differences, there existed in societies throughout the world some universals that characterized human nature everywhere. He was attracted to the concept of behaviorism in psychology, and this led him to the belief that one universal of all human behavior was that it would recur through **positive reinforcement** and would be discouraged or eliminated through **negative reinforcement**. He believed that sociology should be less concerned with the analysis of social structures and institutions and more focused on the dynamics of reinforcement in order to understand recurrent patterns of human behavior. Let us try on Homans's spectacles and examine his ideas, focusing, along with him, on social behavior in the context of individual choice-making.

The Theory

The essence of Homans's work was to apply the principles of operant learning theory to social behavior. In this process people construct their own behavior through the application of rational thought. They seek to maximize their rewards and minimize their costs. Social behavior is shaped by reinforcement contingencies, where previous experiences (rewarding or painful) in similar situations shape a person's predisposition toward action. In the rational process, the individual assesses the value of rewards as well as the likelihood of obtaining rewards through any given line of action.

Homans predicted that people will be attracted to those who possess desirable qualities or characteristics, such as people who have high income, status, or prestige or people who are physically attractive. Being in the presence of such people will usually be perceived as rewarding.

The qualities or characteristics that are valued in people will differ greatly from culture to culture. In some cultures, for instance, Korea, Turkey, and Tsarist Russia (Monbeck, 1974: 47), blind people were revered for having special powers, particularly prophesy, which is very different from the value system in many western European cultures. Youthfulness is a quality that tends to be valued in the United States, while in other cultures, the elderly are revered for the wisdom they have acquired through their long life experience.

Whether or not a person approaches someone with valued characteristics will be influenced by his or her previous experiences in approaching such people. If those experiences were not rewarding in the past, the person may be reluctant to perpetuate what he or she perceives as negative experiences. One does not blindly seek to maximize rewards in situations. Rather, the search for rewards is mediated by an individual's appraisal of the likelihood of success in obtaining those rewards and his or her experience in similar situations.

Exchange theorists expect each individual in a relationship to maximize rewards and minimize costs within the limits of what each sees as attainable (Emerson, 1976). However, the expectations people have are not exclusively focused on self-interest. People also hold expectations about the relationship. They expect it to be fair, just, and nonexploitive or abusive. The concept of distributive justice introduces the expectations that people hold about the interdependence and interrelatedness of the parties in a relationship.

Distributive Justice

Homans focused on interpersonal relationships between people, and he found that the expectation of each party is that both will be mutually rewarded; these norms of reciprocity prescribe that the relationship should be mutually gratifying. Homans also cited his **rule of distributive justice**, which is an expectation that the rewards to each person in a relationship will be proportional to the respective costs of each and that the net result for each person will be proportional to each's investment in the relationship. If this rule is perceived as having been violated, the disadvantaged person will feel angry and the advantaged person will sometimes feel guilty. For both parties, their feelings will reduce their positive experience in the relationship and will, therefore, adversely affect the stability of the relationship. Stability of relationships, for Homans, is dependent upon each party's perception that the rule of distributive justice is being maintained in the relationship.

Teenagers or young adults may choose to leave their parents' home when they perceive that their rewards are not equal to their investments in living with their parents. The parents may ask the child to leave when the rewards they are receiving as a result of the child's living with them are not commensurate with what it is costing them. From younger people's perspective, rewards may include a place to live rent free or, if they are paying rent, a residence for a significantly better price than they could otherwise obtain. There may also be a reward in the fact that food is purchased and available for them at little or no cost. A further reward may be that laundry is often done for them. The companionship of parents is also available when and if they need it. Further for some young people, it might be more comfortable to live with parents rather than to find a roommate, a stranger, with whom they would have to co-exist amicably.

Living with one's parents, however, may come at considerable cost. Freedom and autonomy are lost by living with parents who ask too many questions about a child's comings and goings. Children may believe that if they were living apart from the parents, they would not have to endure aggravating questions. Further, there is the cost of receiving negative sanctions when things occur of which the parents do not approve. Such sanctions may be seen by the young adults as attempts by controlling parents to keep them children. Such sanctions are a cost of living with parents who cannot or will not stop being parental. Another cost of living with parents may involve living by parental rules, including not leaving dirty dishes in the kitchen sink or not leaving dirty clothes on the bedroom or bathroom floor. When such rules are violated, there is negative feedback by the frustrated parents, which the young people would not have to endure if they moved out. If, in the mind of the teenager or adult child, the costs of living with their parents exceed the rewards of this arrangement, he or she will leave the parental home and seek residence elsewhere.

From the parents' perspective, the rewards of having the child live with them may include the satisfaction of playing the nurturing parent, having someone to care for so that one feels competent, worthy, needed, and appreciated. Another reward may be having the companionship of the child, someone to interact with in the absence of an available, compassionate, intimate spouse. A reward may also come from living with someone who brings enthusiasm, energy, optimism, and fun to the household. The child's friends coming to the house may provide the household with entertainment and diversion that would otherwise be absent.

On the other hand, living with the child may come at considerable cost to the parents. There is the frustration and aggravation that comes from rules being consistently broken. There also may be the cost of frustration and aggravation that comes from a feeling of being taken for granted, unrecognized, and unappreciated for all one does for the child. There are the financial costs of greater utility bills, phone bills, clothing and food bills, which are even more costly emotionally when the child is being wasteful through negligence, not caring, or incompetence. The cost may come when loss of control leads to a feeling of low self-esteem, particularly with a child who is openly defiant or hostile. Emotional costs may translate into physical ones, such as when tension results in high blood pressure, sleep disorders, or digestion troubles. When the parent feels that the costs of having the adolescent in the home outweigh the rewards, the parent may ask the child to leave. The co-residential arrangement will only be maintained when rewards are seen as at least equaling costs by both parents and children.

From a social exchange theory perspective, children living with their parents is a voluntary arrangement that is made by all parties. Urban centers are filled with teens who either opted to leave the parental home or who have been kicked out. Children live with their parents when both children and parents perceive that this arrangement has more rewards than costs to each of them, when each perceives that there is distributive justice in the arrangement.

Other aspects of relationships that exchange theorists consider are profit, fairness, and equity. How much profit to each participant is a relationship generating? How fair is it to each person? Are there rewards for each of the parties?

Profit, Fairness, and Equity

The work of Peter M. Blau (1964) is built upon and extends the work of Homans. Blau worked more with economic principles than with operant conditioning. He saw people in a competitive marketplace where they would enter into relationships that were seen as maximizing their profit. **Profit** was defined as rewards minus costs. In Blau's concept, the consideration of rewards, costs, expectations, and available alternatives are all part of the process. People select relationships and behavior from potential alternatives by mentally ranking actual and expected experiences and selecting those that will maximize their profit.

In the profit theory, rewards exist in four categories: money, social approval, esteem or respect, and compliance. Esteem and compliance are generally more valued rewards than are money or social approval.

Fairness theory, on the other hand, involves norms that govern social interaction. Blau, for example, cites a **norm of reciprocity** and a **norm of fairness**. Early in a relationship, people share rewards. Over time, expectations develop that they should also share obligations, such as to be available for support. The more people interact, the more they expect a mutual sharing of obligations and rewards. These expectations constitute a norm of reciprocity. If, over time, obligations and rewards are mutually reciprocated, trust develops between the parties. If reciprocity is not an ongoing part of the relationship, suspicion and distrust occur, which can adversely affect intimacy and stability. Expectations also exist between parties that there will be fairness in the proportion of rewards to costs in the relationship. This is the norm of fairness, much like Homans's concept of distributive justice. Negative sanctions may result from a violation of this norm, which may adversely affect the quality of the relationship for both parties.

Distributive justice and fairness exist for both Homans and Blau when one person's perceived investment in another is equivalent to the profits derived from the relationship, irrespective of the other's perceived or actual ratio of investments to profits. The evaluation for Homans and Blau is intrapersonal, not comparative, between people in the relationship.

Equity theory, on the other hand, involves an interpersonal analysis of investments and profits. There is a difference between Homans's use of "distributive justice" and Blau's use of "fairness" and the way that equity theorists use "equity" (Adams, 1965; Walster et al., 1978). For the latter, the unit of analysis is the comparison of each person's ratio of investments to profits. **Equity** exists when the ratio of investments to profits is similar or proportional for all parties. The comparison is, thus, interpersonal.

Let us now turn to an exploration of the relationship between costs, rewards, profits, and power. The distribution of costs and rewards in a relationship influences the power structure in that relationship.

Power

Blau refers to the ability to extract compliance through the control of rewards and resources as power. The person in a marriage who has the most resources generally has greater access to power, particularly in the area of decision making. Robert Blood and Donald Wolfe (1960) and Wesley Burr (1973) show how husbands generally have control over their wives because of their greater access to the valued resources of money, occupational status, and prestige. Generally, women who are gainfully employed have greater decision-making power in their families than do women who are not gainfully employed, because these working women provide resources of money and occupational status that legitimize their right to say how money is to be spent.

The work of Thibaut and Kelley (1959) adds complex concepts to exchange theory. Their concept is that in dyadic relationships, in addition to concern with maximizing his or her own rewards, each person also has to consider contributing to rewards for the other. In order to obtain rewards for oneself in a dyadic relationship, some of the needs of the partner must also be fulfilled, and thus concern for meeting the partner's needs must be taken into account. Since neither partner can afford to be self-centered and selfish, for a dyadic relationship to work, both partners must be mutually reliant on each other in order to achieve rewarding outcomes.

Dependence and Power

Issues of dependence and interdependence become very important because all exchange relationships involve dependence. **Dependence** relates to stability in relationships. The more a person perceives that the rewards they receive from a relationship cannot be obtained in any alternative relationship, and the more a person wants those rewards, the more dependent that person is. The more dependent a person is in a relationship, the less likely he or she is to leave.

Dependence also relates to power (Emerson, 1962). The more dependent a person is on a relationship to meet his or her needs, the less power he or she is apt to have in the relationship. Safilios-Rothschild (1977) discusses love power by stating that in all dyadic relationships one person is more emotionally invested than is the partner. Rarely do two people have an equal emotional investment in a relationship. Usually one loves more, the other less. The one who loves more, the one who is more emotionally invested in the relationship, needs the presence of the love object more than does the person who loves less. The one who loves more is more dependent and thus more likely to be submissive. Submission is a resource for keeping the loved one happy, for keeping that person around, and for maintaining the stability of the relationship.

Jean E. Veevers (1988) used the principles of dependency and power to explore demographic data in Canada that showed the life expectancy of men to be considerably shorter than the life expectancy of women. As women get older, the pool of available single males becomes smaller. This lessens the likelihood that women who terminate their marriages can expect to find an alternative marital partner and increases the dependence of women upon their current husbands. This dependence, Veevers states, is apt to make women submissive in their marriages, as a method of keeping their husbands from leaving them. Veevers's work is based on the perception among women that married life carries more rewards than does life as a single person. The issue of dependence raises the suggestion that people will stay in unsatisfying relationships if there is little likelihood that a better alternative is available.

Thibaut and Kelley (1959) discuss strategies that people can use to reduce an imbalance of power created through dependence. Less powerful people can seek alternative sources of rewards that are not supplied by their partner, or they can reduce their partner's alternative sources of reward; they can also improve their ability to provide rewards, or they can reduce their partner's ability to provide rewards; finally, they can persuade the partner of the value of the resources that they bring to the relationship, or they can downplay the value of the resources that their partner brings to the relationship.

For example, a person might seek gainful employment or volunteer work as an alternative source of companionship and stimulation thereby reducing dependence on a partner for these. The advantage of gainful employment or of a better job, which offers more income, status, or prestige, is that it would enhance the value of the resources that person brings to the relationship, thus enhancing his or her power in the relationship.

Another approach might be to suggest that the partner reduce his or her involvement in external activities, thereby reducing the partner's alternative sources of reward, increasing the partner's dependence in the marital relationship, and ultimately weakening the partner's power in the relationship. Jealous partners tend to do this. The person who expresses jealousy is dependent, needing the love object around to meet his or her own needs. To equalize the dependency in the relationship, the jealous person seeks to increase the dependency of the partner in the relationship.

When a person expresses the existence of jealous feelings, the revelation is usually accompanied by an implicit command that the partner not trigger those feelings. There is an implicit or explicit demand that the partner not associate with people who might cause the mate to experience jealous feelings. This reduces the field of acceptable friends and associates, making the partner more dependent on the relationship to meet his or her personal needs, which, in turn, enhances the power of the jealous person. The jealous partner is needed more in the absence of others who might have met the partner's needs. The more that the jealous person is needed by his or her partner, the less likely it is that the partner will leave the relationship, in part, because there are fewer alternatives available that are better than the relationship.

PERCEPTION AND EXCHANGE THEORY A critical part of exchange theory is that what constitutes costs or rewards, in addition to their value, is a matter of *perception*. Even if the value of costs or rewards could objectively be measured, it would be irrelevant because people base their behavior on a subjective assessment of how important a reward is or how painful a cost is. As Thibaut and Kelley (1959) maintain, a person's perception is subject to change over time, and perception between two different people may be at considerable variance.

A husband may perceive that bringing in an income is a huge reward that he contributes to a relationship. His wife may see the income as less rewarding, because to earn it her husband has spent a great amount of time away from home. In addition, when he was at home, the husband often might have been preoccupied mentally with thoughts of his work; or he might have been stressed, frustrated, and fatigued because of it. The quality of the time he did spend with his family, therefore, could have been affected adversely by his work.

Also since, as a woman, she values affiliation—time spent together interacting, relating—much more than she values money, the time her husband spends working, away from family, and the emotional stress and fatigue that result from work are huge costs for her that are subtracted from the monetary rewards. Because he, as a man, values affiliation less (Tannen, 1990; White, 1989; England, 1989), our hypothetical husband does not see things in the same way. If the couple would take the time to discuss this conflict, each from his or her own perspective, each would be able to influence the other about what value money has in their relationship.

Expectations

People bring to new experiences their expectations that are based on similar past experiences. Furthermore, their expectations are influenced by the experience of other people—family and friends—in similar relationships. These expectations will influence how people interpret and define the goodness of a given outcome. Thibaut and Kelley (1959) developed the concept of a **comparison level**. This is a standard by which people evaluate the rewards and costs of a relationship in terms of what they thought the relationship should bring them.

Relationships are evaluated as falling above the comparison level if they are more rewarding than was expected or if they are more rewarding than most other people's experience. Relationships falling above the comparison level are experienced as satisfying and attractive. Relationships that are evaluated as falling below the comparison level have fewer rewards than was expected or fewer rewards than in other people's experience. These are experienced as unsatisfactory and unattractive.

Expectations for a relationship are related to a person's level of satisfaction with the relationship; each influences the other. The greater one's level of satisfaction with a relationship, for instance, the more one is apt to invest in it—in terms of time, money, emotional energy, and self-revelation. The more one emotionally invests in the relationship, the more one's expectations are apt to increase. If the relationship is to be stable, the rewards from the relationship must also increase to match these high expectations. If they are not met, the person will be disappointed and frustrated and begin to invest less in the relationship. Farson (1974) maintains that extremely good relationships are often fragile because the partners establish such high expectations from their experience in the relationship that those expectations are eventually bound to be frustrated.

CULTURAL ISSUES AND LEVELS OF EXPECTATION Cultural issues affect levels of expectation relative to marital relationships. It has been noted that African Americans exhibit high divorce rates and high rates of marital separation compared to white Americans (Cherlin, 1981: 99, 107; Collins & Coltrane, 1991: 240–250). Wilson and Neckerman (1986: 237) cite that 22 percent of all married black wives are separated from their husbands. Collins and Coltrane (1991) primarily attribute this to the overrepresentation of African Americans in the working and low-income classes. It is much easier for African American women to find gainful employment than it is for African American men. The economic hardships faced by African American families contribute to stress and conflict in these families, leading to increased separation and divorce (Scanzoni, 1977: 336).

Given this, African American women tend to have low expectations for marital success. Partly as a result of these low expectations, they are apt to marry later than do whites and they are more apt to have nonmarital childbirth than do whites. (Low expectations are also due partly to an unbalanced sex ratio among young African Americans—fewer males are available as potential partners to the number of available females.)

If African American women have low expectations for the success of marriage, based on the experience of their friends and relatives, they may be less willing to make substantial investments into romantic relationships, because they see little likelihood of these having much permanence. By the norm of reciprocity, if the women are not willing to invest much in the relationship, the men may not make much investment either, which will adversely influence the level of intimacy between them. If neither makes high levels of investment, neither is apt to experience significant rewards in the relationship, which adversely affects the stability of the relationship. The situation is almost a self-fulfilling prophecy. This scenario is enhanced by the fact that as a legacy of African culture, the role of mother in African American families is often valued more than is the role of wife.

A counter argument, based on the work of Thibaut and Kelley, is that if expectations for success in marriage are low for African American women, there is, then, a greater likelihood that they will experience their actual situation as better than what they thought it would be. When their experience of reality, therefore, lies above the "comparison level," they should experience their relationship as satisfying. This may explain the relationships that maintain stability.

Romantic Love in the Marriage Marketplace

What makes for what we call a "good marriage" for an individual, when analyzed by a social exchange theorist? What does it mean when we say he or she "married well"? Often it means that in our estimation, the individual in question married someone with at least equal if not more status, prestige, or power than the individual we have as a point of reference. Blau created an exchange theory based on economics. People have a market value, on the basis of qualities they have that are advantageous or detrimental. Everyone comes to the marriage market with a value, based on family background and the status one's family holds in the community. Market value is also guided by one's physical appearance (handsomeness, beauty, ugliness all have their values). One's career potential and training affect one's market value. Marriage can be seen as an exchange of market values that each party brings with them.

Mate selection thus involves maximizing one's likely rewards by considering alternative partners and the likely, anticipated costs and rewards that would exist for us with each of those partners. We interact with many people, some of whom are more valued than others. We may not seek out the most highly valued people available, based on an assessment that we probably would not have a very successful long-term relationship with such a person. Our prospects of success coupled with the risks of being hurt, abandoned, rejected, or exploited by such a person may discourage us from seeking the highest alternative partners that might be available. Thus we may not seek to maximize our rewards for fear of incurring likely costs. Rather, we may seek out someone slightly less desirable, but someone with whom a successful, mutually satisfying, long-term relationship is more likely to occur.

Applying the Theory

An important advantage of exchange theory is its versatility. It is widely applicable to a variety of phenomena. In this section, we will use the theory to analyze many of these life situations. Let us look first at romantic love through the eyeglasses of the exchange theorist.

Romantic Love

Romantic love is seen by exchange theorists as following from a person perceiving that he or she is getting a high ratio of rewards at very little cost. The following example explains how this works out in practice. When Marcia first begins to date John she has the experience of feeling great. She has a wonderful time on dates. Feeling excited and enthusiastic, she experiences an emotional high. She feels good about herself and her life. This all seems to come at relatively no cost to her.

To exchange theorists, the ratio of rewards to costs affects how we *feel* about people. We come to like or love someone who brings us maximum rewards at minimal cost. Our emotions and feelings about people follow from our perception of the costs and rewards they bring us. We like people who maximize our rewards.

The rewards that accompany feelings of being romantically in love are similar to the feelings one sometimes gets when under the influence of mind-altering drugs. There are feelings of a high energy rush, excitement, and euphoria. Love, like drugs, can become addictive (Brown, 1990). One can crave those feelings. When one is addicted to the feelings love brings, there is a tendency to move from relationship to relationship in a very unstable fashion. One gets the high intensity feelings as a relationship begins to develop, but, over time, as those intense feelings begin to diminish, the love addict seeks out a new relationship to keep the emotional high going. Also, like alcohol, love can be intoxicating; and, like the alcoholic, the love addict seeks a perpetual state of intoxication because it feels good.

The Process of Mate Selection

Just as structural-functional theorists tell us that romantic love does not exist in a vacuum, but rather is influenced by the appraisals and pressures of close family and friends, so exchange theorists point to the significant influence of our social environment in determining whom we will marry. Gary Lee (1979) maintains that in conjugal family systems with neolocal residence, newly married adults create a new family, separated from either partner's family of origin. However, within extended family networks, marriage means the addition of a new family member for both partners' families of origin. Who will be recruited as a new family member is thus more apt to be a familial rather than a personal decision the more that the family of origin is an extended family system.

Because the family in an extended family network will be interacting with the new member with considerable frequency, the family has an investment in seeking out its collective rewards without incurring unnecessary costs. The family thus is interested in having some control over who will be included as a new family member. Nye (1979: 28) creates a related proposition stating that "the greater the anticipated economic and social interdependence of the conjugal pair and their families of orientation, the greater control exercised by the family of orientation over the choice of spouses."

Upper-class children have less freedom of mate choice than people in other social classes. Because wealth, power, and prestige is passed down from the eldest to the younger generations, the elderly wield more power in an upper-class family than in any other. Since there are great rewards to pass down to those who comply with their wishes, grandparents can exercise control over their grandchildren in the area of mate choice. Grandparents can threaten that "If you marry her, so help me I will disinherit you, leaving you with nothing." The costs of this marriage thereby become considerable. Thus, according to Nye (1979: 29), "The greater the control of economic and status resources by the family of orientation, the more effective the control of spousal partners by the family of orientation."

A Disposable Society

This country can be described as a "disposable society." People keep things until they are no longer useful and then they dispose of them. They do this with diapers, razors, cigarette lighters, batteries, automobiles, clothes, cans, milk cartons, plastic bags, and furniture. They also do this with people. Children abandon parents when they are no longer useful; corporations discard older employees who are no longer as useful as younger staff or cost more than younger staff; and spouses leave their partners when they perceive that partners have less "value."

There is an absence of loyalty, an absence of appreciation for things done in the past (structural-functional theorists would call this a problem of latent pattern maintenance). History doesn't count for much. This is a present-oriented perspective, based on the well-known question "What have you done for me lately?" This involves a continuous appraisal of cost and reward, and actions tend to be based on perceptions of value in the here and now. Just as we discard objects, so we tend to discard people in our lives based on our perception of their current utility to us, what they can do for us and their value to us in our present lives. Some examples of how society disposes of what it no longer needs follow.

DISPOSABLE EMPLOYEES For people who have been laid off by their companies after many years of service, feelings of anger, hurt, disappointment, and betrayal arise from a sense that the rule of distributive justice has been violated. Costs have been incurred in overtime work, loyalty to the company, anxiety over the company's success, and perhaps illnesses as a result of physical or emotional stress from work. Years of their life have been invested to help the company succeed and prosper, and suddenly they find themselves unemployed, often with very little warning. Very few severance benefits and very little help from the company in finding alternative means of financial support are forthcoming.

DISPOSABLE PARENTS In many Vietnamese communities in the United States, elderly people are sometimes outraged at the ways in which they are abandoned by their children. Vietnamese society values **filial piety**. Children are expected to honor and care for their parents in their old age. One has sons, in part, for this reason.

Affairs

When people who are married have affairs, they recognize that the affair comes at some risk. Should the spouse discover the existence of the affair, marital dissolution may occur. Exchange theorists may account for affairs by making the interpretation that the short-term rewards of the affair were more powerful than were its potential long-term costs.

Rewards and costs can vary in time. There can be short-term and long-term rewards as well as short-term and long-term costs. If the possibility of an affair is imminent and likely, the short-term pleasures may, in the minds of the people, outweigh the possible long-term consequences. Part of the equation is that while the likelihood of the affair is strong, there is considerable uncertainty as to whether or not the affair will be discovered and, once it is discovered, what will be done about it.

The more dependent that the partner is on the marital relationship, the less likely it is that the partner will initiate a termination of the marriage based on knowledge of the affair. The level of dependence that exists for the partner may well enter into the equation of likely consequences should the affair be discovered.

As part of their acculturation into this country, the children have adopted values of individualism instead of the collectivist orientation that existed in Vietnam. As part of that individualism, there is an expectation that each person has the responsibility of taking care of him- or herself rather than of others. Also, children have been known to tell their parents that in Vietnam there was no government-sponsored Social Security system whereby the government took care of the elderly, but that such a system does exist here in the United States, which the children see as letting them off the hook. Since there is an alternative available, let the government do it. When this abandonment happens, the elderly parents are outraged. What accounts for the outrage?

Again, in exchange theory terms, these people believe that the rule of distributive justice has been violated. The elderly parents' rewards are not commensurate with the costs they incurred in raising their children, and their rewards in their old age are not proportional to the investments they made for their children while they were growing up. These elderly parents think back on the hardships they incurred and the sacrifices they made for their children and they believe "It's not fair!" When they perceive that the rule of distributive justice has been violated, feelings of anger, hurt, disappointment, and betrayal arise.

The experience of the elderly Vietnamese parent is similar to the experience of most elderly parents in the United States, namely, that children care less for their elderly parents today than they did in the past, because, increasingly, government programs such as Social Security and Medicare provide some sources of support to elderly parents. One might well ask why parents should make such costly investments in the care and socialization of the very young

How one defines the costs and rewards of a sexual experience is partly a function of the era in which one lives. The ways in which sexual behavior is defined and interpreted have undergone significant changes over the twentieth century in this country. Until the 1960s, a sexual act was perceived as being primarily for procreation. One significant risk of an affair would be impregnation and the complications produced by that event. In the 1960s and 1970s, engaging in sex was defined as more recreational than procreational, and sex therapists informed people about how to make sex fun (Hunt, 1974). In the 1980s and 1990s, sexual intercourse was defined as a potentially lethal activity that could kill people should they contract certain fatal sexually transmitted diseases. In the mid-twentieth century, there was fear of contracting gonorrhea or syphilis but these became treatable over time; they were embarrassing and uncomfortable but rarely fatal. In our contemporary climate, fear of contracting AIDS is an additional potential cost of engaging in sexual affairs, a cost that people in earlier decades did not need to consider.

---

when they will probably not receive many rewards from those children when they grow up?

Why Care for the Young?

First, there are costs of *not* investing in the very young that might include guilt over not spending as much time with a child as one thinks one should. There is a potential cost of negative responses from friends and relatives that parents are not doing as much as they think that the parents should do. There is a potential cost of interference from social service authorities who might arrest a parent or remove a child for parental neglect or abuse. There is a potential cost that if a child is not socialized sufficiently well—does not know manners or how to read or write or do mathematics—he or she will not be able to become gainfully employed and autonomous, and may therefore be economically and emotionally dependent upon a parent for much longer than a parent might wish (Nye, 1979). If a child cannot become financially autonomous, there are costs to society in financially supporting this dependent adult through social services, which ultimately cost all citizens through higher taxes. Furthermore, if a parent is negligent in the socialization of a child, the child might get into trouble with the law or might do damage to property or people, for which the parent could be liable.

Second, there are potential rewards to the parent for treating a child well. Perhaps, if parent and child maintain a good supportive relationship, the parent will have a place in the adult life of the child, particularly as an involved grandparent, who has easy and frequent access to grandchildren, which is seen as an important reward to many adults.

An alternative argument can be made that, regardless of these potential costs and rewards, parents in the United States are abandoning their responsibilities to care for and socialize their children. As they increasingly work to support their own survival needs, these parents give the care and socialization of their children to schoolteachers, school nurses, neighbors, relatives, and friends. The argument can be made that the costs of raising children today are so high, in terms of money, time, and energy and the likelihood of success so low, given the prevalence of drugs and violence, that parents are overcome by the imbalance and reluctantly give up what appears to be an uphill battle. Both arguments have some empirical validity, depending on which parents are being observed.

Spousal Abuse

Exchange theory has been used to explain the existence of persistent spousal abuse in relationships. The argument has been made that spousal abuse is maintained in a relationship when rewards exceed costs for the abusive spouse (Gelles & Straus, 1988; Straus, Gelles, & Steinmetz, 1980). The primary *reward* for the abusive spouse is *power* attained through intimidation. Force or threats of force allow abusive spouses to get their partners to do what they want them to do; they can get their own way. As one wife, who had been abused for two years, stated in an interview:

> I would do anything. I would try to anticipate his moods. Cook his favorite dish. Dress the way he liked. I would have the kids washed and in bed when he got home from work so there wouldn't be any stress at home. I gave up my first job so I could be home, but then he got too worried about money, so I got another job as a teacher. I think I spent twenty-four hours a day either doing things to please him or thinking ahead to prevent his getting mad. (Gelles & Straus, 1988: 34)

A second *reward* abusive spouses often get is an emotional rush through the abusive behavior. It is a high much like the high one might get on drugs. As such, abusive behavior can become addictive, so that the person seeks that emotional rush of energy and excitement and suspense about the unknown—what will happen? Because of the rewards, it is rare that violence abates in a relationship once it begins. It usually escalates with each recurrent episode.

Why does a woman often stay in an abusive relationship? This can partly be explained in exchange theory terms. She often feels that she has nothing to offer another person. Her spouse may have convinced her that she is worthless or stupid or not worthy of another's love, and thus she holds on to her spouse for fear that she would never attract anyone else. Furthermore, she may fear that she cannot make it on her own because she has little or no skill or work experience by which she can become economically self-sufficient and independent. Also, if she were to bring the abuse to the attention of authorities, it might adversely affect her husband's earning power because he could lose his job as a function of going to jail. If the spouse were to become unemployed, there would be no child support to supplement her income, even if she could find a job. Such women also fear adverse repercussions from their spouses should they try to leave (Pagelow, 1981).

On the other hand, the costs to the abusive spouse are usually minimal or nonexistent. Law enforcement agencies are often reluctant to intervene in domestic disputes, in part because more injuries are incurred by law enforcement personnel during domestic violence calls than in any other offense investigation. If an abused spouse does call a law enforcement agency and it does nothing to intervene, this often acts as an official condonation of the violence for the abusive spouse and places the abused spouse in a much more vulnerable position. What has been demonstrated is that the abused spouse will receive no institutional or societal support.

There is some evidence that increasing the *costs* of abusive behavior acts as a deterrent to its continuance. In one study, Minneapolis, Minnesota, police were randomly assigned one of three ways of handling domestic violence calls from abused wives: give the male a warning, order him to leave the house, or arrest him (Sherman & Berk, 1984). A six-month follow-up study indicated that the males who were arrested were far less likely than the other abusive men to have been rearrested or reported as abusive by their partner. Another study in southern California (Berk & Newton, 1985) also showed that arresting a husband for spousal abuse lessened the likelihood that this male would be rearrested for subsequent abusive behavior. Increase the costs of a particular behavior and the likelihood that it will recur is reduced. As one law enforcement officer put it, "Arrest is best."

In the next section, let us examine divorce using an exchange theory framework. The decision to divorce is based upon an assessment of justice in the distribution of costs and rewards for each partner in the marriage.

Divorce

It seemed to Marcia that dates were frequent and unendingly enjoyable and fun. Eventually John and Marcia married. After the wedding, it seemed that the dates became less frequent and, increasingly, less fun. Time spent together was less enjoyable and her emotional highs seemed less high. Little gifts that used to be given—flowers, candy, cards—were no longer given.

Marcia also noticed that not only were rewards less intense and frequent, but now that she and her husband were living together, there were increased costs to her in the relationship. Now she cooked not because she wanted to but because she felt obligated to, and the products of her cooking thus brought her less enjoyment and satisfaction. Now there was laundry to do, not to mention ironing, vacuuming, and general cleaning, and she didn't seem to be getting much help with these chores. Increasingly she felt as if this relationship was costing her more than it used to. It cost energy to perform these chores. She experienced frustration and anger at not being appreciated and not having the costs shared by her partner. She began to feel exploited and taken for granted and to feel less good about herself and the relationship.

As she began to perceive that she was incurring more costs and getting fewer rewards in this relationship, she began to think of getting out of it. She discussed her thoughts and frustrations and disappointments with her husband, but these discussions seemed to have no effect in changing what went on in their division of labor. She was no longer being courted, no longer being complimented, no longer being hugged or caressed, and she anticipated that this was not going to change for the better.

From an exchange theory perspective, any person or group will seek to terminate a relationship when they perceive that the costs of the relationship exceed the rewards for them and when they also see that this will continue into the future. They will seek to terminate a relationship when they perceive that they are incurring most of the costs and that the other is getting most of the rewards, or when they perceive that their rewards are not proportional to the investments being made in the relationship.

Divorce: Duration of a Marriage

We have seen how the assessment of costs and rewards can influence decisions to divorce. Let us focus now on how the duration of a marriage can affect the distribution of those costs and rewards. It is more likely to be the husband rather than the wife who initiates a divorce in marriages of long duration. Why is this?

For some men, women seem to be most valuable in the earlier stages of marriage, in the roles of procreator, mother, and caretaker to the couple's children, for which she has often sacrificed her career.

After the children grow up and leave the nest, these women are sometimes perceived by their husbands as being less desirable because the work that their husbands most valued them for is over. Couple this with society's emphasis on youth and glamour, and the husband may not give high value to his aging wife. Should she return to her career, her efforts may not be highly valued by her husband. She is often seen as contributing relatively little financially to the household, since her wages are apt to be significantly less than her husband's, whose career has continued without such interruption. Because she has been out of the labor market for some time, the wife is sometimes seen as obsolete and thus often cannot earn wages that are comparable to her skills or knowledge.

The husband, in this later stage of marriage, sees himself as having much more value than he perceives in his wife. He brings home most of the income and has status in the community by virtue of his career position and earned income. He can give a partner decent lifestyle and leisure experiences. He sees his working wife as a liability for himself because she is less accessible and available to serve his needs, problems that increase as he begins to cut back working hours and to spend more time at home. Now, when he is at home, his wife is away working, and he perceives her absence as a cost to him. From this husband's perspective, if he terminated the marriage, he would have little to lose. He could keep most of his income, his lifestyle; and since his wife isn't around that much anyway, there would be little time lost spent with her. He might even find someone younger and more physically attractive who would add energy and intrigue to his life. So, he is more apt to seek a divorce than is his wife.

The wife may perceive her vulnerability at this time of her life, where, at a societal level, men tend to be more highly valued than are women. This may be enhanced by the fact that, because women outlive men, there are fewer men in older age cohort groups. The wife is also apt to be vulnerable financially. However, she may also perceive a prospective departure of the husband as an advantage in her life. She may understand that she has devoted her life to serving others: her parents, her children, her spouse. A marital termination would free her for the first time to live her life, attending to her own needs rather than the needs of others.

The decision by either party to terminate the marriage will be based on an assessment of the alternatives. According to exchange theorists the marriage would only be terminated if the party who initiated the termination believed that there would be more rewards in terminating the marriage than in staying in it, and that the costs would be less than the costs of staying married.

Divorce: Class and Gender

Costs and rewards of terminating marriages are determined, in part, by social class. Divorce rates are inversely related to social class—the higher the social class, the lower the divorce rates. There are high costs involved in the divorce of upper-class people because if property is evenly divided by the parties, each loses a considerable amount. With so much property to be divided, the attorney and court costs become astronomical, discouraging divorce. Because there are assets available, the alternative choice—both parties maintaining separate residences and living apart—often involves less cost than actual divorce. People of lesser means would not have this option available to them.

Nye (1979: 27) suggests that there is a considerable gender difference in the divorce rates of financially successful men and women. Financially successful men are less likely to divorce than are men of average social status, while financially successful women are more likely to divorce than are women of average social status. Men who earn high incomes are often above the "comparison level" with regard to income, so their wives are relatively satisfied with their standard of living. They may also be economically dependent upon their husbands to maintain that standard of living, which discourages them from initiating a divorce. Women who earn high incomes are not economically dependent upon their husbands and thus are freer to initiate a divorce in an unrewarding relationship. In a divorce, they probably would not have to share the rewards of their employment with their spouse.

Critique

Social exchange theory acknowledges the ability of people to construct their own behavior through a process of defining and interpreting the costs and rewards that exist in any situation both for themselves and for others. The theory posits a premise that people assess costs and rewards, and that they are aware of the balance of costs and rewards in situations. The theory proposes a context for how people think.

When you ask yourself what you should do in a particular situation or how you should act in an uncertain or ambiguous predicament, do you mentally go through a rational process of weighing possible and likely costs and rewards that may arise for you? Do you find yourself weighing long-term and short-term costs and rewards? One critique of the theory is that too many people, when they learn about the theory, have difficulty relating it to their everyday lives because their own experience leads them to say, "But I just don't go through all that prior to acting." Many people fail to see a correspondence between the theory's construct and the experiential reality of what they do prior to responding to another person or situation. They may be able to identify with the process for some of their important decisions, but they do not usually identify going through an analysis of costs and rewards most of the time.

The theory is critiqued for being very narrow in scope. People may rationally consider factors relative to their behavior, but they do not think only in terms of costs and rewards. Many other considerations lying outside this narrow context may enter into their thought process. They may consider how the feelings or actions of others will affect them other than in a cost-reward equation. Thus, the theory is critiqued for imposing too narrow a context for analyzing the ways people think.

Other situations that sorely test the theory include cases where behavior seems to stem from an emotional response, rather than a rational thought process; some cases of religious behavior where asceticism, sacrifice, and denial of rewards are preferred over maximizing rewards; and altruistic activities where people behave for the benefit of others with no concern for payback or reward to themselves.

The theory also has some problems dealing with situations where there is no consensus among numerous people over the presence or absence of rewards and of the extent to which something is rewarding or not. Rewards can exist in an objective reality and not be perceived by actors in that reality. They can be perceived as existing by the people involved and yet not be seen as existing by external observers. They can be perceived by one person in a group but not by another in that group. Rewards influence behavior when they are perceived; however, not everyone sees rewards in the same way.

A FEMINIST LOOK AT MASCULINE BIAS Paula England (1989), a feminist theorist, has criticized the theory as having a strong masculine bias. The theory assumes a "separative self" rather than a "connected self." The individual is seen as autonomous from a collective group, as an individual focused on self-interest. Autonomy and independence are seen as male values, while females are seen as valuing connectedness, affiliation within a collective structure of others, integration and interaction with those others from whom one receives support and to whom one gives support and nurturance. England critiques the theory as being incapable of understanding behavior that supports group solidarity at the expense of individual profit or reward. The theory so assumes individuation and maximization of individual gain that it ignores altruistic behavior that may promote the maintenance of interpersonal relationships. It is also masculine in focusing on the influence of rational thought on behavior at the expense of focusing on the effect of emotions on behavior. The theory is a reflection of male values and male styles of behavior, and thus males may well find the theory more palatable than females would.

CULTURAL BIAS The focus on a separative self and on autonomy and individuation are all themes that are a part of western European culture. The theory can thus be accused of having a cultural bias that may limit its applicability in other cultures and in other parts of the world. Particularly in preindustrial societies, people do not tend to differentiate themselves as separate from groups in which they exist. What is good for the group is all that cognitively exists, and separation of oneself from the group in thought is unfathomable.

In structural-functional theory, one of the pattern variables was self-collectivity. Here people have a choice of behaving out of self-interest or sacrificing self-interest for the welfare of the collectivity. The structural-functional theorist at least acknowledges the existence of alternatives. Exchange theorists, however, assume that people only behave out of self-interest. With such a focus, they are blind to the possibility of people acting to promote the welfare of the collectivity.

In the next chapter, looking through the glasses of the symbolic interaction theorist, we will see that, unlike the social exchange theorist, this theorist has no preconceived ideas about how people define and interpret themselves and others. The social exchange theorist provides a specific context in which people operate in their world. The symbolic interactional theorist takes it away.

Summary

Exchange theorists believe that all social interaction comes at a cost. The cost is at least time and energy, but it can also include money, anger, frustration, depression, physical injury, or negative feelings, such as the sense of being exploited. Interaction also brings rewards such as fun, a good feeling about life and self, a sense of energy and enthusiasm, a feeling of usefulness and being needed. The ratio of rewards to costs determines how we feel about others—whether we like them or not—and whether we are inclined to continue or to terminate our interactions with others. People subjectively assess the costs they incur in a relationship as well as the rewards they receive from it, and from this assessment they construct their behavior relative to other people. So long as people perceive that the rewards of a relationship outweigh the costs, interactions are likely to continue.

Exchange theorists see people as behaving out of self-interest. People seek to maximize their rewards and minimize their costs—maximize their pleasure and minimize their pain. They are willing to incur some cost as long as there is perceived fairness. This fairness must come from either a perception that their own rewards at least equal their costs or that their rewards and costs are proportional to the rewards and costs incurred by others in the relationship.

Chapter Five

Symbolic Interaction Theory

The Focus

All of the eyeglasses that we tried on in the discussions of the first three theoretical frameworks showed us people being powerfully influenced by forces external to them. These forces, called "social facts" by Durkheim (1895/1964), and called norms, status, and role expectations by other social scientists, are powerful. Wearing these glasses, we saw people as socialized in order to internalize values and norms, we saw people who acted the way they did because they had been taught to act that way. Furthermore, sanctions (in the form of rewards and punishments) were exercised in the social settings in which people acted that exerted their influence to cause people to conform to norms.

In addition, the social exchange theory, which we just examined in chapter 4, imposed a specific context within which people interpret their world—a system of costs and rewards was the given of this theory. Symbolic interaction theory, which we will now explore, presents an alternative to all of these images of people. This theory assumes only that people will define and interpret objects and events in their environment (Stryker, 1959, 1967, 1972). It has no preconceived ideas about how people will do this or how they will define and interpret themselves and others.

In this theoretical framework human behavior is seen as a function of a people's ability to think critically and analytically, to make indications to themselves prior to acting. The symbolic interactionist focuses on the reflective nature of people. These theorists assume that people have the autonomy to carve out for themselves patterns of action that may violate social norms and expectations. People are not seen as powerless against structural forces. Rather, they can and do violate social norms, something that can be explained in terms of their ability to interact with social structures, not just conform to them.

The Theory

The founding father of symbolic interaction theory is George Herbert Mead, a philosopher at the University of Chicago in the first decades of this century.

Mead wrote very little in his lifetime, but he was a popular and dynamic teacher. The tenets of symbolic interaction theory are found in a book called *Mind, Self and Society* (1934), which names Mead as the author, but which is really a combination of his students' lecture notes, compiled after his death. Mead's students transcribed their notes into this book, which they credited to Mead since it reflected Mead's ideas.

The two basic concepts underlying symbolic interaction theory are the "self" and the "mind." In the next section, we examine the first of these concepts.

The Self

The **self** refers to people's capacity to step outside themselves and treat themselves as an object in their own environment. Look at a chair and describe its height, weight, color, shape, and possible functions. Sit on it, use it to defend yourself against adversaries, or use it as a weapon or as an instrument for vandalism by throwing it. Whatever you can do with objects in your environment you can do with yourself. You can describe yourself, including your height, weight, color, and shape. You can describe yourself in terms of how you usually act, using personality concepts such as shy or outgoing, active or passive, light or serious, spontaneous or controlled. You can act toward yourself, dress yourself, prod yourself, praise yourself, and talk to yourself, which is what thinking is—talking to ourselves.

A great deal of what people know about themselves they internalize from their interpretations of the appraisals of others. People tell us what we are like, and we internalize these appraisals. Charles Horton Cooley (1964) wrote of the **"looking glass self,"** referring to the fact that our image of ourselves is a mirror image, a reflection, of what others tell us about ourselves. For Mead, this was too passive a view. He saw people not as sponges, who absorb the views of others, but rather as filters. We take the appraisals of others and interpret them, giving them meaning, discarding some that seem unfavorable, such as expressions of envy or jealousy. We tend to keep, if not accentuate, the favorable appraisals given by others, as we define those people who praise us or admire us as being insightful or bright. This selectivity, by which we accentuate the positive and de-emphasize the negative, allows most people to create positive images of themselves.

The concept of "self" is not to be confused with the concept of "self-image." Self is the capacity to step outside ourselves and both see ourselves as an object in our own environment and act toward ourselves as an object in our own environment. Self-image is a part of a more inclusive concept of "self"—namely, self-image is what we see when we step of outside ourselves and look at ourselves as others see us.

THE "I" AND THE "ME" OF SELF For Mead the self consisted of two parts, the "I" and the "me." The **I** is the impulsive, spontaneous, unpredictable part of the self; the "me" is the thinking part of the self. The **me** constructs action by interpretative thought, taking into account personal goals and competencies as well as the expectations of others in the environment.

The vast majority of our behavior is **meaningful behavior**, behavior preceded by thought, which means something to the actor. Mead was only interested in studying behavior that was constructed by interpretative thought processes.

A very small segment of behavior is not preceded by thought; it is spontaneous, reflexive behavior, sometimes driven by emotion. It is created through the "I" without direction from the "me." We are aghast when we realize that, in response to verbal abuse, we have hit another person with a right hand to the face. On receiving bad news a person cries hysterically. There was no thinking about these behaviors. Consequences or what others might think were not considered. The behavior just occurred spontaneously. These are **nonmeaningful behaviors**, which are not preceded by thinking. Although these actions at times do occur, Mead believed that they are very rare. Nor was Mead interested in studying these non-meaningful behaviors.

It is critical to understand Mead's concept of the mind in order to comprehend the dynamics of constructing meaningful behavior. In the next section we explore that concept.

The Mind

The **mind** refers to the ability that people have to make indications to themselves, to think before acting. Making indications to oneself involves talking things over in one's mind, or as some people call it, "thinking." People must make indications to themselves prior to action. To illustrate this, think of individuals who are really concentrating on something that they are doing—reading a book, building something, sewing, cooking—something in which they are deeply engrossed. Suddenly they finish it and realize that they are phenomenally hungry. They were in fact hungry well before this recognition; however until now, they had not indicated to themselves that they were hungry. Without making the indication to themselves that they are hungry, they will not seek food, even though physiologically they may be in need of food.

A person may experience going to a neighbor's house to borrow something. The neighbor has just finished baking a delicious-looking cake and invites the visitor in to have a piece along with a cup of coffee. The visitor indicates to himself that he is not very hungry, so he says, "No thank you." But the neighbor is very excited about her cake. The visitor does not want to hurt her feelings, so he compromises and says, "Just a small piece." A piece is cut and after a short time, the visitor looks down at his empty plate and exclaims, "Gee, I guess I was hungrier than I thought." This translates to mean that he was actually hungrier than he had indicated to himself. If a person does not indicate that he is hungry, he will not seek food. Making indications to oneself is a necessary precursor to action.

What are these indications that one makes to oneself? They consist of a "definition of the situation." They also consist of the consideration of alternative lines of possible action that can be taken relative to the situation. Finally, they include the anticipation of probable consequences of each possible line of action and how those consequences fit into one's system of values and goals.

Defining Situations

The **definition of the situation** is one of the most useful and meaningful concepts in the social sciences. In defining this concept, W. I. Thomas and Florian Znanecki (1918–1920/1958) said, "If men define situations as real, then they are real in their consequences." What does this mean? It means that the way in which people define a situation will affect the action that they take in relation to that situation. Some examples are in order.

A safari hunter is talking with a native shaman in a village hut when a clay doll, which is on a shelf, falls to the ground, breaking the doll's arm. The shaman is visibly disturbed by this. He exclaims that this is an omen that one of them will soon break an arm. He says, "I don't know about you, but I'm playing it safe and staying in bed for the rest of the week." The safari hunter sees this as native superstition in which he does not believe and decides to go about his regular activities. The shaman defined the doll's breaking as being a "real" event, as having a specific meaning. The hunter defined the event as being of no consequence; thus the event had no consequence in altering his proposed behavior. By defining the situation as he did, the shaman did alter his previously planned behavior for the week. If men define situations as real, then they will be real in their consequences.

A man walks along the ground, which is strewn with scraps of metal that used to be his airplane. He could define the crash of his plane in a number of ways. He could define it as a miscalculation on the part of his pilot, who, crashed the plane into the mountain. He could define it as a blunder by his pilot, who because he was an incompetent navigator, flew the airplane over enemy territory, where it was shot down. Alternatively, he could define the incident as an act of unprovoked aggression on the part of the enemy. How he defines this situation will affect what action he takes—whether or not he retaliates against his enemy.

People also make snap judgments of others, often based on very little evidence. From quite casual observation, one person might discredit another as being too serious, too intellectual, too snobbish, too boring, too immature, too superficial, or too crude. These labels lead the observer to believe he or she knows all about the other. This definition of the other, whether accurate or not, will influence the behavior of the person making the assessment. With the confidence that the assessment is accurate, a person making a negative assessment of another will be disinclined, for instance, to ask the other out for a date. Thus, if men and women define their negative assessments as accurate, they will be real in their consequences because no further interaction with the other will be sought.

Herbert Blumer (1969), a student of Mead's, a past all-American football player, and a past president of the American Sociological Association, coined the name of this theoretical framework. He called it "symbolic interaction" to depict the process of interpersonal interaction. A symbol is anything capable of having multiple meanings.

BEHAVIOR AS SYMBOL Words are symbols. The word "stardust," for instance, could mean a song, a hotel in Las Vegas, or the Milky Way. Behavior can also be a symbol. Action has to be defined; meaning has to be given to it. When one person acts, another has to define and interpret that action. The interpretation of the behavior in part depends on the situation in which the behavior occurs. The action could be defined as hostile and antagonistic or friendly and supportive. Once the action is interpreted, this affects the alternatives that can be considered in responding to it. Once a line of action is constructed and the reaction occurs, the reaction then has to be defined and interpreted by others, who will, in turn, respond by carrying out their action. Interpersonal interaction becomes a continuous stream of response where actors, in turn, define the actions of others and construct appropriate responses, which are then interpreted and responded to by others.

BEHAVIOR AS CHOICE Symbolic interactionists do not exclude the existence of structural forces, such as norms and role expectations, that externally impinge upon the individual. They say, however, that the individual does not automatically conform to these forces. The individual has the capacity (mind) to reflect on, interpret, and define these norms and expectations as acceptable or not; and he or she has the power to reject them, to violate norms, to deviate. It is in the area of explaining deviance that symbolic interaction theory has been extremely useful. An illustration follows.

A person is driving home from a party. It is 2 A.M. This person is extremely tired and comes to a red traffic light. He looks around and sees absolutely nobody in sight, not a car, not a pedestrian, nothing. What flashes through his mind is that he is supposed to stop for red lights (the norm). However, he also acknowledges that he is very tired and wants to get home to bed. There is obviously no danger of a collision (these are the indications made). If there is a policeman watching, a ticket is probably inevitable. He knows he cannot afford a ticket. Looking around, he sees no police car. Despite the existence of the norm that he should stop, he drives through the red light.

If he does not go through the red light, then he probably has indicated to himself that saving a few minutes is not worth the risk of getting a ticket. Deviance just doesn't happen. It is often mentally constructed through a reflective thought process, which symbolic interactionists call "the mind."

The symbolic interactionist believes that people construct their own actions. They act the way they do by making indications to themselves. These indications include defining the situation and giving meaning to objects and people within the situation, assessing alternative courses of action that are available options of response, and anticipating consequences for all alternatives considered. When social scientists seek the causes of human behavior, they must look within the actor, to the actor's thoughts and feelings. People interpret the norms and expectations that are imposed upon them. They can choose to conform or to deviate from them. People have a choice—autonomy over their own lives.

Methodology

Methodology follows from theoretical perspective. Each theoretical framework makes assumptions about the major causes of human social behavior and the processes involved in creating behavior. Each framework informs a researcher of what to study, whether norms, sanctions, or other external constraints that impinge on the behavior of individuals (which the structural-functional theorist studies), or indications that people make to themselves (which the symbolic interactionist studies). The theoretical framework informs researchers as to what information is important to look for, what kind of data is needed. Researchers then adopt a methodology that enables them to procure the needed data.

COLD FACTS Structural-functional theorists, believing that external social forces such as age, sex, race, religion, education, or social class affect a person's behavior, seek the determinants of behavior by administering questionnaires in survey research, which is an efficient way of obtaining this kind of information. They assume that if one knows the age, gender, socioeconomic status, religion, race, and marital status of persons, predictions can be made with considerable accuracy about how they will vote in elections and what products they will buy. These theorists to some extent borrow from Marx's belief that economics affects ideology (beliefs and values) and ideology affects behavior. Their questionnaires usually are constructed with forced-choice questions of the kind that exist on a multiple-choice test.

WARM BODIES Symbolic interaction theory leads to a distinctive methodology. If we want to know why people behave as they do, we have to "understand" (the German sociologist Max Weber used the word **verstehen**) the subjective states of mind of the actors. This takes intensive, in-depth interviewing. Understanding involves trying to feel what actors feel, know what actors know, perceive as actors perceive. One must try to step into the actor's shoes, to **take the role of the other**, to know what is going on in his or her heart and mind, if we are to truly understand the individual's action and what it means to him or her. If behavior is a function of the indications that people make to themselves prior to action, then to understand the action a researcher must comprehend the indications that preceded the action.

Symbolic interactionists seek particular kinds of information in order to examine the causes of behavior. Their methodology requires field work including **participant observation** and intensive **interviewing** (Blumer, 1969). Using participant observation, they can capture the indications that people make to themselves by interacting with them in a natural way, by becoming part of the very groups that are being observed. Using the interviewing technique, they can capture the indications that people make to themselves through the use of semi-structured interview schedules. These schedules have questions that are to be asked, but the interviewer has the flexibility to probe, elaborate, and embellish the questions on the schedule in order to better comprehend the meaning of what the actors think and feel. Written presentations of the research often offer significant direct quotes from respondents or informants rather than statistical composites. In doing research on families, symbolic interactionists would present direct quotes from respondents that best illustrated a trend or response pattern. The data thus have a richness because they reflect the humanness and subjective reality of the respondent's existence. The people are presented as real thinking, talking, and feeling human beings rather than as cold statistics.

We have thus far primarily dealt with symbolic interaction theory as it pertains to an individual's behavior, because this is usually how symbolic interaction theory is used—for microanalysis of interpersonal interaction. The theory can, however, also be applied to explain the behavior of groups, such as families. A **social group** is defined by Mead as a collectivity of people who share common definitions of objects and events in their environment.

We see how this applies to families in the next section, where we use symbolic interaction theory to analyze romantic love, parenting, life in families with an alcoholic, and child custody issues.

Applying the Theory

How can symbolic interaction theory be applied to the study of family life? In order to answer the question of why a husband beats his wife or child, it is important to understand how he defines this wife or child. What indications did he make to himself prior to his action? Why does a husband desert his family? It can be understood by understanding the indications that the man made to himself prior to fleeing. Some insight is gained by understanding how this man has defined his relation to his wife and children, both in terms of what he considers to be an ideal relationship—what he would like—and what he realistically can have, given his capacity (or lack thereof) to physically support them. Why does a woman seek out an abortionist? In order to understand this we must ask her: What alternatives did she see as available to her; what else did she consider; what did she perceive as the probable consequences of her action?

Symbolic interaction theory will first be applied to an analysis of romantic love. The theory uses the concept of mind to focus on the fact that, prior to action, people think, make indications to themselves, defining and interpreting objects and events in their environment. Someone in love defines the love object as terrific and wonderful, interpreting and giving meaning to the other in a very positive way.

Symbolic interaction theory states that behavior is constructed from a definition of objects and events in our environment. How parents perceive and define children influences how those parents will punish those children. We explore how a parent's perception of a child might encourage physical child abuse and how a parent's perception of acceptable punishment and the legal authorities' perception of acceptable punishment are often at variance.

An important concept in symbolic interactionism is role. People carve out roles relative to each other in the process of social interaction. Dysfunctional families often exhibit roles that are distinctive, and we explore roles often exhibited in families where one member is chemically dependent.

Lastly we explore how making indications to oneself is an integral part of the divorce process, involving a definition of the marital situation as unchangeable and painful. The process involves considering alternatives to divorce and anticipating the consequences of the alternatives considered.

Romantic Love

The concept "definition of the situation" involves giving meaning to objects and events in our environment. When one person loves another, the love object is defined as being extraordinary.

The popular expression "Love is blind" means that early in a relationship, a person focuses on another's assets, strengths, and positive traits. The partner is often blind to the other's liabilities and shortcomings, which only become visible later in the relationship. What accounts for this selective perception early in a relationship?

ACTORS ON A STAGE Sociologist Erving Goffman (1959,1963,1974) raises the question, "To what extent is the image one person has of the other manipulated by that other, constructed and contrived in the courtship process? To what extent do we marry a fiction, a false image of the partner, that is created by the partner for us?"

Goffman is often linked to the **dramaturgical approach** in sociology. He saw all the world as a stage and all the people as actors, playing out performances for an audience. When people get up in the morning, they go to their closet to pick out the clothes they will wear for their day. They think to themselves about the performances they will execute in the coming hours, and they select their costume for playing out those performances. They create images of what they are like in the minds of others. They construct an identity for others to see. If their agenda includes a job interview, they may seek a costume that will lead the interviewers to see them as responsible, dependable, mature, efficient, neat, and organized. If they are going to a picnic or party, they may seek a costume that leads others to perceive them as "ready to play."

SCENE CHANGES In his book *Presentation of Self in Everyday Life* (1959), Goffman describes the world as constructed with **back regions**, the bathrooms and bedrooms and kitchens where a person prepares for the performances of life, and the **front regions**, the living rooms or dining rooms where those performances are played out. Sometimes back regions can become front regions, as when guests congregate in the kitchen to watch their host prepare dinner, in

Romantic Love—Words as Symbols

A **symbol** is anything that is capable of having multiple meanings. Words are symbols. When someone says "I love you" he or she can mean many things. The wide variety of meanings is summarized by Meerlo (1952: 83):

> I love you. Sometimes it means: I desire you or I want you sexually. It may mean: I hope you love me or I hope that I will be able to love you. Often it means: It may be that a love relationship can develop between us, or even I hate you. Often it is a wish for an emotional exchange: I want your admiration in exchange for mine, or I give my love in exchange for some passion, or I want to feel cozy and at home with you, or I admire some of your qualities. A declaration of love is merely a request: I desire you, or I want you to gratify me, or I want your protection, or I want to be intimate with you, or I want to exploit your loveliness. Sometimes it is the need for security and tenderness or parental treatment. It may mean: My self-love goes out to you. But it may also express submissiveness. Please take me as I am, or I feel guilty about you, or I want through you to correct the mistakes I have made in human relationships. It may be self-sacrifice and a masochistic full affirmation of the other, taking the responsibilities for mutual exchange of feeling. It may be a weak form of friendliness, it may be the scarcely even whispered expression of ecstasy. "I love you," wish, desire, submission, conquest, it is never the word itself that tells all the meaning.

So given all the diverse meanings of "I love you," lovers must decipher what their partners mean when they say these words. They assess the meaning not only from the tone of voice, the pitch, resonance, intonation, muscle tone, and body posture of the speaker but also by analyzing, giving meaning to their behavior, their actions, in the past and present. They must decipher whether "I love you" means I want to own you, have sex with you, have you around to abuse verbally and physically, parent you, have you parent me, take care of you, have you take care of me, protect you or have you protect me, admire you because you are so much like me, change you, mold you as I want you to be, dominate you, exploit you, and so forth. "How do I love thee? Let me count the ways," wrote Elizabeth Barrett Browning in her sonnet (XLIII from *Sonnets from the Portuguese*). Here we have counted some additional (if less poetic) ways in which some people love.

---

which case the preparation is part of the "show" and the kitchen becomes a front region. Bedrooms can become a front region in the playing out of a sexual performance. Whether a place is a front or back region is defined "in context."

In his book *Stigma* (1963), he states that all people have **stigmas**, facts about themselves that have the potential of discrediting their identity in the eyes of others. This could be that the person's parents are divorced or that the person has had an abortion or was once arrested, or that the individual is a member of some religious, racial, or ethnic minority group. It could be that the person was once sexually molested or fired from a job or, as a child, held over to repeat the fifth grade. The book explores how people deal with these stigmas to manage their identity in the eyes of others. Do they hide the existence of the stigma or do they acknowledge it? If people acknowledge it, how do they present it to others so that they can be seen as all right in the eyes of these others? Goffman subtitles his book *Notes on the Management of Spoiled Identities.*

THE PLAY'S THE THING Goffman's ideas, applied to the courtship process, show that courtship first involves getting the attention of a potential mate. This may be done by wearing flamboyant clothing or through flamboyant behavior or by any other way that the person devises to attract someone's attention.

Once someone gets the other's attention, he or she engages in impression management. From Goffman's perspective, courtship sometimes involves manufacturing an image in the mind of another as to what he or she is like. That image is constructed. People usually present themselves as somewhat different from what they are "really" like—as nicer or wittier or more polished than they see themselves to be—all in the name of trying to create a good impression.

If the suitor is fortunate, the love object buys (consumes) the image that is created. The love object likes the pursuer and may eventually experience love. The two people marry; each person has married an illusion, a manufactured creation of who the other is. Then indeed marriage becomes a journey to find out who it is that one has *really* married.

ACTORS ALL The image that a suitor has of another does not occur in a vacuum. It is not self-created. Rather it occurs as symbolic interaction. An individual is given a presentation of self by the other that is then interpreted as being real or somewhat distorted, as being something likeable or not. The person creates a response to the other, conveying a message of interest and availability or of disinterest. The message may be perceived as it was intended to be or not, but the response will be molded by the interpretation that the person makes of the partner's response.

The appraisals that significant others make of the love object are a further guide to the suitor. If people who are valued and respected—parents or friends—define the love object as worthy, then the person's own definition of the love object is supported, and this gives the person confidence to continue, perhaps more boldly. This is not always the case, however; sometimes parental opposition will also heighten commitment to a relationship (Romeo and Juliet), perhaps as a way of asserting autonomy and independence from the parents.

Love as a Socialized Phenomenon

The lifelong process of socialization is an important element of symbolic interaction theory. The definitions and interpretations of objects and events in a person's environment come to be learned, acquired through interaction in the socialization process. The definitions we hear are often inconsistent. Peers, parents, teachers, media, and neighbors do not always send the same messages. They do not define objects and events in the same way. This leaves individuals to resolve these inconsistencies and construct their own interpretations. The theoretical eyeglasses of the symbolic interactionist would focus on romantic love as a socialized phenomenon.

People learn that romantic love should precede marriage and be a basis for marriage. They learn, through books, magazines, movies, and their parents and peers, what a person experiencing romantic love should feel and how he or she should act. Romantic love is a phenomenon that is socially created. People, in United States culture, are taught to look for it, long for it, and are encouraged to experience it. There are, however, other cultures in which romantic love is unimportant, or has nothing to do with marriage. Here, marriage is arranged between families, and the bride and groom may not even know each other prior to the arrangement.

Romantic love is given meaning in our culture. It tends to be defined as something for the young but not necessarily for the old. Elderly people who marry thus often say that they marry for companionship (Bulcroft & Bulcroft, 1991) rather than out of romantic attachments they feel for their partner. Romantic love is often defined as something that should exist between people of similar social characteristics but not between people with different social characteristics. In a socialization process, people are taught the rules of romantic love, as well as how to express that love and behaviorally manifest its existence.

Love is defined as irrational and emotional. That definition leads to some very bizarre expressions of romantic love, expressions that might be equated with madness. Stalking the love object, shooting the love object, killing oneself when the love is not reciprocated are all ways in which romantic love has been behaviorally demonstrated. Being in love can be used as an excuse for irresponsible, unpredictable behavior. The termination of a love affair can result in severe depression. The irrational, emotional behavior that surrounds love is consistent with its definition in this culture.

In the box on page 139, there is an exploration of the meaning of words, such as "I love you." Words are seen as symbols, which connotes that they are capable of meaning many different things.

Making Indications to Ourselves

Indications that lovers may make to themselves do not focus just on the love object but also on themselves. They recognize that when they are with the other they feel great, have high energy, have a wonderful time, feel good about themselves; they recognize that food tastes better, the world looks brighter, and life seems great. They may also indicate to themselves that if they marry this person, these feelings will last forever and that the relationship will continue for the rest of their lives. They may perceive marriage as an option among others, and they may anticipate that if they marry, they will both live happily ever after.

Children of divorce are apt to indicate to themselves that they know marriages often do not last forever and that all marriages are risks. They may indicate that taking this risk with their partner is probably better than taking the risk with anyone else they know and that it is a reasonable risk to take with a possibly favorable outcome.

Childrearing

The definition that parents have of children influences the ways in which parents relate to those children, particularly how they discipline the children in the process of socialization. If infants are perceived as being angelic or innocent, there is some likelihood that they will be treated in a nurturing, protective way. If the essential nature of children is seen as being evil or wicked, they will be treated harshly.

DEFINING CHILDREN AS EVIL In the early New England colonies in America, children were defined as innately evil and sinful (Kenkel, 1977). They were seen as being born with "original sin." It was thought that children had a natural inclination toward evil. Only through rigid and harsh discipline, through beating, could the sinful inclinations of children be curbed. If they were not curbed, not only would this have disruptive consequences for the community but for the individual child as well, for upon his death, he would surely be damned to spend eternity in hell.

The sinful nature of children was impressed upon these children in church, school, in the home, and in the children's books that existed at the time. In the book *The History of the Fairchild Family,* Lucy, a young child, repeats the following as a portion of a prayer (Earle, 1889, 238):

> My heart is so exceedingly wicked, so vile, so full of sin, that even when I appear to be tolerably good, even then I am sinning. When I am praying, or reading the Bible, or hearing other people read the Bible, even then I sin. When I speak, I sin; when I am silent, I sin. (Quoted in Kenkel, 1977: 177)

At home children were constantly reminded of their wickedness. Any offense, whether major or minor, reminded parents that within their children there was an innate evilness that had to be suppressed. In beating their children, parents were cleansing the entire community of the evil in their midst, and thus they went about their disciplining with dedication and force.

Some towns gave commissioners the power to sentence boys to be whipped when they misbehaved. Occasionally incorrigible youths would be brought before magistrates for their evil ways. Children were clearly to be seen and not heard.

The early New England colonies were not unique in viewing children as essentially evil. In sixteenth century Russia, a code of family practices called the Domostroy urged parents (Elnett, 1926, 32–33) as follows:

> Beat your son in his youth, and he will comfort you in your old age and will give beauty to your soul. And do not weaken in beating the child. Beating with a rod will not kill him, but will make him healthier for hitting his body you are saving his soul from death. Loving your son, inflict more wounds on him and you will rejoice afterward. . . . Bring your child up used to denials and you will find in him rest and blessing. Do not smile at him when playing with him, if you will be weak in his childhood, he will make you suffer when he grows up, will set your soul on edge. And give him no power in youth but crush his ribs when he is growing, because when he is big he will not obey you, and you will feel annoyed and ill at heart, and your house will be ruined, and your neighbors will reproach you, and your enemies will rejoice at your misfortune. (Quoted in Kenkel, 1977:98–99)

From these examples we can see that "if men define situations as real [children are innately evil and wicked], then they are real in their consequences [the sinfulness must be beaten out of them]." How people define situations will produce the behavior that they use in those situations. How children are defined influences how parents relate to those children.

TODAY'S DISCIPLINE In our contemporary society, there is considerable diversity about how children should be disciplined. Many people believe that because there are such strong pressures in the external environment for children to be violent and disrespectful of authority, harsh measures are needed within the home to reinforce respect and obedience as valued behavior. They believe that harsh physical punishment of children is appropriate at times as a deterrent to negative behavior. Such discipline might involve the use of spanking or hitting, or the use of belts, wooden spoons, or what are euphemistically called "love paddles," wooden or plastic boards, sometimes with holes in them (to reduce wind resistance), which are used to physically punish children.

. . . OR CHILD ABUSE? The use of such instruments is defined as "child abuse" by district attorney offices in many jurisdictions. In the county in which this author lives, it is permissible to spank a child on the buttocks with an open hand, so long as the person doing so is in control of his or her emotions. However, it is abusive behavior, and liable for prosecution, if any adult hits a child anywhere other than on the buttocks and with anything other than the open hand.

The legal definition of the situation is clearly at odds with the definition of the situation of many parents, who believe that to spare the rod is to spoil the child. Consistent with their respective definitions of appropriate and inappropriate discipline, the parents who believe in corporal punishment will use it, and the district attorney will prosecute such punishment, particularly where it leaves some physical evidence (bruises that can be photographed, broken bones that can be x-rayed) that can be presented to a jury.

When these parents are arrested, a common reaction is moral indignation, signified by the statement, "How dare you tell me what I can and cannot do with my children. They're *my* children!" These parents define their children's bodies as being theirs, the parents', and they feel they can do with them as they wish. To the contrary, the legal authorities define the bodies of children as belonging to the children, with the parents having no right physically or sexually to injure them.

These discrepant ways of defining who owns the bodies of children have parallels in the arguments over abortion. Pro-choice advocates tend to define the fetus as within the body of the woman, who has the right to do with her body as she sees fit. Pro-life advocates tend to define the body of the fetus as belonging to the fetus, not to the parent. When the parent violates the fetus's right to life, they call it murder. These discrepant definitions of pregnancy will influence the holder of one perception to be willing to have an abortion and be a political activist for pro-choice causes, while the holder of the opposite perception would never have an abortion and would be a political activist for pro-life causes. If men and women define situations as real, they are real for them in their consequences.

Roles

When people interact, they carve out roles in relation to one another. The concept of role has many different definitions. One can see **roles** as patterns of behavior that exist around some theme. This behavior is greatly influenced by expectations that exist in one or more persons regarding how someone will behave in relation to them and to others. These expectations influence behavior because we tend to want to conform to them.

The patterns of behavior that constitute roles are created in a continuous process of interaction. Furthermore, expectations between people as to how they will act toward each other may change over time. Likewise, behavioral expectations toward one another may be different in one setting than in another; people cannot be expected to act the same way in all social settings.

SELF-FULFILLING PROPHECIES Roles tend to be created in a circular process of interaction. One person behaves in a certain way toward another, and that other generalizes that behavior and comes to expect the person to act that way consistently. Once the expectations exist, they exert an influence of their own, so that the person senses those expectations and feels a need to conform to them in order not to disappoint the other. The expectations thus create a self-fulfilling prophecy that this is the way the person is; the expectations will generate evidence that the image the other has of the person is correct.

This evidence is created in a two-way fashion. Pressure exists for the recipient of expectations to conform to them; but also, the person who holds the expectations will selectively see behavior that conforms to his or her expectations of the other and will be blind to behavior that is not congruent with these expectations. People thus tend to create their own data to support theories they have in their own minds about people and events.

A child may, at an early age, be caught shoplifting. From this experience, people may come to define this child as trouble, as deviant, as a thief. People then act toward the child with suspicion. They do not trust the child, who becomes labeled and identified as troublesome. The child feels some pressure, at an unconscious level, to conform to these expectations of others. Sometimes the only time the child gets attention is when he conforms to the expectations of others, for when he is compliant and obedient, he is ignored. It is only when he conforms to the negative expectations of others that his existence becomes recognized by others. The expectations thus help create the expected behavior. When the expected behavior is produced, it reinforces the image of the child as trouble, and the others are confirmed in perceiving the child as they did.

ROLE RECIPROCITY Sometimes people act in **reciprocal roles**, such as when one person is dominant and the other submissive, where one is a giver and the other a taker, where one person is a caretaker and the other is taken care of, or where one person acts as a responsible parent to an irresponsible child. Reciprocal roles exist when people behave in opposite and complementary positions relative to each other. The complementarity of the parties binds them in an interdependent way, because a person cannot be parental unless there is someone playing the role of child. An individual cannot be a caretaker unless there is someone to be cared for. People who play reciprocal roles do so in a covert collusion, each participating in a process and perpetuating that process by dutifully playing his or her role.

This process is enhanced by each person's definition of the other. The caretaker perceives that he or she cannot stop being a caretaker because the person cared for would surely suffer. The person cared for believes he or she cannot survive without the assistance of the caretaker. The definitions each holds serve to maintain the structure of their relationship. Likewise, the person who parents believes that the person who is the child needs guidance and support, believes that the child would stumble without this help. The child also believes this. Through the shared definitions of their situation, each maintains this reciprocal relationship. Although their behavior may be reciprocal, their definitions of the situation are often consistent. It is when the definitions change and become incongruent that change in the relationship becomes possible. When the dependent person comes to believe that he or she could succeed independently, he or she may try to do so. Such attempts hold the possibility of breaking the complementary and reciprocal relationship.

Scapegoating in Families

Scapegoating is a process by which members assign one person or group more responsibility for evil than is warranted by the facts. The word "scapegoating" comes from the Bible (Leviticus: 16:20). God tells Aaron to take two goats and to sacrifice one and to put all the sins of the people of Israel onto the other goat, which is to be led out into the wilderness by a pure man. Structural-functional theorists would say that the function of scapegoating is to purify members of a group. In our example, once all their sins were put onto the goat, the people of Israel were left with clean hands and pure hearts—they were purified. Scapegoating is a purification ritual.

Families often engage in scapegoating. In symbolic interactionist terms, family members share a common definition of the family's situation when they place the blame for all of the family's problems and troubles onto one member. When they do this, others in the family are absolved of any responsibility for the trouble. Scapegoats in families frequently include stepparents, chemically dependent people, physically disabled or emotionally disturbed children, or unemployed adults.

ALL AGAINST ONE Families that scapegoat often feature a social structure of all against one (Vogel & Bell, 1960). The dominant coalition pattern has everyone supporting each other against a socially isolated scapegoat. This social isolation of the scapegoat is important, because having no allies reduces the power of the scapegoat to counter the collective's definition that he or she is responsible for all family problems. Symbolic interaction theory holds that the process of socialization involves learning how to define and interpret objects, events, and people in a person's environment. When scapegoating exists, family members learn the shared definition and interpretation that the scapegoat is responsible for the family's major problems and that everything would be fine if it weren't for the scapegoat.

Ways of changing the existence of scapegoating thus involve a change of social structure. The scapegoat is given allies to enhance his or her ability to fight the collective definition that he or she is primarily responsible for all the family's troubles. Symbolic interactionists would argue that if scapegoating is to be eliminated, the way the scapegoat is collectively defined within the system must be changed.

ACCENTING THE POSITIVE In Milan, Italy, family therapists change the definition of the scapegoat through a process they call positive connotation (Goldenberg & Goldenberg, 1991). The assumption is made that the scapegoat serves a positive function for each and every member of the family. Family members come to understand the positive function that the scapegoat serves for them and each member is asked, on at least a weekly basis, to thank the scapegoat for performing that function for them. Siblings thus may thank the scapegoated child for being the family villain, which helps them look good in comparison. Many of their transgressions are ignored because the parents are focusing on the behavior of the scapegoat. Not only do siblings thus see the scapegoat as being helpful and not just troublesome, but the scapegoat is also less likely to think, "Why should I do that for my brothers and sisters?" As symbolic interactionists believe, perception changes result in behavior changes.

ELIMINATING THE NEGATIVE Other family therapists seek ways in which the family's negative definition of the scapegoat might be altered to bring about a better balance to the perception. The scapegoat can be seen as a person having faults and deficiencies but also as having strengths and assets, a person who contributes to the family in positive as well as negative ways. A therapist might ask the family when and under what circumstances the scapegoat does *not* cause trouble, is not a problem, so that the family might begin to look for instances where the scapegoat does behave well and does exhibit positive, constructive behavior. The therapist looks for the exceptions, the situations when problematic behavior does not occur (de Shazer & Berg, 1988). When an individual is labeled as troublemaker, delinquent, paranoid schizophrenic, or truant, such labels usually generalize that person's behavior. These people are not trouble, delinquent, schizophrenic, or truant all of the time. There are exceptions when they do not act in accordance with their label.

Recognizing and focusing upon the exceptions can lead to a significant change in the definition of the problem. If the problem behavior is not continuous, then the problem exists not within the individual but rather within the situation that sometimes exists to elicit the problem behavior. As the situation changes, the behavior changes. Family therapist Jay Haley (1980) focuses on behavior as arising out of situations. He sees most behavior that is labeled as psychopathology as appropriate behavior that is an adaptive, reasonable response to an impossible situation in which the actor finds himself.

Indeed, problematic behavior can be defined and interpreted in numerous ways by mental health professionals. If the behavior is seen as arising within an individual, it is reasonable to alter the behavior through some form of individual psychotherapy or drug therapy. If the problematic behavior is seen as arising out of difficult situations or out of interpersonal interactional dynamics, those interactional dynamics can be changed without drugs, which is what family therapists do. How the problem is defined will influence how the attempt is made to change it. The following example shows the process in action.

A couple comes in for therapy complaining about the behavior of their child. They plead, "Fix him, he's driving us up the walls!" A mental health practitioner who believes that behavior is created from within an individual, as a function of an individual's thoughts and feelings, will probably do individual psychotherapy with the child in an attempt to change the child's thoughts and feelings, which will then result in altered behavior. Another mental health practitioner may believe that the child's behavior is an adaptive response to the behavior of others in that child's environment. The child's behavior may be seen as a response to the way the parents act toward the child or, even more, how the parents behave toward each other. A practitioner with this definition of the situation would do family therapy, hoping to change the behavior of the parents so that the behavior of the child would change as a result. This is systemic family therapy, based on systems theory and the belief that a change in one part of a system (parents) will effect change in other parts of the system (children).

From a symbolic interactionist perspective, agents of change, like therapists, have different interpretations and definitions about what brings about behavior (Nichols, 1988). Their individual beliefs will influence the kinds of interventions they make and the kinds of therapists they are; for, as we have stated earlier, "if men [and women] define situations as real, then they are real in their consequences."

We next turn to a discussion of how symbolic interactionists might analyze the process of divorce. This process is seen as arising from a definition of the marital situation, held by at least one of the parties, as being something negative, something from which to be extricated.

Divorce

Definitions of objects and events are always subject to change over time. The love object, who was formerly defined as wonderful, may later come to be perceived differently. Often the very things that initially attract one person to another become problems for a couple over time. If someone is attracted to the physical appearance of another, the very beauty or physical attractiveness of that love object can be a source of jealousy later in the relationship. The thinking might be that if you found the partner attractive, other people may find him or her attractive too, and the partner may be the object of looks or stares, advances, and invitations that may prove difficult for a possessive, jealous partner.

A person may be attracted to another's apparent stability, reliability, and maturity initially. Over time, that may lead to a perception of the partner as being dull, boring, and unchanging, or inflexible and unexciting. A person may be attracted to another's humor, energy, vivaciousness, and zest for life. In time, this may lead to jealousy over "friendliness" to others or a wish that at times the other could slow down, be calm, or serious or intellectual. It is possible to have too much of a good thing.

FROM THE THOUGHT TO THE DEED As an individual increasingly defines a situation as undesirable, thoughts of alternatives may lead to counseling, discussions about discontent, marital separation, or divorce. If one person has already been divorced before, thoughts may include, "I know I can survive divorce, I've proven that already once before" or "I don't want to become a two-time loser." There is an internal dialogue that proceeds over time. After counseling and discussions have been tried, this dialogue may include indications such as "I know now that things are not going to change. I know I can't live like this any longer. I know that this will be bad for us financially and bad for the kids emotionally, but I owe it to myself to lead a better life than this." Divorce is "understood" by the symbolic interactionist, who grasps the internal dialogue of people who enter into divorce, comprehending the indications they made to themselves—which alternatives they considered and what they anticipated the consequences to be of the alternatives that they took into account. Divorce is seen as behavior stemming from the thoughts and feelings of the individuals; it is constructed behavior created by the individuals involved.

THE IDEAL OF MARRIAGE People usually carry in their minds very high expectations for what marriage ought to be like. They expect marriage to be exciting, rewarding, and fulfilling; to have energy, and passion; to meet their needs for companionship, sex, intellectual stimulation, recreation, and emotional support. This may be one of the reasons for high rates of divorce. People have such high expectations for marriage that they are bound to be disappointed by its realities.

People compare their expectations with the reality of their lives, and the reality falls far short. Yet they are committed to the idea that marriage, as they perceive it, is possible, attainable, out there waiting to be discovered. So although they do not have a terrible marriage, they are willing to terminate it for the ideal marriage that they carry in their heads. Divorce, then, is a commitment to the ideal of what marriage might be.

DEVITALIZED MARRIAGE Cuber and Harroff (1968) identify many couples in the United States as having what they call a "devitalized marriage." It is so-so, ho-hum, boring, dull. It has lost its zest, energy, and vitality. It is not a terrible marriage, which raises the point that divorce is not necessarily a good index of the quality of a relationship. We cannot assume that people who divorce have worse relationships than people who stay married to each other. Many couples with terrible relationships cannot terminate them; their relationships are poor but stable, perhaps the worst kind for children, who get trapped, with no way out of the conflict and abuse. Very often these couples have such ineffective interaction that they cannot negotiate their way to a termination of their marriage.

Child Custody Issues

Prior to World War I in this country, fathers were usually awarded custody of children when there was a divorce. Children were defined as economic assets. They were free labor on farms, and they often worked in factories and sweat shops. They were valued commodities. At about the time of World War I, child labor laws were passed that regulated the ability of children to work. These laws helped change the definition of children from economic assets to economic liabilities. If children could not work, they were economic dependents, costing the parents their food, clothing, and shelter. In cities, space was expensive, so the more children, the larger were the quarters that were needed to house them and the more expensive children became. Since children were less desirable, men became less interested in having custody of them. After child labor laws were passed, women increasingly received custody of children in divorce. Today, there is a preference for some form of joint custody, awarded to each parent, but usually women are still given primary physical custody of children.

In a joint custody arrangement, each parent is ensured of having the children some of the time. Usually, there is a primary custodial parent who has physical custody of the children most of the time, while the other parent has the children for a lesser time period. Children of divorce exhibit great loyalty to both of their parents, but this loyalty can prove problematic for divorced parents.

THE BIRTH OF A CUSTODY BATTLE In the following hypothetical situation, the primary custodial parent is the mother, who has remarried, meaning that there is a stepfather. The biological father, who has also remarried, has the children on alternate weekends. Out of loyalty, the children may tell their biological father what they think he wants to hear, what they think will make him happy—how much better he is than the stepfather and how much they love him. Perhaps the children may sense some jealousy on the part of the biological father. The biological father may perceive the stepfather as a competitor for the children's affection. He may be fearful and insecure in this perceived competition, because the stepfather has much more access to his own children than he has. So to relieve dad's concerns, they talk of how terrible their stepfather is. They share with their father how they are harshly disciplined by the stepfather, how unfair and unreasonable the stepfather is, and how much he yells at them. What will make the biological father happy, the children think, is hearing how much they miss their father and how much they wish they were with him. The children are selective in the information they give their biological father, avoiding all references to good times that they have with their mother and stepfather, all the good things this new family group has done for them, because information about the fun, support, warmth, and nurturance would only heighten their father's anxieties about his role in their lives.

Through his children's selective portrayal, the biological father comes to adopt a definition of the situation in which the children are miserable, the victims of psychological and physical abuse in their mother's household. He is, however, reluctant to check out the accuracy or completeness of his children's accounts. Through his definition of the situation, he files a motion with the court for a change of custody on the grounds that the best interests of the children would be served with him, given their miserable existence in the other household. He assumes the role of rescuer, whose mission it is to eliminate the victimization of his children.

His definition of the situation is subjective, and may or may not accurately or completely reflect an objective reality. If this father defines the situation as abusive, his definition will be real in its consequences, and a motion for change of custody will be filed. A custody dispute arises and the entire family is thrown into turmoil. The children meant well—they only wanted to please their dad—but the consequences for them can be traumatic, as they are put in the middle of a custody dispute. The courts then must determine the extent to which the father's definition of the situation is or is not an accurate reflection of the children's real world.

LANGUAGE AND REALITY The use of **language** is important, as it is the vehicle by which reality is created. Each single word we use connotes a meaning in the mind of the listener. Change words, and the reality for the listener may be altered significantly.

Salvador Minuchin et al. (1978) at one time advocated that family therapists should never label children in families as being "sick." When this word is used or implied, it often has a paralyzing effect on family members who perceive that sick people are cared for and dealt with by professionals. By defining children as sick, the implication is that parents have little power to do anything in altering the behavior of their children. Rather, Minuchin advocated defining children as powerful or, for young children, naughty. If children are defined as powerful, they exist within a province that parents can manage. The definition further contains within it the suggestion of how to deal with this child, namely, having the parents coalesce and support each other in maximizing their power to change the child's behavior.

What a different reality is created if a person is labeled "crazy" on the one hand or "creative" on the other! Crazy people might be candidates for drugs or institutionalization. Creative people are unusual, distinctive, often valued, and defined as potentially useful. They are tolerated and usually kept within family systems.

In the next section, we will continue our discussion of language as it applies to the words that people use when characterizing their relationships to other family members.

Defining Families

The words that people use to describe others reflect the definitions and interpretations that they make in relation to those others. This is illustrated when people use a kinship term to identity someone as being a family member, even though they are not related by either blood or marriage. Carol Stack's (1974) research on urban, African American families shows how people who live in these households are identified as **fictive kin**. Academic texts generally say that any people referred to as kin are related by blood; they share a consanguineal (blood) bond. Yet many urban African Americans refer to people as "my cousin" or "my nephew" even though there are no ties of blood or marriage between them. The subjective reality that exists by calling someone "my cousin" or "my nephew" is that the speaker feels so close to this person that he or she is like "family" and is given a family title.

The scholar of family life, who uses words that have carefully constructed definitions of concepts, would not define and interpret these fictive kin as true kin. To the symbolic interactionist, the definitions and interpretations academic social scientists make are no more real or accurate or truthful than the subjective definitions and interpretations of the urban African American who refers to someone as "my cousin" when there are no blood ties. The job of the symbolic interactionist is to understand the reality of others, to respect that reality, and not to impose his or her own reality on others who might not share it, for that would constitute a kind of academic tyranny. The job of the symbolic interactionist is to understand and describe the subjective states of minds of actors, which requires taking the role of the other.

Two different people sometime have very different definitions and interpretations of a situation. How these discrepancies are sometimes resolved is illustrated by Gubrium and Holstein (1990: 59–60) when they described the proceedings of an involuntary commitment hearing. The judge was predisposed to commit Conrad Moore to a hospital, where he would get love and attention, which he would not get living on his own because he did not have family to care for him. Moore was living in a board-and-care home. He considered the people there very much family, and he referred to them as such when he told the judge:

> You can't tell me they [hospital staff] care about me like my people. I got people at Briarwood [the board-and-care facility], man. They care. They're my family, man, my people. We're all in the same boat out there. We got each other, man, just like a family. Why can't you just let me stay?

The judge could not accept Moore's definition of his situation that the board-and-care members were family. The college-educated judge was taught that family members, to be family, had to be related by blood and/or marriage, and none of the people in the board-and-care facility were so related. Thus the judge could not conceive of these people as constituting Moore's "family." In Moore's subjective reality they were, and he called them his family.

Similar problems arise when a man and a woman live together as husband and wife. They refer to each other as husband and wife, introduce their partner to others as "my husband" or "my wife" even though they have never been legally married and even though they live in a state that does not recognize common-law marriage. In their reality, they are husband and wife. In the reality of the law, they are not. Should one partner die, leaving no will, and should the surviving spouse seek the partner's assets as "next of kin" by virtue of being "the spouse," the objective reality of the law would probably supersede the subjective reality of the surviving spouse, with the law denying access to the property because he or she was not, by legal definition, a spouse. When two different realities conflict, the concept of power becomes relevant. Judges have power to impose their definition and interpretation on others.

What is a family? Is it a social group whose members are related to each other through blood and/or marriage? Or is a family any social group defined by one of its members as a family? Whose reality should dominate? The symbolic interactionist states that reality is whatever people define it to be, and that there are millions of different subjective realities, all correct and truthful for the people holding to them. The role of the social scientist is to observe and record those realities and how they influence peoples' behavior; it is not to define some realities as being more right or more sane than others.

Critique

Symbolic interaction theory tends to be used to study the interpersonal behavior of individuals rather than groups. The theory works best for the microanalysis of interpersonal behavior and usually is not used for the macroanalysis of larger social structures.

Because this theory focuses on the role of interpretations and definitions in guiding behavior, and because there are no general principles or laws that allow one to predict how people will think, such as social exchange theorists provide, the theory tends to be idiosyncratic, with little predictive value. There is no way of predicting how any individual will interpret or define a situation; that has to be described only after a person gives meaning to an object or an event. Once a person gives meaning to the object or the event, alternatives must still be considered and consequences anticipated. This is done in a unique way for each individual, which means that the theory does not permit the anticipation or prediction of the behavior of anyone—particularly not the behavior of large numbers of people. This would present a problem for a theorist interested in building theory at a macrolevel.

Mead tried to overcome this by defining a social group as a collection of people who share common definitions of objects and events in their environment. This definition leaves much to be desired. Even dyads, as groups, do not contain people who share common definitions of objects and events in their environment, sometimes by virtue of the fact that this dyad may contain two people who are of different genders, family backgrounds, or social classes. Families are multigenerational, so that by adding diverse ages of people, there is even less likelihood that all members will share common definitions of objects and events in their environment.

Where people in families have different ways of defining and interpreting objects and events in their environment, symbolic interactionists would study the discrepant perceptions and interpretations and analyze how family members cope with these discrepancies—how they coordinate their actions in light of them. For instance, do family members avoid areas of discrepancy and only interact in areas of shared perception and interpretation?

Methodologically, symbolic interactionists run into some problems. A pattern of behavior that exists prior to baseball games is that people stand up for the playing of the "Star Spangled Banner." Suppose 1,000 people at a game were asked what indications they made to themselves that would allow a person to understand why they stood up for the "Star Spangled Banner" when it was played prior to the game. Some people would bark, "I don't know; leave me alone!" Others would say they couldn't remember. It is only a very few highly insightful, introspective people who can retrieve, in any meaningful way, the interpretative thought processes that they used prior to action, which would allow a researcher to "take the role of the other." These few introspective people act as informants, allowing a researcher to form working hypotheses that then have to be tested on the less introspective people. The testing of these hypotheses, however, is very difficult, because people generally do not recall all they thought about prior to their actions.

People stand when the "Star Spangled Banner" is played in part because they often choose to conform to the demands of the situation. And because they take into account the probable reaction of others in interpreting their own behavior, they may well conform to the behavior of others so that they are seen by the others as "normal." In this regard, the situation has some power in guiding their behavior.

Methodologically, symbolic interactionists, when they observe people behaving in situations, tend to see themselves as external observers, external to the situation being observed. They often perceive themselves as outsiders looking into situations. This stance can be critiqued, however, on the grounds that the observer is always, even as an observer, a participant in the situation being observed and may, indeed, influence the behavior of others. Thus, there are no boundaries in terms of being in or out of a situation.

This theory, which focuses on the process of defining and interpreting objects and events in an external world, overlooks the role of emotions as a component of behavior. Some level of emotionality is possible through the "I" part of the self, as are nonrational thought processes, such as might occur in the unconscious, but the "I" part of the self is relegated to a minor role in the theory. Because of its focus on how interpretative thought rather than feelings affects behavior, symbolic interaction theory has a masculine bias, just as exchange theory did.

Symbolic interaction theory presents a stark comparison to structural-functional theory. Where structural-functional theorists focus on how human behavior is externally controlled by structural factors such as social class, age, gender, religion, ethnicity, occupation, and level of education, symbolic interaction theorists focus on the autonomy of individuals in constructing their own lines of action. They acknowledge the existence of norms and sanctions. These are taken into account by actors, who may opt to conform with or deviate from the norms. With their focus on individual autonomy and their resistence to seeing individuals as externally constrained by structural forces, symbolic interactionists do not delve into concepts such as social class, ethnicity, age, religion, or gender as influences on the ways in which people define and interpret objects and events in their environment. The approach tends to overlook the external forces that impinge upon the individual and exert their influence on human thought and behavior.

Individual autonomy is important in both social exchange theory and symbolic interaction theory. The frameworks differ, however, inasmuch as social exchange theorists articulate a context by which people interpret objects and events—through an analysis of costs and rewards. Symbolic interactionists may consider it presumptuous to impose an analytic context on the perceptual processes of actors. Rather, they seek to understand just how actors perceive, define, and interpret objects and events. They approach their quest for understanding in a value-neutral way, without prejudging what they will hear.

Conflict theorists are social activists. They have a commitment to social action to remove inequality and injustice in the world. These theorists are apt to be impatient with the symbolic interactionist, who is interested in understanding why people behave as they do by theoretically interpreting the subjective states of minds of actors. The conflict theorist may well ask, "So, once you understand why people behave as they do, what are you going to do about it?"

For symbolic interactionists, the understanding exists for its own sake. Understanding is the goal, the objective. Conflict theorists would want understanding to lead to change and control. They would take a utilitarian position in relation to this knowledge. The symbolic interactionist generally has no such interest.

The conflict theorist would ask what symbolic interaction theorists would do with their understanding of why people behave as they do. Some symbolic interactionists would respond, "Nothing." They would define social action as not their job as social scientists. They would respond that their job is to understand human behavior, not to change it.

It could also be argued that if the way people define and interpret their environment guides their behavior toward objects and events in their environment, then to change the way people define and interpret their environment will alter their behavior. The symbolic interaction theorists may seek to change the ways in which people define and interpret others in order to promote different actions toward these others. Some interactionists may seek more favorable interpretations of, say, racial and ethnic minorities, to promote more tolerant, compassionate behavior toward these groups. Others may seek less favorable interpretations of, say, violent criminals, to promote less tolerant, compassionate behavior toward them.

Symbolic interactionists cannot just study the interpretations made by people outside of themselves. They must also define for themselves what is appropriate and inappropriate behavior for them as sociologists. They must define whether their job is to study human behavior or to change it.

Summary

Symbolic interaction theory focuses on the autonomy of individuals to carve out, to construct, their own behavior through a process of defining and interpreting objects and events. The thinking process involves giving meaning to objects and events in a person's environment—interpreting and defining the behavior of others—as well as considering alternatives of action that are available and anticipating probable consequences of each of those alternatives. Norms exist, impinging upon people, but individuals have the ability to take those norms into account and decide whether it is in their best interests to conform to those norms or to deviate from them.

In the process of social interaction, people construct roles relative to one another that create expectations in the minds of actors as to how people will behave in specific situations. These roles constrain people to act within the limits of those roles, restricting them from access to the full range of behavior that is available to them. People often assume roles within their families, and it is often difficult for them to break out of those roles. The roles they play in their family of origin influence roles they play in their families of procreation, in part because the roles they play become integrated into how they define themselves. Their images of themselves influence the indications they make to themselves, which in turn has an effect on the way they act toward others.

Symbolic interactionists react against the power of external constraints on individual behavior that are integral to developmental, structural-functional, and conflict theories. They give people the power to define their external world and to construct their own lines of action toward others. They give individuals the power to react against forces external to them, when they see those forces as being unjust or harmful.

Part Three

Attempting a Synthesis

We turn, in the final chapter, to a summary of the ideas put forth so far. We explore the ways in which they are different. The focus of each theoretical eyeglass is illustrated by employing each framework in the analysis of single-parent households and stepfamilies. We conclude with the recognition that each of these theories is accurate in portraying some dimension of the real world. Anyone trying to make sense of a segment of reality should use the framework that best fits the qualities of the reality that is being observed. The frameworks are not right or wrong, but rather more or less useful when they are applied to any reality. Ultimately, it is a utilitarian standard that sociologists adopt when they choose one framework over another.

Chapter 6

Putting It Together

Chapter Six

Putting It Together

The Focus

Our discussion of frameworks for studying families began with a discussion of how complex our world is, and with our understanding that it contains both change and resistance to change. Our world also contains external pressures to behave one way or another, people with autonomy to overcome pressures and construct their own behavior, and conflict as well as consensus, harmony, and integration.

Because no single framework exists that is capable of encompassing this vast complexity, there are many different theoretical frameworks that focus on specific elements of reality. With some of our theorists' glasses, therefore, we have a wide-angled view; with others we focus more narrowly. There is so much to look at, from so many perspectives, that it is no wonder that each theory must focus on a different dimension, and that all of them are needed to help us understand relationships in our familial and societal world.

In addition, sociologists in the last two decades have put forth additional frameworks that constitute the next stages of theoretical development in this dynamic field, which we will examine briefly.

The Theories

The theories that have been presented are very different in the approach each takes in presenting a view of reality. Developmental theorists focus on change and see the world as being in constant change, developing over time through stages. Sometimes the change is so slow that it is imperceptible except over a very long time span.

Change and Resistance

Developmental theorists can be compared to structural-functional theorists who generally see systems as resisting change and try to maintain a structural equilibrium by adapting to the forces that encourage change. Those individuals and subsystems that have the most status in a system will be particularly invested in resisting change to maintain their status.

Developmental theory and structural-functional theory seem to take antithetical and irreconcilable positions on the issue of social change. The irreconcilability may be more apparent than real. When a scenario is envisioned where a family is in a continuous and gradual process of change, there are forces seen within that family that attempt to resist the change and maintain a structural equilibrium. Were the resistance not present, the change might have been more rapid. But the resistance is not totally successful, because some slow change does exist. The question for a theorist in this situation is what to focus on, the change or the resistance to it. Developmental theorists would focus on the change; structural-functional theorists would focus on the resistance to the change. Both accurately represent a part of reality.

Conflict

The structural-functional theorist focuses on the ability of systems to integrate members into a cooperative, harmonious whole, bound together by a consensus of shared beliefs, values, and perceptions of reality, which they call "culture." Conflict is seen as dysfunctional, interfering with integration and latent pattern maintenance within a system. Conflict leads to change. The structural-functional theorist sees conflict as dysfunctional because the resultant change is antithetical to a system's ability to maintain a structural equilibrium.

The conflict theorist, on the other hand, sees conflict as natural, normal, and inevitable within all social systems. There will always be conflict over scarce resources in any system. There will always be conflict over power. Conflict is seen as functional, important, and even necessary to the survival of social systems. Systems can collapse from an absence of conflict. Can conflict be both functional and dysfunctional at the same time? How can these apparently discrepant perceptions of conflict be reconciled?

Indeed, conflict can be functional in some ways and dysfunctional in others. The structural-functional theorist focuses on the dysfunctional aspects of conflict. The conflict theorist focuses on the ways in which conflict is functional. Both accurately represent a part of reality.

Similarities

Despite these apparent differences between the theories, there are also some similarities that exist for them. Structural-functional theory's concept of a "cultural system" recognizes that people in systems are integrated by a shared system of beliefs and values. This is very similar to symbolic interactionist George Herbert Mead's definition of a social group as a collectivity of people who share common definitions of objects and events in their environment. What makes for a group in Mead's work is their shared definitions, their shared perceptions—in structural-functional terms, their culture. The postmodernists, whose theory will be discussed shortly, focus on language as a critical part of the culture of a group. For them, language is a crucial vehicle for constructing reality. As people within groups tend to speak the same language, as they are integrated by the language they share, they tend to share perceptions of reality.

UNDERLYING CONSENSUS Conflict theorists maintain that underlying conflict is a consensus over the ground rules under which the conflict will be waged. In structural-functional terms, the consensus functions to integrate the system of combatants.

When sports teams enter into conflict, there is a shared consensus on the rules by which the game will legitimately be played. Those rules are established by a league, which provides umpires and referees to enforce the rules and apply sanctions when the rules are violated. Even war, as conflict, is waged with a consensus of rules under which the war will be fought. The Geneva Convention Accords, which consist of rules governing the treatment of prisoners of war and the waging of chemical and biological warfare, have been agreed upon by signing nations as conditions under which wars shall be fought. The United Nations and the World Court are bodies that impose sanctions upon countries that violate those agreed-upon rules of warfare. Thus there seems to be some consensus between the conflict theorists and structural-functional theorists in relation to the normative structure under which conflict is waged. There are norms that govern the behavior of combatants and there are sanctions that are imposed to ensure conformity to those norms.

UNANTICIPATED CONSEQUENCES In structural-functional theory, exchange theory, and symbolic interaction theory, people are believed to have the ability to think rationally. In all three theories, part of the rational process involves the anticipation of consequences relative to alternative behaviors that are available to people. In all three theories, people may, and often do, predict incorrectly the consequences of their actions. Merton's concepts of manifest and latent function formalized the idea of "unanticipated consequences" more completely than this idea exists in the other theories. The idea that our thoughts affect our behavior but that we may incorrectly anticipate the consequences of our actions exists in all three theories.

Constraint and Autonomy

In most social systems, whether families or whole societies, a struggle (conflict) can be seen between the forces that seek to control the behavior of individuals and the force that individuals exert in their effort to maintain their autonomy.

Families seek to control the behavior of their members to achieve integration. That integration can be achieved if the family members share core values and exhibit behavior that is consistent with those values. Shared cultural values are the cement that binds the members of a family together.

The existence of norms influences the manifestation of behavior that is consistent with values. Compliance to norms is ensured through sanctions. It is through the sanctioning of behavior that people in families most directly experience external control of their behavior.

Norms function to ensure the order, structure, and predictability of behavior that is critical to the mental health of family members. If there is order and structure and predictability of behavior, the levels of stress and anxiety that people experience in their lives are reduced.

Although Freud (1929/1961) wrote that habitual anxiety or neurosis is created by an excess of order and structure, anxiety can also be created by too little order and structure. The absence of order and structure makes people in a family wonder whether or not critical tasks will be performed. If people have to worry about whether groceries will be purchased and by whom, whether dinner will be cooked and by whom, whether there will be clean clothes available, and if these worries exist on a regular basis, they will feel less happy, less secure about their lives. The more people worry, the more anxious and stressful they become.

Although order, structure, and predictability are necessary in families, there can be too many demands for conformity, so that there is no room for individuals to develop their own personal behavioral styles. There has to be some individual autonomy to explore and experiment in the world. This self-exploration is an important ingredient in personal development.

The struggle for autonomy is often exhibited in the form of deviant behavior, behavior that violates norms. If the norms are to be maintained, the deviant behavior must be negatively sanctioned. Deviant behavior does not always have to be negative behavior, however. Brilliant creativity is also deviant and can lead to innovative, constructive change. This behavior challenges the system to change and adapt. Deviance creates a stimulus for change so that the family does not remain static.

Deviant behavior exists in all social systems. People may engage in it because they want to feel a sense of personal power over the forces of the system. They may engage in it as a form of self-expression, a way to identify a part of themselves that is truly free of external constraints. They may engage in it in conformity to competing alternative norms that exist.

When looking at families, a struggle can usually be seen between forces demanding conformity and control and forces seeking individual autonomy and self-determination. Theorists emphasizing external constraint focus on the importance of order and structure and the energy that is put into preserving it in families. The exchange theorists and symbolic interactionists focus on the struggle to overcome these external forces that enables individuals to create and construct their own behavior.

In exploring the writings of Toynbee, we discussed the idea that all social systems must face and overcome challenges that exist to potentially threaten the viability of the system. All families must face and overcome the challenge of maintaining order and structure while at the same time permitting levels of individual autonomy. In facing this challenge, families often move in pendulum-like fashion toward having too much order and structure, or too much autonomy, and then they must adapt and change to create better balance.

Contemporary families in the United States increasingly feature parents who are working long hours and who are away from home most of their waking time. Children are increasingly unsupervised. Families in the United States may well be characterized as having, in structural-functional terms, an integration crisis. The contemporary family may well be seen as becoming, in postmodern terms, deconstructed. The contemporary family is currently at the far end of the pendulum swing to individual autonomy.

Whether this is interpreted as good or bad, desirable or not, is a matter of politics. For political conservatives, the challenging question of our time is how the family can regain order, structure, and integration—structural-functional concepts—and still find a way to survive economically. For them, order and structure require that parents regain hierarchical control over their children that would enable them to successfully transmit cultural values: honesty, obedience to authority, respect and tolerance for others (particularly for others who are different from us), education and knowledge, the attainment of economic self-sufficiency through legitimate gainful employment, and a spiritual transcendence to a supreme beneficent power that some refer to as God. They insist on the hierarchy and control existing in family systems, but not in government, which they think should be reduced in controlling the lives of individuals, while families should increasingly control the lives of their own members.

From a structural-functional perspective, this argument does not promote integration between families and the political system. It creates an anomic situation, where families are left unsupported to effect significant changes. From where does the family get support in its struggle to regain control of children? Families cannot do it alone and, especially if they live in poor neighborhoods, neither the community nor its churches will have the resources to lend the level of support that is needed to get the job done.

For the politically liberal, individual autonomy is seen as beneficial in lifting the constraints of patriarchy. Women are freed from the dominance of men, and children are freed from the often abusive control of parents. The liberation of the human spirit, enabling people to be what they choose or aspire to be, is seen as socially desirable. The withering away of hierarchical control is particularly liberating to the disadvantaged and oppressed in the society: women, the poor, ethnic and racial minorities. In this mode of thought, families should be egalitarian and facilitate individual autonomy and self-actualization, while the role of government should be to enhance the ability of the disadvantaged and the oppressed to gain greater autonomy over their own lives. The challenge of government becomes how to facilitate individual autonomy through social programs that do not create dependency and control over those served. Programs that impose control of their "clients" reinforce the "status quo" and do not teach these clients to gain control over their own lives. Of course, governments do not want to give money without maintaining control.

AUTONOMY AND ANOMIE Individual autonomy, particularly as expressed in symbolic interaction theory, is facilitated by incongruities that exist within any social structure. The existence of ambiguous or incongruent norms in a social structure is called anomie by structural-functional theorists. These theorists perceive anomie to be dysfunctional (Merton, 1968). However, anomie exists to some extent in all social structures.

Sometimes the anomie exists as an inconsistency between ethical norms and statistical norms (Bierstedt, 1957). **Ethical norms** are "shoulds," injunctions to behave in particular ways. **Statistical norms** are indices of what people actually do in their behavior. There are ethical norms that forbid jaywalking (crossing the street in the middle of the block, not at a corner, or when the sign reads "Don't Walk"). Despite the ethical norms, which often exist as city ordinances or laws, the statistical norm is that most people jaywalk. This situation illustrates anomie, the incongruity between ethical and statistical norms. Another familiar example involves the ethical norm that forbids the use or possession of marijuana, even though many studies indicate that most college students at some time in their lives have experimented with the drug.

When anomie exists, the individual finds the opportunity to be autonomous. No social structure is a perfectly integrated, well-meshed blend of norms and values. All social structures have incongruities and inconsistencies that reduce the power and determinism of the social structure. This, in turn, allows people the freedom to create independent action.

In a large, industrialized society, the socialization of children is shared by parents, schools, churches, peer groups, and mass media. The values and norms that the individual is exposed to by these various socializing agents leave the individual with choices, because the values and norms espoused by these agents differ. From all of the choices and alternatives presented, the individual can select one system or a combination of value and normative systems to serve as the model for behavior. The social structure does not contain within it singular standards of right and wrong, desirable and undesirable.

Honesty may be espoused by clergy, and it may be verbalized by parents; but this is countered by children's hearing their parents brag, for example, about cheating on their income tax filing. Though honesty is verbalized as a value, a peer group in actuality may show prospective members how to shoplift merchandise and may demand that this be done by the children as a prerequisite for gaining entry into the group. So the children are left with a difficult choice, to obey their parents or obey their peers.

In school a child is told by a teacher, "Don't cheat" on exams, yet the child may also be taught by peers that "everyone cheats." He or she may be taught five alternative methods of cheating, and thus be faced with making an autonomous decision presented by rival participants in the social structure; cheat or don't cheat, and if cheat, how?

Symbolic interaction theorists believe that people construct their own lines of action. Structural-functional theorists provide the concept of anomie that explains the source of autonomy as coming out of the incongruities within the social structure. Anomie tends to intensify in a postindustrial world as large groups fragment into smaller special-interest groups.

In a postindustrial world, individual autonomy also increases as a function of the great heterogeneity and diversity that exists in that world. The problem for these societies, and for social institutions within them, is how to attain integration.

We already see this in family structures where children have gained significant autonomy, particularly in dual-worker families or single-parent families. The problem in these families is how to attain integration so that each person is not functioning alone but interacts with other family members with enough frequency to feel a sense of belonging to the group and to feel support and nurturance from the group. When integration is not achieved, people seek the resources of other groups, such as gangs, for support. Autonomy and integration must exist in a delicate balance. It is the challenge of all social systems, and essential for families, to create that balance.

As with members of a family, adherents of each of the theoretical frameworks we have studied often seek to maintain their autonomy in a family of sociologists. The purity of their analytic approach enables them to be distinct within the discipline of sociology. Yet it is possible to integrate many of these frameworks into a mosaic of the social world. In the next section, each framework will be shown as unique and distinctive in its focus, yet able to be combined to create a comprehensible *gestalt,* a wholeness that explores diverse aspects of reality.

As our example, the postdivorce experience of families will be analyzed, using the concepts and perspective of each theoretical framework. It is hoped that this format will enable the reader to comprehend how the eyeglasses of each framework enable the wearer to see different aspects of life, in this case, in single-parent families and in stepfamilies.

CULTURAL BIASES IN THEORY Before going on to the application of the theoretical frameworks, there is another observation, important to our discussion, that should be made at this point. This author had the opportunity to teach sociological theory for one year at United College, which is part of the Chinese University of Hong Kong. The eye-opening experience of teaching theory in a non–Western European culture led to the realization that each of these theoretical frameworks tends to be consistent or inconsistent with basic principles of a particular culture.

For example, the three theories of external control in Part I were easily understood by Chinese students, because Chinese culture is filled with deterministic beliefs (Hsu, 1970; Winton, 1975). Individuals are seen as being governed by gods, spirits, deceased ancestors, astrology, parents and grandparents, educators, and hot and cold foods. Parents in Chinese families are often authoritarian with their children. Teachers are authoritarian with their students, and governments are authoritarian with their subjects. People are seen as tightly controlled and governed by forces external to them. The theories emphasizing external control of the individual were consistent with these Chinese students' experiences of the world.

The two theories in Part II, however, were totally foreign to them. Concepts such as individual autonomy, self-determination, equality, and democracy are all Western concepts (Winton, 1975). They are sometimes incomprehensible to the Chinese mind. The notion that people construct their own lines of action as a function of their own internal thought processes was inconsistent with their experience of the world. They were very skeptical and critical of these theories.

Each of these theories is predicated on the notion of individual autonomy and self-determination. They are products of the Western European mind. This means that they are apt to be received better in Western European countries than they may be in societies in other parts of the world. The cultural beliefs in non-Western societies may include more deterministic principles, making the theories in Part I more attractive and consistent. The veracity of any theory, therefore, may lie in the extent to which it is congruent or incongruent with people's experience of the world and with the principles of their own culture. It is not that one theory is right and another wrong. Rather, the attraction to one theory over another is, in part, because of its consistency with cultural values and beliefs that have been internalized in a process of socialization.

Applying the Theories

Although the incidence of non-marriage is increasing in the United States, Arthur Norton and Jeanne Moorman (1987) estimate that 90 percent of women born after 1950 will eventually marry. Approximately half of the first marriages will end in divorce (Ihinger-Tallman, 1988). Slightly more, 60 percent, of second marriages will end in divorce. Approximately 80 percent of divorced men and over 75 percent of divorced women will ultimately remarry (Schoen, R. et al., 1985).

Using Developmental Theory

The developmental theorist, portraying change over time as occurring in stages, might depict a three-stage process of divorce. The first stage might be labeled "marital separation and divorce." The developmental tasks that are performed in this stage would include acknowledging the unsatisfying nature of the marriage for at least one of the parties and negotiating the marital separation (Wallerstein & Blakeslee, 1990). This negotiation includes who will leave the family household and with what possessions they will leave. When children are involved—and they are involved in approximately 60 percent of all divorces (Weitzman, 1985)—negotiations must be entered into regarding the custodial arrangement for each parent during the separation period. One of the parties files for a legal dissolution of the marriage. The parties must then negotiate a settlement agreement, specifying all the terms and conditions of the divorce.

The marital separation creates the second stage, the "single-parent household" (Wallerstein & Blakeslee, 1989: 9). The developmental tasks of this household include surviving economically on limited funds. If the single parent is not gainfully employed, he or she must become so in order to obtain the physical necessities of life: food, shelter, and clothing. If the single parent has been employed part-time, he or she must usually seek full-time employment. The family must create a new division of labor, so that needed tasks get done. Child care must be arranged. The family must also cope with fatigue, as the combined demands of school, work, and the household create exhaustion.

The remarriage of the single parent creates the third stage, the "development of a **stepfamily**" (Visher & Visher, 1990). Formerly married people select mates from a generally wider pool of eligible partners than do those marrying for the first time (Sacks & Suitor, 1992; Wilson, 1989). For instance, there is a greater age difference between the spouses in second marriages. In first marriages, the groom is usually two years older than the bride. In second marriages, he is usually four years older. People who are marrying for the first time usually marry in their mid-twenties. Those who marry for a second time are usually in their mid-thirties. As a function of being older and more experienced, people in second marriages add pragmatic criteria in deciding whom to marry. In addition to love, mate selection is based on instrumental needs, such as assistance with parenting, household labor, and financial responsibilities. Almost two-thirds of remarriages involve children from a former marriage (Cherlin & McCarthy, 1985).

The developmental tasks required in the stepfamily stage include bringing the new spouse into the fabric of family life. The parents must coordinate their parenting styles and philosophies. If both spouses bring children from a prior marriage with them, the children must bond with one another. New relationships must be created between people who have never lived together before. The children must reconcile their biological parent's wish that they have a good relationship with the stepparent with their own sense of loyalty to the noncustodial parent. The stepfamily must establish a workable interaction with the noncustodial parent.

Stepfamilies in the United States today are probably no more prevalent, as a percentage of total families, than they were 300 years ago. What led to the creation of stepfamilies has changed, with divorce replacing widowhood as the vehicle creating marital separation. In colonial America, widowhood was frequent; life expectancy was limited by the risks of childbirth, war, disease, and inclement weather. Because of the harshness of their existence, people remarried because they needed helpmates to survive. Their remarriages created stepfamilies.

Using Structural-Functional Theory

The social structure of most single-parent families features a female head of household. Approximately 90 percent of single-parent households are headed by women (Mulroy, 1988). Most single-parent households are created as a function of divorce, but some are created through widowhood, and others exist as a function of a nonmarital pregnancy. The structural-functional theorist focuses on how the social structure of the single-parent household affects interpersonal dynamics within that system.

Talcott Parsons made a distinction between people who perform an instrumental function in a family and those who perform an expressive function. When people perform an instrumental function, they meet the family's physical needs; they provide food, clothing, and shelter through their gainful employment in the outside world. Through their work they relate the family to the outside world. The person who performs an expressive function meets the family's emotional needs, making sure that everyone is happy. This person relates family members to each other, making sure that everyone gets along and that the family is integrated. In a single-parent household, the single parent must perform both functions. This can lead to role overload.

ROLE OVERLOAD It is not that single parents cannot perform both functions; it is just that they are operating at the height of their capability on a daily basis (Sanik & Mauldin, 1986). The usual routine calls for single parents to awaken in the morning at 6 or 6:30, get themselves ready for work (most single parents work full-time), wake up their children and get them ready for school, give them breakfast, go to work themselves for a full day, return from work, prepare dinner, serve, eat, and clean up after dinner, spend some time interacting with the children, helping them with schoolwork, bathing them, getting them ready for bed, and, finally, putting them to bed. Then there is a magic hour, the only hour in the parents' day when they can attend to their own needs, rather than meeting the needs of others. Single parents often try to protect this special time, which, of course, can be intruded upon by children who will not or cannot go to bed. Finally, the parents go to sleep just to awake the next morning and repeat this routine, day after day after day.

Because these parents are working at maximum capacity, there is little energy or flexibility left to cope with unusual crises: a sick child, a car breaking down, malfunctioning equipment. Such emergencies sometimes result in an emotional breakdown—a sense of being overwhelmed, overpowered, overburdened, helpless, hopeless—and paralysis in coping with the crisis. This is **role overload**.

In times such as these, friends, who normally lie outside the boundaries of the family system, could be important sources of assistance and emotional support. However, because single parents often do not have the time or energy to nurture friendships, they are often **socially isolated**. It is difficult for them to maintain friendships given their time constraints (White & McLennan, 1987). Family and work demands for their time and energy leave single parents with little left for the maintenance of friendships.

ESSENTIAL CHILDREN Children in single-parent households assume a role in which their labor and cooperation are essential ingredients for the physical and emotional survival of the household. They are assigned more responsibilities and chores than are children in intact nuclear family units (Wallerstein & Blakeslee, 1989; Weiss, 1979). This has sometimes been labeled a "loss of childhood" for these children, who are apt to be asked to assume what are sometimes thought of as adult responsibilities, such as cooking, doing laundry, cleaning, and so forth. This is particularly true for older adolescent girls (Greif, 1985). More responsibilities in the household usually earn children in single-parent households a higher status than children might have in intact nuclear families. To outsiders, this may look like a very permissive household in which decision making is shared by all family members.

Life in single-parent households is often a struggle, since there is frequently a shortage of money and energy. This shared struggle functions to bind family members into a tightly knit, highly integrated unit. This high level of integration can be dysfunctional.

PROTECTIVE CHILDREN It is sometimes harder for children from single-parent households to launch out of the family, as independent, autonomous adults, than it is for children from intact nuclear family units (Gerstel & Gross, 1989). The last child, particularly, can find that leaving mom by herself causes considerable guilt and concern. Sometimes the protective inclination is such that children are willing to sacrifice their autonomy to stay home and care for their mother.

Graduating seniors in high school, formerly excellent students who are on their way to attend a college or university away from home, will suddenly start failing a course that is required for graduation from high school. At a less than conscious level, these students know that if they fail the course, they will not be able to leave home to attend college. They can stay home and care for their needy parent. Should the students pass the course, they may then do poorly in college in their freshman year, because they could not concentrate on their studies out of worry and concern for mother. The latent function of flunking out of college is that students can return home to care for their mothers.

STEPFAMILIES If a divorced single parent remarries, a stepfamily is created. The social structure of this system consists of a stepparent, a biological parent, and children from the previous marriage. Because in the vast majority of divorces, women have primary physical custody of the minor children, the stepparent is usually male and the biological parent is usually female (Gerstel & Gross, 1989: 216; Basow, 1986b).

One of the functions of stepfamilies is that they add kin to family networks. Particularly for children, this extends the potential for warm, nurturing relationships with more people. It provides children with a broader network of support and interaction than they had in a single-parent household. In the box on page 170, we will examine how a structural-functional theorist would do a structural analysis of stepfamilies.

Conflict Theory

The conflict theorist will focus on conflict within single-parent families and stepfamilies, conflict arising from power differentials and conflicts over scarce resources. This theorist can explain why children in single-parent households have as much power as they do. Their labor is essential to the survival of the system (Krissman, 1992). Their labor thus becomes a valued resource, which is used as a base for power. Because they do almost as much work in the household as does the single parent, older adolescent girls particularly gain al-

A Structural Analysis The social structure of the stepfamily leads to integration problems. How can the single parent and her biological children, bound together by their shared history and struggle for economic and emotional survival, allow this stranger, this outsider, to integrate into their tightly knit system?

The stepparent, as an outsider, sees the children as having higher status than he believes they should have. He believes they need to return to their roles as children. He sees the biological mother relating to them as equals. He believes that the biological parent disciplines the children neither well nor enough, so he often adopts the role of stern disciplinarian (Wallerstein & Blakeslee, 1989: 251). When a stepfather disciplines, the children run to their mother for nurturance and support. When she gives them support, she sabotages the disciplinary efforts of her spouse. The parents work against each other. They assume complementary roles, with one being a nurturant parent and the other being a disciplinary parent. What develops is a **fragmented parental subsystem**, where mother accuses the stepfather of being too harsh and he accuses the biological mother of being too soft. A latent function of the fragmented parental subsystem is often that the children gain more power than either parent, which can result in out-of-control children.

---

most as much as power in the family as the single-parent head of household. They usually do not have as much power as the mother, since the mother controls more of the system's resources because of her paycheck.

As we have seen earlier in this chapter, the labor of children in single-parent households is a more valued resource to those families than is labor of children in intact nuclear family units. Children in single-parent households, therefore, also have more power than do children in intact nuclear family units because, as a resource, they are so critical to the family's survival. The work done by these children is sometimes a source of conflict within the system. The eldest daughter may well complain that she is expected to do more work in the house than are her younger siblings. She may complain that she is expected to do more work at home than are her high school peers. When children are negligent in doing their chores, the issue cannot be ignored by the single parent because of the necessity for everyone to pull his or her own weight in the household. The parent must, therefore, confront children for their negligence. As a result, conflict may sometimes occur.

UNREALISTIC CONFLICT A single-parent mother who holds considerable anger toward her former spouse may displace this conflict onto a son. She selects a son because, as a male, he symbolizes the father. Conflict between the mother and son would thus be nonrealistic conflict, since the mother's anger is manifested toward the son but is really felt for the father, who may be inaccessible.

Salvador Minuchin, Bernice Rosman, and Lester Baker (1978), structural family therapists, argue that when there are problems with children, whether those problems are truancy, delinquency, poor grades in school, or psychosomatic illness, it will often be found that one parent is enmeshed (overinvolved) with the problem child. This means that the enmeshed parent will have a closer relationship with the problem child than with the spouse. The disengaged parent then feels that all the attention, affection, energy, and concern are being directed by the spouse to the problem child and thus feels neglected and withdraws emotionally. The disengaged spouse accuses the partner of being excessively involved and concerned with the child, and, at the same time, the enmeshed spouse feels no support from the partner. The enmeshed spouse resents having to deal with the problem child all alone. There is again a fragmented parental subsystem. It is only when this parental subsystem becomes integrated and the parents work together as a team that the child's symptoms will begin to disappear.

What structural family therapy implies is that there is an ideal structure for family systems. Parents should have more power than children. The only way they can generate more power than their children is by working together and supporting each other.

This may be one reason why sons often do better in their postdivorce adjustment in father-custody, rather than mother-custody, households.

In stepfamilies, conflict arises between the stepparent and the stepchildren when the children compare the stepparent with the noncustodial parent. The children usually have great loyalty to the noncustodial biological parent, who does things differently from the stepparent. To them, different equals wrong. Of course, different is not wrong, it is only different, but children do not see things this way. Particularly when the biological parent is deceased, children can have an idealized vision of the missing parent with no reality to which to compare it. The stepparent is then compared to an idealized ghost and may well have to fight hard to be evaluated on his or her own terms.

One kind of stepfamily is a blended one. A **blended family** is formed when two parents marry and each brings with them children from a previous relationship. The box on page 172 describes some of the problems of the "blend."

Social Exchange Theory

Social exchange theorists will look at single-parent households and stepfamilies by focusing on costs and rewards, gains and losses that are incurred by family members in these structures. The exchange theorist will see that single-parent

Conflict in Blended Families

The Brady Bunch was a blended family. When children from previous families are joined together to make a new nuclear family household, there will be conflict over many scarce resources. There will be conflict over space and territory. When two children have to share a bedroom, there will often be conflict over who gets which bed, who gets which side of the closet, who gets which drawer in the chest. The beds, sides of closet, and drawers are not perceived as being of equal value, but as having particular qualities, some of which are more preferable than others. These differences cause the children to fight over space and territory.

Marriage into a stepfamily is sometimes described as having a honeymoon in a crowd. The parents feel that they are being drawn and quartered by family members' demands for time. First of all, the parent must spend time with the new spouse in order to establish a new marital relation. Then the parents' biological children expect time alone with their parent, in a nostalgic attempt to maintain the former single-parent household. These biological children want time together with their biological parent as the old single-parent unit, and each child also wants time alone with his or her biological parent, time that does not have to be shared with siblings. Each parent must, in addition, spend time with his or her new stepchildren, both together and individually, in order to establish a unique relationship with each of them (Basow, 1986a: 231; Visher & Visher, 1990). And the parents must spend time with the entire stepfamily as a unit, with all members together so that they can establish the sense of a new family unit. There just is not enough time

---

households are usually created through the experience of some loss. The loss may come through the death of a spouse or through divorce.

The loss in the minds of the children involves the loss of the family as they have known it. It involves the loss of daily contact with both parents and of sharing a household with both parents. It involves the loss of an identity for themselves as they adopt a new identity either as a child of divorce or of bereavement. These losses are synonymous with costs.

Often children of divorce are not told about the change prior to the departure of a parent from the household. They wake up one morning to find one parent gone. This can lead to sleep disorders for children, because the message from their experience is that if they sleep, a parent will disappear into the night. With one parent already gone, the children cannot sleep for fear of losing the remaining parent. They know that this can happen unexpectedly; it has already happened to them once.

SABOTAGING ADULT RELATIONSHIPS Children in single-parent households will often sabotage relationships that their custodial parent has with potential

to devote to all these diverse permutations. Meanwhile, the children's jealousy helps them keep track of the time parents spend with other family members. They demand equity, perhaps accusing a parent of loving another child more than themselves.

The same issues relate to the spending of money. Children often keep a mental account of how much money each person in the family is allowed for spending on clothes or entertainment. They may compete with one another so that they do not come up short in the accounting.

One function of this conflict is to establish a power structure among new family members. Through the conflict, the children are creating a hierarchy of those who have more and those who have less power (Haley, 1986). They are discovering tactics that work and tactics that do not work in getting what they want. They invite the parents into the conflict to assess whether or not the parent will intervene and with whom the parent will side. If the parent does intervene and if the parent does side with one child against another, the parent will be sought in future battles as an ally by the children with whom the parent coalesced. Furthermore, a latent function of parents intervening to interrupt the conflict may be that the conflict is prolonged. The interruption does not allow the conflict to become resolved, so the conflict may be initiated anew to establish a resolution between the children. When the children do battle among themselves, they can see who is more or less powerful. They can see where they stand in relation to the others. Once the hierarchy comes to be established, the level of conflict usually subsides, flaring occasionally as one or another child retests that hierarchy.

---

partners. An exchange theorist would interpret these sabotaging attempts as occurring from fear of further losses. In the single-parent household, the children have mother's undivided attention, affection, time, and money. A new person in her life is a competitor. The enemy must be vanquished so the children can have their mother to themselves. From this author's experience as a therapist, it is only when children are older that this sabotaging ceases. When the children are 16 or 17, it is to their advantage that both parents have partners, because with someone to care for their parents, with someone else responsible for them, the children are off the hook for these caretaking responsibilities. They can launch themselves out into the world guilt free.

Children in stepfamilies see the remarriage of the custodial parent as involving losses for themselves also. Certainly the remarriage is a threat to their hope and belief that mom and dad will eventually get back together again and reconstitute what the children believe is their "real" family. Even though a remarriage occurs, the belief in the reconciliation of the parents does not die. The children often believe and hope that the forthcoming marriage will be short-lived so that then mom and dad will become reconciled and live together again.

There is the loss of the single-parent unit. There is a loss of status that the children have if the stepparent issues rules and regulations and takes an authoritarian, disciplinary posture. There is often a loss of territory and privacy if more persons occupy the same dwelling than lived there before. If the children perceive that stepfamily life will incur more costs than rewards for them, they will not easily participate and cooperate in having the new family system run smoothly and happily.

Symbolic Interaction Theory

Symbolic interaction theorists will focus on the interpretations and definitions people have of objects and events in their lives and on how those perceptions influence behavior. Children of divorce generally love both their parents and usually want to be loyal to both. If, in the single-parent household, one parent bad-mouths another in anger, the child often internalizes this as anger toward him- or herself. If the anger is directed toward a biological father, the child, realizing that he or she is a part of that father, may perceive the anger as directed toward him- or herself. A son who sees the anger directed toward his father may internalize the anger as being directed toward males generally, particularly if he identifies strongly with his father, has a close bonding with him, or strongly loves his father.

KEEPING THE PEACE Children of divorce sometimes define themselves as the family messenger (Wallerstein & Blakeslee, 1989: 189), the peacemaker, the person who is in charge of seeing that mom and dad get along. This sense of responsibility results in feelings of crisis and failure when the parents do not get along well. Children may also come to define themselves as responsible for their parents' happiness, and thus may take parental depression and pain as their own personal failure. They may feel the need to play the role of clown to cheer up the parent, or they may feel the need to take on adult responsibilities in the home (sometimes tackling potentially dangerous jobs) so that the parent will not be so tired. Increasingly, children in this society are taking the role of caretakers of their needy parents rather than that of people who are cared for by these parents.

LIVING WITH MYTHS When stepfamilies are initiated, each of the parties tends to make different indications to themselves. These indications constitute fantasies each has as they enter this new family. The biological parent is apt to think, "Finally, I'll get some help." The stepparent is apt to think, "We'll be one big happy family." The children are apt to think, "This will not work out (and we'll help it to not work out so that mom and dad will eventually get back together again)." This is the **myth of reconcilation**. Note how the indications made by the stepparent and the children are antithetical to each other.

This situation is complicated by the **myth of instant love**, usually held by the biological parent. This parent believes that the new spouse is a terrific and wonderful person and that the children cannot help but quickly love this person, too. This is an expectation that is very likely to be dashed by reality.

Why should the children love this person? The stepparent is a stranger. He or she has not shared the history of struggle and hardship that they have endured. The stepparent is the competitor, victorious in the struggle with the children for the biological parent's time, attention, and affection. He or she is the heavy, who is disciplining the children and "putting them in their place."

As a result of the fantasy that "we will be one big happy family," the stepfather sometimes attempts legally to adopt the children. He figures that if they all have the same name, there will be a unifying effect (Wolf & Mast, 1987). These attempts will often be met with resistance by the children, who are apt to think to themselves, "I already have a fine last name that has served me very well all these years. I don't want your name." The attempt at adoption is interpreted as more than the loss of a name for the children; it is the loss of their identity. The children believe that if they do not resist this adoption attempt, they are being disloyal to their biological father, who will be furious upon learning about this. The shared name is often identified as an important link the children have to this parent, a link that is in jeopardy of being broken.

Sexual behavior between the stepparent and the stepdaughters sometimes occurs in stepfamilies (Wallerstein & Blakeslee, 1989: 249). This is facilitated by a popularly held definition of incest as being sexual behavior between people who are related by a consanguineal bond, such as biological parents and their children. The stepparent and stepchildren are not bonded by a blood tie, and thus the stepparent can rationalize the sexual activity as not constituting incest. Legal authorities may also define it not as incest but as sexual abuse, punishable by imprisonment. Others may define the behavior as incest, if they define incest as sexual behavior between any members of a family who are not married to one another.

Reality is like a multifaceted diamond. Each of the theories that sociologists employ focuses on a particular facet of the whole. By using all the theories, one still does not grasp the whole, which is more than the sum of its parts. Through their interaction, the parts are in a continuous process of change. As the parts change, the interaction changes. The reality that exists at one point in time is different from the reality existing at another point in time. This is one of the factors that makes the analysis of the social world so difficult.

Critique

Developmental, structural-functional, conflict, exchange, and symbolic interaction theories are considered modernist frameworks because they derive from basic assumptions that have their roots in the European Age of Enlightenment. Sociology is often thought to have begun in the mid-nineteenth century with the work of the French social philosopher Auguste Comte (1855; 1877), who is often cited as the "father of sociology."

Comte and his followers believed that social life was governed by "natural laws." They believed that the real world had a structure, a pattern, a consistency that could be articulated through theory. The development of theory was the way social scientists ordered and structured their knowledge about the world. Through theory building, the natural order of social life could be known. If it could be known, then this knowledge could be used to improve the quality of human life. In Comte's words (translated from the original French), "To know in order to predict, to predict in order to control."

Following from this intellectual tradition, developmental theory posits that it is the natural order of all social systems to change gradually in an orderly direction through stages over time. So-called "developing societies," societies that are preindustrial or in the early stages of industrialization, change toward greater urbanization and industrialization. Families in these societies change toward nuclear family units. As postindustrial societies develop, nuclear families exhibit an increasing array of diverse forms, including single-parent households, stepfamilies, gay and lesbian families, communes as families, and cohabiting, nonmarital families.

Structural-functional theory portrays the natural order of the social world as containing systems that are interrelated and interdependent. These systems have a definable social structure, where coalitions, a division of labor, and a hierarchical power structure can all be described. These systems attempt to maintain a structural equilibrium. To survive, the systems must feature latent pattern maintenance, adaptation, and integration; and they must be able to attain at least short-range goals.

Conflict theory portrays conflict as a natural, normal, and inevitable part of the social world, functional in many respects, and indeed a critical component to the survival of social systems. Conflict occurs within a framework of ground rules under which the conflict is waged. Conflict exists because all social systems have scarce resources that are fought over. All social systems also have social stratification (assuming that people will inevitably create a hierarchical organization with some people having more power than others and further assuming that all equalitarian social structures are inherently unstable until a clear hierarchy is attained). This breeds conflict, because those with less power will seek more and those with more power will seek to maintain that power.

Exchange theory assumes that behavior is affected by thoughts and feelings that lie within individuals and that all people think in terms of an exchange of costs and rewards. Costs and rewards can be quantified, but the ultimate determinant of behavior is an individual's subjective appraisal of costs and rewards.

Symbolic interactionists assume that the vast majority of human behavior is constructed through interpretative thought. To understand human behavior, the process by which that behavior is constructed must be comprehended, which includes defining situations and self (a person's capabilities and competencies), considering alternatives of action, and anticipating the probable consequences of each alternative.

The prediction of behavior is based on assumptions that there are repetitive patterns of behavior in the world. Behavior can be predicted if the patterns and repetitive processes that are part of the basic structure of reality can be understood. All of the theories that have been explored thus far are modernist theories, because they assume that there is a "real" objective world out there. They assume that the world has a knowable structure and that it contains processes that recur over time.

Modernist theories articulate a pattern of "truths" that exist, enabling the theorist to understand and predict human behavior in social groups. A truth for the developmental theorist is that everything is in a process of change. For the structural-functional theorist it is that systems seek to maintain a structural equilibrium. A truth for the conflict theorist is that conflict is natural, normal, and inevitable in social systems. For the exchange theorist the truth is that people will seek to maximize their rewards and minimize their costs. Finally, a truth for the symbolic interactionist is that people are rational beings, constructing their lines of behavior through a process of making indications to themselves.

Postmodernism

Postmodern theory, which has developed within the past two decades, asserts that there are no organizing principles that structure the world. Indeed, the world is seen as having no structure. Any structure that seems to exist does not exist in the world but rather in the mind of some analyst. The analyst's idea is then imposed or projected onto the world, as if the world had that structure. If the real world has no structure, the search for basic "laws" governing social behavior and the prediction of behavior according to those laws is folly.

THE SEARCH FOR PATTERN Adherents of postmodernism believe that there are no "natural laws" to be discovered. They believe that in the quest to find the inherent dynamics of human social behavior, theorists of the past have made the error of seeking regularities (repetitious patterns) of behavior. The theories and assumptions we keep in our heads tend to bias our observations. If we assume that there are regularities of human behavior that exist to be discovered, we will look for those regularities. What we look for, we will find.

We have spent the past century searching for regularities of behavior and theorizing about those regularities. Our theories and assumptions have enabled us to create data to support our theories and assumptions. However, each of the theories has exceptions in the real world. Developmental theorists tell us that change is ever-present, yet some things tend to be very resistant to change, such as the ideology and dogma of the Catholic Church. As most family therapists will tell you, some families, and some people, are very resistant to change. Some alcoholics, drug addicts, and criminals are very resistant to change.

Structural-functional theorists maintain that social systems resist change and try to keep a structural equilibrium. Yet some social systems change a great deal, as we know by reading daily newspapers. The old Soviet Union is no longer; it has changed. Czechoslovakia and Yugoslavia are no longer; they have changed. Haiti, China, South Africa, and Cuba are all changing dramatically.

Conflict theorists focus on conflict as natural, normal, and inevitable, yet not all couples fight. Exchange theorists say that we operate out of self-interest, yet some people are very altruistic, making great personal sacrifices to improve the welfare of others. Symbolic interactionists say that we construct our behavior in a process of rational thought, yet many people cannot recall that they thought anything prior to acting.

The postmodernist will say that just as these modernist theories are true in some cases, so they are untrue or inapplicable in others. This becomes apparent if one focuses on the diversity in the world, the exceptions to which theories or principles do not apply.

REALITY AS SUBJECTIVE Postmodernists critique modernist theories on the assumption that the real world has no inherent order or structure. Scientists cannot ever come to know a basic structure if structure does not exist (Seidman & Wagner, 1992). There are no basic truths about the world. There are only perceptions imposed upon the world. The only realities are subjective realities, what actors believe to be the truth. There are an infinite number of subjective truths, and each social group that exists tends to be a special-interest group with its subjective truths and its agendas that it wants to promote. Truth, according to the postmodernists, can never be discovered objectively because it does not exist (Brannigan, 1992; Frank, 1990).

Each of the members in a family has his or her own perception of the family's dynamics. For example, the grandparents' perception of family dynamics may be very different from the parents'. These, in turn, will probably be different from what the siblings perceive, which is different from what neighbors or church congregants or friends perceive. Even within the generational groups, not all members will see things in the same way. The males may see things in the family very differently from the way the females see them.

The reality that exists in any family is constantly changing over time. The family can be seen as creating a story. The story is continuously evolving, and the members have the ability to create the next chapter of the story. Each family's story is in a dynamic process of being told.

For postmodernists, the language that is used to tell the story greatly influences the reality of the story. It can be told in language that is sad and powerless or hopeful and empowering. The language one uses in telling the story is of critical importance, and changing the language can change the story that is told. Postmodern therapists see their role as changing the language with which a family tells its story, for in changing the language, one changes the reality that the family experiences (Goolishian & Anderson, 1987).

COLLECTIVE REALITY Reality is not "out there" to be discovered. Rather, it is created through a linguistic process of interpersonal interaction. It is created collectively in groups. The reality that is constructed by one group will be different from the reality constructed by another group. Some postmodernists label themselves as **constructivists** (Hoffman, 1990; Sluzki, 1985), to highlight their belief that reality is constructed through a process of interaction in groups.

This makes reality relative; it takes multiple forms for different groups. It also makes reality very political, as one will construct reality to serve the group's particular interests. If a black teenager is killed by police in a large city, the reality of the black community may be that this is an example of police brutality and inherent racism in the society. The reality of the police is that this was necessary force to maintain law and order and was warranted to protect the life and health of the police officer.

Likewise, an abortion will be seen by a group of pro-choice advocates as a woman exercising her constitutional right to choose a medical procedure that will terminate her pregnancy. A group of pro-life advocates will perceive the abortion as an act of murder that does not take into account the right of the unborn fetus to life, liberty, and the pursuit of happiness.

To the postmodern theorist, the truth does not exist in any objective reality (Bauman, 1988; Frank, 1990). What is right or wrong can never be ascertained. Groups have opinions and perspectives on right and wrong, and they vie for political power to impose their beliefs on others. What is perceived in any era as right or wrong is the result of powerful groups imposing their cultural beliefs on less powerful groups. The beliefs of the powerful are no more or less right or accurate than the counter beliefs held by others.

Foucault (1980) accuses academics in a modernist era of generating great power by convincing those who control society that it is a worthy endeavor to pour huge sums of money into universities in the quest for knowledge about the essential, inherent structure of the physical and social universe. Academics construct systems of ideas that constitute the cultural beliefs of academics at any given moment in time. Through this tyranny of ideas, those who conform to the beliefs held by those in power in a particular discipline are rewarded with hiring and promotion, while those who disagree are punished and ostracized. The same thing has happened in corporations.

POSTMODERNIST ALTERNATIVES? Although postmodern theorists have critiqued modernist theories on diverse grounds, it is sometimes difficult to ascertain exactly what postmodernists propose as alternative theory. If all perspectives and narratives are equally real, then every point of view can be heard, with none more privileged than others. With this position, the postmodernists are hard-pressed to accept some points of view and reject others. It leaves them accepting all positions and perspectives as equally valid. All are real reflections of the holder, given the believer's situation. Postmodern theory, which is essentially antitheoretical (since theory imposes pattern and structure), leaves few criteria for selecting a preference for some perspectives over others.

DECENTERED STRUCTURES Centralization of power in social systems is a structural characteristic of institutions in societies that are industrialized. The tyranny of ideas is made possible as a function of structural centralization, in which those few people who control a university department or a company can impose their worldview on others who are below them in the structure, resulting in the powerful group's domination of values and material life, which marginalizes the other groups.

In postindustrialized societies, the centralization fractures as power becomes more evenly distributed throughout the social structure (Lyotard, 1984). Postmodernists call for **decentered structures** as a vehicle for countering the tyranny of ideas imposed by the most powerful. When structures are decentered, the situations and voices of many different groups, including women, children, and racial and ethnic minorities, must be taken into account. These formerly ignored groups are granted the privilege of entering into a discourse about constructing lines of social action.

Decentered structures exist throughout the contemporary world at diverse levels. The fragmentation of whole countries such as Yugoslavia, the Soviet Union, and Czechoslovakia can be seen as political and ethnic decentering (Harvey, 1989), despite a new international integration of nation-states into a globalized community. The restructuring of large corporations into smaller, more specialized companies can be seen as economic decentering, even though the decision to fragment is usually made at the top, by a power elite. The loss of power that parents have over their adolescent children can be seen as part of family decentering.

Most postmodernists see the decentering of structures as good, since it permits an efflorescence of ideas that are diverse, allowing those groups with less power to hold and espouse views that are contrary to the views of the more powerful. They feel that the political and social world must be decentered in order to free people to experience and understand the differences in social reality, especially the differences experienced most acutely by those who hold less powerful positions in this country: women, homosexuals, the poor, the working class, nonwhites, the third world (Lemert, 1992; 38–39).

To be consistent with postmodernist theory, these often disenfranchised people cannot be seen as homogeneous groups, because these groups become fragmented and decentered also. Feminist theorists, for instance, can be accused of being "modernist" in approach, when they lump all women into one group and write of *a* feminist perspective. Such an approach overlooks the heterogeneity of women and fails to recognize the diversity of their situations and perspectives (Lemert, 1992; Nicholson, 1992).

FRACTURED FEMALE IDENTITIES Donna Haraway (1985) and Sandra Harding (1986) write of "fractured identities." The status of women is fractured by race, class, and world position. There is no abstract total woman, just as there is no abstract total man. There are black, Baptist, married, childless, working-class women; or white, nonreligious, divorced, middle-class women with school-aged children; or Mexican American, Catholic, never-married, childless, working-class women; but even within each of these groups, women are not all alike; they think differently and act differently by virtue of being different people with different life experiences that have molded them at any given point in time. The decentralization of the feminist movement, feared by movement leaders, would result in fragmentation into more homogeneous special-interest groups.

REALITY DECONSTRUCTED One consequence of decentered structures is that reality becomes **deconstructed**. The different groups present alternative views of reality that make reality less "real" and more visible as constructed to accomplish specific goals (Lemert, 1992). The diverse special-interest groups, offering competing views of reality, allow people to see that reality depends upon how it is looked at. In some ways this book deconstructs reality, by presenting competing theoretical perspectives. Through those perspectives, reality depends upon how it is viewed, which theoretical eyeglasses are worn to look at the world. There is not one truth "out there" in the world. Reality thus becomes relative.

The different perceptions of reality that exist among different subgroups are facilitated by their use of language. If thinking is really talking to ourselves, then the language we use in order to think structures the very things we can and cannot think about. The study of how language influences our perception of reality is an important element of the postmodern framework.

In the concept of decentered social structures, there is a political ideology that promotes greater power throughout organizations and discourages centralized power from the top of an organization. This concept can be linked with political liberalism, populism, or even communism. With less power at the top of a structure, individual autonomy is maximized. Politically, postmodernists and structural-functionalists strike a sharp contrast. Structural-functional theorists value control through hierarchy. Postmodernists value individual autonomy, which arises through the withering away of centralized control.

TODAY'S DECENTERED FAMILY A decentered social structure exists in many dual-worker families today. Many adults have lost control of their adolescent children. Many families have become so structurally fractured that there is little integration and everyone looks after himself or herself. There is so little verbal interaction between people in these families that home is little more than the place where everyone usually sleeps at night. The breakdown of structure is illustrated by the fact that increasingly in this postindustrial society, more and more people are living alone. Much of what exists in postmodernist theory can be seen as occurring in the real world today. Social structures are becoming decentered.

Postmodern theory in many ways reflects conditions that exist in a postindustrial society. This society is heterogeneous and fragmented into many competing special-interest groups. Postmodern theory tells us to focus on that diversity, to be aware that reality is different to people in these diverse groups. The eyeglasses of a postmodern theorist may well resemble a kaleidoscope. A person looking through it would see a mosaic of different colored fragments that coexist in a colorful, constantly changing whole.

A contemporary theoretical framework that reflects both the complexity of postmodern society and the complexity of postmodern theory is the life course perspective, and it is to this framework that we now briefly turn.

The Life Course Perspective

In response to diverse criticisms made of the family development model, which we explored in chapter 1, a new framework has been developing over the past two decades called the **life course perspective**. This new approach is multidisciplinary. The framework incorporates the work of developmental psychologists, who focus on the cognitive, emotional, and physiological development of individuals throughout the life span from cradle to grave.

This framework incorporates the work of family developmental theorists and incorporates a comparative analysis of how a family's life course might change within a society over time. For instance, the parenthood stage occupies a reduced percentage of an individual's total life span as compared with 100 years ago in this country because of people's increased longevity. Likewise, the empty-nest stage occupies an increased percentage of a person's total life span compared to what it did 100 years ago (Glick, 1990).

The framework includes historians who use historical documents from diaries and letters to statistical records of towns, villages, cities, counties, and other government agencies (including federally generated census figures). In addition, the work of demographers who study population trends, such as birthrates, death rates, rates of morbidity (disease), and migration patterns, is used in this framework, which also includes analyses by economists, biologists, and anthropologists.

USING A MULTILINEAR APPROACH This approach takes a unilinear idea—human development—and gives it the richness and complexity that exists in the world. It introduces a multilinear dimension to human development. Adherents of the approach show how human development is influenced by historical events, such as wars or economic depressions, and how family dynamics are influenced by demographic phenomena, such as differential rates of mortality or morbidity within racial, ethnic, or social groups. What they demonstrate is that, as a consequence of historical events, human development has a different course for different cohort groups. Family development is different for different social groups as a consequence of demographics. These theorists overcome the simplistic developmental models of unilinear theorists by analyzing how any social group in a given time and place is uniquely influenced by forces that other groups in other times and places did not have to confront.

Methodologically, using a life course perspective, sources of data are much more diverse than they were using the family development approach. Each theory that is explored tends to have a **methodology** that is consistent with that theory. With the life course perspective, there is content analysis of the diaries and letters, use of census data, and interviews with people, asking them to recall their family experience (an approach with marginal validity because the recall of people is very subject to error). There are, also, longitudinal studies of families, done over many decades, that involve both questionnaires and interviews.

COMMON LIFE COURSE THEMES Despite this eclectic diversity, there are some common themes that characterize the life course approach (Bengtson & Allen, 1993). First, these theorists use multiple contexts for analyzing the developmental process. They consider the physiological health, the cognitive development, the emotional development, and the moral development of an individual (Featherman & Lerner, 1985).

What happens in a person's life at an earlier point in time may well have an effect on that person's thoughts, feelings, and behavior in the present and in the future. For instance, it has been suggested (Forest, Moen, & Dempster-McClain, 1994) that women who did not experience childhood stressors had higher levels of adult depression when confronted with undesirable life experiences than those who had encountered stressful childhood experiences. The ability to survive childhood stress—such as father's absence due to business, parental unemployment, parental illness, or parental alcoholism—may have given these women the experience that such stressful, unpleasant events can be overcome as well as the confidence to overcome them. Having these experiences seems to have trained these women to cope with stress as adults. They were thus less apt to experience depression as adults as compared to women who did not experience this childhood training. Life course perspective adherents might also ask how other childhood experiences, such as being physically or sexually abused or being sickly as a child, would affect the ways in which such victims might parent their own children or interact with peers in deep emotional relationships.

A second tenet of the life course perspective is that individuals must be seen in a sociohistorical context. The individual's biographical life span is seen in the context of his or her place generationally within a family. As individuals age, how do their kin obligations change within the family and how is their interaction and relationship with other family members affected (Rossi & Rossi, 1990)?

A further tenet of the life course perspective is that cultural factors as well as a family's place in the social structure of a society affect how events in the family life cycle are socially defined (Clausen, 1986). Different social classes maintain different expectations regarding the age at which a person should marry. Lower-class families expect marriage to occur earlier than do middle-class families. What is considered appropriate or possible behavior by elderly people may be very different among people in tightly knit retirement communities such as Sun City, Arizona, Venice, California, or Miami Beach, Florida, than among elderly people who are more integrated into nonretirement communities with greater age diversity.

HISTORY'S IMPACT ON HUMAN DEVELOPMENT The concepts of childhood (Aries, 1962) and adolescence (Kett, 1977) are culturally created and accepted as discrete stages in the life cycle in some historical times, but not in others. The meaning that is given to life cycle stages dynamically changes over time within a culture (Demos, 1986). Childhood was not always defined in western Europe as a separate status. Medieval children were often expected to work with adults. They served with adults in armies and navies. They often dressed like adults. In the fifteenth through seventeenth centuries in western Europe, there was no notion that it was the job of parents to care for children physically, emotionally, or morally. Children did not have to be cared for because they were not perceived as being dependent. Cultural changes in the meaning of statuses in the life cycle are part of what intrigues life course theorists.

The adherents of this perspective ask how historical time—events in history such as a depression or a war—impact upon an individual's experience of life. Historical events interact with human development. Thus, one might ask how adolescence was similar or different in different historical time frames—during the Depression, during World War II, during the prosperity of the 1950s, and in the 1990s. How was life in a person's 60s the same or different in the 1790s, the 1890s, and the 1990s in the United States, in terms of work, family relationships, and community involvement?

In the next section, we explore how these questions might be addressed using a life course approach. We look at how the perspective is used to understand differences in families at different points in time.

Applying Life Course Theory

The role of history in influencing family dynamics is often examined through the use of cohort analysis. A **cohort group** includes people who have been born within a specified period of time, sometimes in the same year, sometimes in the same decade. Rossi's (1985) book presents an array of studies using the life course approach. Many of the studies reported in this book use cohort analysis.

An example of cohort analysis exists in Glen Elder's (1974) research. He used longitudinal data to study the effects of the Great Depression on children born in 1920–1921. His initial data were taken from studies of individual development. He enlarged these data to include interviews with the children's mothers at three different points of time in the 1930s. He administered questionnaires to the children both in junior and senior high school. There were staff ratings of the children's development and of family behavior and follow-up surveys in the 1940s and 1950s.

Peter Uhlenberg (1980) compares the effects of increased longevity on the experience of children born 75 years apart, in 1900 and 1975. Vern Bengtson and Katherine Allen (1993: 488) summarized the Uhlenberg data. Many more children born in 1900 would lose one or both parents to death before they reached age 15 than children born 75 years later. Likewise, in 1900, almost twice as many spouses would lose their partners through widowhood before their 40th anniversary as spouses in 1976. Divorce replaced widowhood as a primary termination of marriages of 40 years or less by 1976. In 1900, less than one in five 15-year-olds would have three or four grandparents living, while by 1976 over half of the 15-year-olds had three or four grandparents living. In 1900 only 10 percent of middle-aged couples had at least two of their parents still alive, while 47 percent of couples in 1976 had at least two of their parents still living. These data are summarized in Table 6.1 on page 185 (reproduced from Bengtson & Allen, 1993).

Edward Kain (1993) analyzes the data on longevity and applies them to white and African American families. Longevity is significantly lower for African American males than for white males (Kain, 1990). African American women are thus more likely to be widowed at an early age than are white women. Kain speculates that these differentials in mortality may help to explain why there has been, historically, a much greater incidence of gainful

Table 6.1

Changes in American Family Structure as the Result of Improved Life Expectancy 1900–1976

	1900	1976
A child would experience death of parent by age 15	24%	5%
Marriage would end in widowhood before the 40th anniversary	67%	36%
A 15-year-old would have 3 or 4 living grandparents	17%	55%
A middle-aged couple would have at least 2 of their parents still alive*	10%	47%

Data source: Bengtson & Allen, 1993: 488, *adapted from Uhlenberg, 1980. Reprinted with permission.

The impact of increased longevity on the life course and family life experience of individuals, both in their childhood and in later life, has been profound.

employment among African American than white women. Kain hypothesizes that the African American women had to work to support their families in light of their widowhood.

Demographic trends exist at a macrolevel and impact on what happens within individual families at a microlevel. The life course perspective examines the interaction of macro- and microlevel processes. Increased longevity effects changes in interpersonal dynamics in families, and we find sociologists creating new concepts to reflect these changes. One such concept is **midolescence.** Midlife adolescence features rebelliousness to authority, identity crises, feelings of boredom and of being in a rut. Another, the **empty nest syndrome**, refers to problems of functioning as a childless couple once the last child has left the home. The concept **sandwich generation** refers to people, roughly from age 45 to 65, who are sandwiched in between two dependent generations of parents and children, both of which may be dependent on the middle generation both economically and psychologically. Their neediness siphons off resources of money and energy for the sandwiched couple.

These concepts have only come into existence after life expectancies have significantly increased. Whether these are new terms developed to identify truly new phenomena that have come with increased longevity or whether these phenomena have really existed for decades but were not identified by sociologists is a question appropriate to social historians and sociologists participating in the life course perspective.

Consistent with postmodernism, what the life course perspective focuses upon is the complexity and fragmentation of the world. Although all people may have a life course, the objective nature and subjective quality of that life may be very different, affected as it is by the variables of gender, social class, religion, ethnicity, race, the geographical region where the person lives, and the historical events affecting the person's life. It is only by focusing on these variables, which fragment a population, that we capture the true diversity of experience that exists in peoples' lives. Recognition of the importance of these factors serves to decenter broad generalizations about family life. Where modernist theorists focused on the similarity of peoples' experiences in their attempts to generalize about repetitive social processes, postmodernists and life course theorists focus on differences in peoples' experiences. The focuses are very different.

Modernist theories tend to be grand in scope; that is, they are high-level theories that make generalized statements about large numbers of people. Modernist theories make broad, overarching propositions: All social systems exhibit social stratification; all social systems exhibit conflict over scarce resources; all social systems are changing to realize their inherent potential; all people will seek to maximize rewards and minimize costs. Postmodern theorists warn us that the higher the level of theory, the more exceptions exist to those theoretical generalizations, and the more the theory is apt to represent a distortion of reality. Postmodern theorists and life cycle theorists tell us that theories must be low level and specific to very small numbers of people if they are to represent the reality of those people in an accurate, valid way. Increasingly, in our postmodern, diverse world, contemporary sociologists are building low-level theories that apply only to very specifically defined groups in an attempt to portray accurately the reality of those people. Theory building in sociology is reflecting and being congruent with the increasing diversity in a postmodern world.

Using the Theories Today

How can the five modernist frameworks presented in this book be used to make sense of the real world? Do they have any utility in today's world when we consider them from the perspective of postmodernism?

Let us begin by exploring the concept of **reification**. Reification occurs when a distinction fails to be made between an analytic framework and the real world in such a way that the analyst confounds reality with the analytic perspective. Conflict theory, for instance, is an analytic perspective. One applies this perspective by recognizing that even though in the real world conflict is not natural, normal, and inevitable, we are looking at the world as if it were. The framework imposes certain assumptions about reality on the reality being observed. The framework, as a set of eyeglasses, tells us to look for certain things in the world that are important. What the theory tells us to look for we will find; that is, the theory helps us create our data. The theory tells us to look for conflict. If we look for conflict we will find it.

To avoid reification, we must recognize that when we use one of these theories we are imposing its narrow focus on the world we analyze, distorting our view of that world. However, we cannot take in and grasp the real world in its totality, because the real world is so complex. One theory cannot incorporate all that complexity. We can agree with postmodernists that there is no single knowable truth that will allow theorists to grasp reality in its totality. Sociologists must analyze the world in parts (D'Amico, 1992), much like the blind people who try to comprehend what an elephant is by feeling it. Each can feel only a small portion of the enormous animal. None can know the elephant in its totality.

Initially, then, sociologists must observe the world of their subjects. Then, to help further understand and analyze this world, a theory or a framework must be constructed. The framework used is one that best fits the world we see. We select the framework from knowledge of all of the frameworks available to us. If we observe a family steeped in conflict, and the conflict is persistent over time, we may choose to observe and analyze that family using conflict theory concepts and assumptions, which will allow us to understand this family's dynamics in a coherent way. If we observe a family that is resistant to conflict, that never fights but always accommodates and adapts, we may choose to use structural-functional theory as the theory that will best fit the reality we are observing. Each theory presents us with a framework for understanding part of the real world, for making sense of a piece of the observed mosaic.

Each of these frameworks has a distinctive language, a vocabulary of concepts that we impose on the world in order to make sense of it. By using these concepts, we are not depicting the world as it is, but as we see it through whatever eyeglasses we use. The question is not whether our perception is accurate or not but, rather, whether or not it works for us in understanding what is happening. Therapists or other agents of change will also use one of the frameworks to enable them to implement change to improve the quality of life for people. The ultimate question for theorist and therapist alike is whether it works to meet their needs, their objectives, their goals, whether those goals be understanding or the effecting of change.

Clearly, modernist theories do not meet the goals of postmodern theorists, who see that the diversity and complexity of the world must be accurately reflected in the theoretical frameworks sociologists use. To them, modernist theories, in seeking to make generalizations about social processes, have overlooked many exceptions that must be the focus of inquiry. The exceptions are molded by the unique situations in which many small groups exist in the total fabric of life. Their uniqueness is fashioned by the interplay of factors we call social class, ethnicity, gender, religion, age, geography, history, and race. Sociologists are currently struggling with how they can maintain modernist theories, portraying general processes of social life, and not lose sight of the unique reality of people's lives.

Summary

When sociologists are trained to become professionals, they learn all the theories presented in this book. All theories are taught because it is widely accepted that no one theory in sociology is adequate for describing and accounting for the diversity of human behavior that exists.

There are some elements of different theories that are compatible, and these can be combined and synthesized if such synthesis is useful. When synthesizing from different theories, care must be taken not to employ pieces of the theories that are contradictory or incompatible.

Postmodernism reminds us that the theories existent in sociology are not the only frameworks that might exist to understand the world. Each of us, in our everyday lives, creates frameworks or models by which we make sense of the world around us. As observers of social life, we must not be so arrogant as to assume that only those frameworks taught in colleges and universities have validity or utility in making sense of social behavior. If sociologists impose their own models to explain the reality of others, they will inevitably distort the reality of those others. Postmodernists believe that there is a better chance of representing the reality of observed actors by using the actors' frameworks of reality.

Where will the frameworks come from for interpreting and making sense of interpersonal behavior? Will they come from the sociologists, based upon their training and derived from their body of theoretical knowledge, or from the people sociologists study? Or will they come from the interaction between the observed and the observers? These are questions and issues with which contemporary sociologists are struggling.

As symbolic interactionists tell us, reality arises out of an interaction between actors. Social scientists are not just observing reality; they are a part of the very reality they are observing. Because they are in this reality, they have the ability to interact with the people they are trying to understand. In this interaction, the realities of both observers and observed may change.

Glossary

achievement: Norm governing interaction that encourages people to relate to each other based on what they do or how they act rather than on who they are. 68

acute stage: Wallerstein's first stage in divorce where pain and family disorganization are maximized. 38

adaptation: Ability of a system to adjust to change so that the basic structure of the system stays intact. 70

affectivity: Norm governing emotions in interaction, which permits the showing of feelings. 66

affective-neutrality: Norm governing emotions in interaction, which forbids the showing of feelings. 66

affineal bond: Bond of marriage. 57

affines: People related to each other through marriage, eg. one's spouse and one's mother, father, brothers- or sisters-in-law. 57

agency: The power of people to mold and construct social structure. 84

agricultural wave: First technological wave for Toffler, in which societies have an economy based primarily on farming and the harvesting of raw materials (for example, lumbering, fishing, mining). 11

anger: Third stage in Hendrix's model depicting the demise of romantic love in a relationship, in which one partner feels hurt and betrayed. 36

anomie: Existence of incongruent or ambiguous norms in the social structure of a system. 55

antithesis: From Hegel, an idea that arises to challenge and contradict a widely accepted truth. 86

ascription: Norm governing interaction that encourages people to relate to each other based on who they are, their status or kin affiliation, rather than what they do or how they act. 68

back regions: Goffman's term for places where one prepares for life's performances; in houses they are often bathrooms, kitchens, and bedrooms. 138

bargaining: Fourth stage in Hendrix's model, depicting the demise of romantic love in a relationship in which partners offer each other deals to motivate changes of behavior in an attempt to salvage the relationship. 36

blended family: Family that is created when two spouses marry and each brings with them children from a previous relationship or marriage. 171

boundaries: Psychological and emotional barriers that exist to distinguish between the inside and the outside of a system; boundaries can be created through norms. 20

bourgeoisie: In a capitalist system, the owners of the means of production (from Marx). 87

changing identities: A condition that people in the postindustrial world will experience as they move from job to job or marriage to marriage. 33

childless married couple stage: Developmental stage existing for most couples immediately after marriage and prior to parenthood in which the couple works to build their nest. 18

clear boundaries: A definitive boundary exists, but there is interaction across the boundary. 20

closed boundaries: Rigid boundaries that do not allow the outside world into a system and do not permit system members to leave the system in order to get needs met. 52

clown: In a chemically dependent family, person who jokes to give comic relief and call attention to him/herself; is funny and theatrical. 63

coalition: Two or more people who support each other against a third. 90

codependents: Another term for enablers, caretakers. 62

cohort group: People who were born within a specifically defined period of time. 184

collective consciousness: Term Durkheim used to signify a group's shared sense of right and wrong; the group's shared sense of morality. 69

collectivity: Norm governing values in interaction that encourages people to value the interests of the group above self-interest. 67

companionship stage: Burgess saw the romantic stage of early marriage moving to a valuing of companionship and intimacy as passion wanes in the relationship. 35

comparison level: Standard by which people evaluate the rewards and costs of a relationship in terms of their expectations; what they thought the relationship should bring them. 117

conformity: Merton's term for adherence to culturally accepted goals and use of institutionalized means for attaining those goals. 55

conjugal family: A household comprised of a husband and a wife and their children (also called a **nuclear family**). 31

consanguineal bond: A blood tie. 57

conspiratorial avoidance: A group norm to avoid discussion of a controversial or emotion-laden topic. 66

constructivists: People who believe that reality is constructed through interaction and dialogue; that reality can be constructed and reconstructed. 178

decentered structures: In which power in a system is not concentrated at the top in an organization but rather is shared throughout the structure. The decentering of social structures sometimes occurs through a fragmentation of the structure into smaller, autonomous units. 180

decision/commitment: Part of Sternberg's Triangle of Love Theory, involving a short-term decision to love a certain other and a long-term commitment to maintain that love. 35

deconstructed reality: Postmodern term signifying that a belief, generally held by a group and generated from a powerful elite, becomes challenged by the reality of others. The challenge places reality as a relativistic phenomenon. What one perceives as real depends upon one's experience of the world and one's place in the social structure of a system. 180

definition of the situation: Way in which people interpret and give meaning to a reality that they confront. 134

denial: Second stage in Hendrix's model depicting the demise of romantic love in a relationship; this involves denying the negative traits or characteristics of the partner. 36

dependence: When rewards received in a relationship cannot be obtained in alternate relationships and a person wants the rewards. 115

dependent: A role; often a person who is chemically addicted to alcohol or other drugs. 62

despair: Fifth stage in Hendrix's model depicting the demise of romantic love in a relationship, in which parties either seek divorce or outside relationships while remaining married. 36

developmental tasks: Havighurst's psychological concept, applied to family development theory, suggests that developmental tasks arise in each stage and must be addressed. 14

differentiation: Specialization of functions located in different subsystems, which leads to high levels of interdependence between the specialized subsystems. 61

diffuse boundaries: Weak boundaries; people become enmeshed or overinvolved with one another. 20

diffuseness: Norm governing interaction that permits the content of conversation to include everything anyone may wish to discuss. 65

disciplinary father: One role that fathers play, which stresses the enforcement of norms, particularly by negatively sanctioning deviance. 51

disengaged: When a person is emotionally unaffected by the actions of people around them. 21

distancer: Person who actively seeks greater emotional distance in the relationship. 19

dramaturgical approach: Perspective linked to Goffman which views people as actors on a stage, playing out a theatrical performance to manage their identities for an audience. 138

dyad: A two-person system. 22

dysfunctional: Consequences of action that are detrimental for a system. 59

empty nest stage: Developmental stage that exists after the last child has left home to establish an autonomous life. Parents return to being a childless married couple. 25

empty nest syndrome: Problems of functioning as a childless married couple after the last child leaves home. 185

enablers: Caretakers who unwittingly maintain a dependent's symptoms by being nice, sympathetic, and understanding. 62

enmeshed: Overinvolved, resulting in a loss of boundaries between people. 20

equilibrium of conflict: The maintenance and persistence of conflict in a system. 86

equity: When the ratio of investments to profits is similar or proportional for all parties. 114

ethical norms: Shoulds; injunctions to behave in particular ways. 164

ethnocentrism: Belief that one's own culture is more advanced than others or better than others. 11

eufunctional: Consequences of action that are beneficial for a system (also called **functional**). 59

expressive role: Provider of the emotional needs of family members; relates family members to each other, making sure that people get along with each other and support one another. 52

extended family system: All the relatives, kin, and affines existing outside of a nuclear family. 49

extended kin: Kin lying outside the nuclear family unit, such as grandparents, aunts and uncles, cousins, nephews and nieces. 48

family of origin: The family into which one is born and raised, consisting of one's mother, father, siblings, and extended kin. 18

family of procreation: The family one creates through one's own marriage; includes one's spouse and children. 20

fictive kin: People who are not kin or affines but who are treated as if they were family members. 151

filial piety: Expectation in Chinese culture that children, particularly sons, will care for and honor their elders in their old age. 121

first generation immigrants: People who have come to the United States from their homeland; they speak the language and practice the customs of their homeland. 97

formal social structure: Organization of a system that is presented to outsiders. 90

fragmented parental subsystem: Where parents sabotage each other because of their different parenting philosophies and styles. 170

front regions: Goffman's term for places where one plays out performances for others; in houses, often living rooms or dining rooms. 138

front: Presentation of a formal social structure; what people in a system show to the outside world in order to manage an image in the minds of observers about how the system works. 90

function: What happens as a direct or indirect result of a person's action. 59

functional requisites: The tasks that must be performed by all social systems if they are to survive; according to Parsons, they were latent pattern maintenance, adaptation, integration, and goal attainment. 45

functional teleology: Confusion of function and cause when theorists assume a phenomenon exists because it is seen as performing a function. 82

functional: Consequences of action that are beneficial for a system (also called **eufunctional**). 59

general evolution: General direction of change that societies exhibit, part of this process is that preindustrial societies become urbanized and industrialized. 41

goal attainment: Ability of a system to mobilize resources and energy to attain goals they set for themselves. 73

hero: A successful, competent role the eldest child usually takes in a chemically dependent family. 62

homeostasis: The tendency of a social system to resist change outside a range of acceptable behavior to maintain the system's structure. 60

homogamous: Description of the marriage of two people who are of the same social class. 74

I: From Mead, a part of the self that is impulsive and spontaneous. 132

industrial wave: Second technological wave for Toffler, in which societies have an economy based primarily on converting raw materials to manufactured goods. 11

informal social structure: Organization of a system as it really is; how it really works. 90

inner-directed: A concept used by Riesman to depict people who get cues for how to behave by internalizing norms, becoming self-directed. 11

innovation: Merton's term for deviant behavior when individuals accept cultural goals but do not use institutional means to obtain those goals. 54

instrumental role: Providing for the physical needs of family members, usually through gainful employment; this person functions to relate the family to the outside world through work. 52

integration: Ability of a system to incorporate all members into a well-meshed coordinated whole in which all participate and contribute constructively. 72

interdependent roles: A network in which family members are linked to each other as well as to various service personnel who perform needed tasks. 77

interviewing: Research methodology in which the researcher asks respondents open-ended questions face-to-face. 136

intimacy: The mutual sharing of thoughts and feelings—self disclosure—between parties in a relationship. 35

issei: First generation Japanese immigrants. 98

joint family households: Consanguineally linked multigenerational nuclear families sharing a common residence. 30

kin: People related by a consanguineal (blood) bond, such as one's biological mother, father, and siblings, as well as one's children and grandchildren. 57

language: In postmodernism, one critical vehicle by which reality is constructed; the language people use carries meaning, interpretations of reality. 150

latent functions: From Merton, consequences of action that are neither recognized nor intended by actors. 59

latent pattern maintenance: The ability of a system to get loyalty from members, even if those members are not physically present. 70

levels of systems: Similar to micro- and macroanalysis, systems can exist in small scale, such as with families, or in large scale, as with whole societies. 47

lexicon: Words; the vocabulary of a language. 5

life course perspective: A multidisciplinary developmental approach showing how individual development is affected by historical, social, and cultural factors. 182

looking glass self: From Cooley, the idea that our image of ourselves is a mirror image reflecting the appraisals that others make of us. 132

lost child: Role in a chemically dependent family in which the child withdraws, stays out of the way, is inconspicuous. 63

macroanalysis: The study of large-sized groups, such as large corporations or whole societies. 28

manifest functions: From Merton, consequences of action that are both recognized and intended by actors. 59

mascot: The baby in a chemically dependent family; is cute, often immature, and calls attention to him/herself; is always on stage playing a theatrical performance. 63

matriarchal authority: Where the wife has more power than her husband. 28

matrilocal residence: When bride and groom, after marriage, reside in the household or village of the bride. 28

me: From Mead, a part of the self that constructs action by rational thought. 132

meaningful behavior: Behavior constructed from an interpretation of the behavior of others and a definition of the situation; the constructed response and the situation responded to are each given a meaningful context in the mind of the actor. 133

methodology: Ways in which researchers obtain data to create and test hypotheses. 182

microanalysis: The study of small-sized groups. 28

midolescence: Midlife adolescence. 185

mind: From Mead, the ability of people to make indications to themselves, to rationally think and construct their own lines of action. 133

mutual dependency: Third stage of Reiss's Wheel Theory of Love in which partners become emotionally attached. 34

myth of instant love: A belief, usually held by the biological parent in a stepfamily, that the new spouse is such a terrific person that the children will immediately come to love him or her. 174

myth of reconciliation: A belief, usually held by children of divorce, that their parents will reconcile and resume living together, which would reintegrate the family unit. 174

negative reinforcement: Punishing behavior to discourage its repetition. 111

neolocal residence: When bride and groom, after marriage, establish their own residence apart from either set of parents. 29

nisei: Second generation Japanese immigrants. 98

no-fault divorce: A divorce granted without assigning responsibility for the dissolution to either marital partner. 78

nonmeaningful behavior: Spontaneous, impulsive behavior that is not preceded by making interpretative considerations. 133

norm of fairness: Rule prescribing that people in a relationship should mutually share obligations and rewards. 114

norm of reciprocity: Rule prescribing that relationships should be rewarding to both parties. 114

norms: Rules that exist at the social system level. 45

nuclear family: Husband, wife, and their biological or legally adopted children (also called a **conjugal family**). 31

nurturing father: One role that fathers play, which stresses physical and emotional caretaking and support. 51

open boundaries: Semipermeable boundaries that allow the outside world into a system and allow system members to leave the system in order to get needs met. 52

other-directed: Concept used by Riesman to depict people who get cues for how to behave from reading the expectations of others and conforming to those expectations. 11

parental subsystem: Composed of people who relate to each other in the roles of mother and father to their child. 17

parenthood stage: Developmental stage existing after the birth or upon the adoption of the couple's first child; the developmental task is to work together to raise and socialize the children. 13

parentified children: Children whose job it is to be caretakers of parents who exhibit a diminished capacity to parent. 80

participant observation: Research methodology where the researcher is an active participant in the processes being observed; this involves simultaneously trying to be inside the reality as a participant and outside of it as an observer. 136

particularism: Norm in structural-functional theory that governs interaction, encouraging people to relate to others based on the specific relationship they have with each other. 68

passion: Energetic longing for union in a relationship; can be sexual and/or emotional. 35

patriarchal authority: Where the husband has more power than his wife. 28

patrilocal residence: When bride and groom, after marriage, reside in the household or village of the groom. 28

personality need fulfillment: Fourth stage of Reiss's Wheel Theory of Love in which partners confide in each other and support each other to realize ambitions and goals. 34

positive reinforcement: Act of rewarding behavior in order to encourage its repetition. 111

postindustrial wave: Third technological wave for Toffler, in which societies have an economy based primarily on providing human services. 11

power: Ability to get people to do what one wants them to do. 18

premarital stage: Developmental stage existing prior to marriage, in which a primary task is to be able to play well together. 12

primogeniture: State of being the first-born child, almost always the first-born son in societies with patrilineal and bilateral descent systems, who inherits all of the parents' assets. 30

profit: In exchange theory, rewards minus costs. 114

proletariat: In a capitalist system, the working class (from Marx). 87

pursuer: Person who actively seeks greater emotional closeness in the relationship. 19

questionnaires: Research instrument that is consistent with structural-functional theory, which normally uses forced-choice questions to obtain data (which is analyzed quantitatively) from large numbers of people. 46

rapport: First stage of Reiss's Wheel Theory of Love in which people become attracted to one another by virtue of shared social characteristics and cultural values. 33

rebel: Child in a chemically dependent family who acts out as an incorrigible child, deflecting attention to himself/herself and away from the dependent. 63

rebellion: Merton's term for a form of deviance that exists when an individual rejects both cultural goals and institutionalized means to attain goals and replaces them with an alternative set of goals and means. 55

reciprocal roles: Complementary roles that people take toward one another, such as giver and taker, leader and follower, or parent and child. 145

reification: Taking a mental construct and assuming that this concept or framework actually exists as part of the real world. 186

resources: Characteristics or qualities, skills or knowledge, objects of value that people have, which enable them to generate power over others. 87

retirement/widowhood stage: Developmental stage that occurs either upon retirement from gainful employment or widowhood, whichever occurs first. 26

retreatism: Merton's term for a form of deviance that exists when an individual rejects both cultural goals and institutionalized means to attain goals. 55

rigid boundaries: Strong, impermeable boundaries leading to disengagement between people. 21

rituals: Routine patterns of behavior. 50

ritualism: Merton's term for a form of deviance that exists when an individual follows institutionalized means to attain the goals but does not seek goals accepted by the dominant culture. 54

roles: Patterns of behavior that exist around different themes. 144

role overload: A feeling of paralysis, a sense of being overwhelmed and helpless in the face of having too much work to do and too many demands. 168

role set: According to Merton, the totality of different roles that one plays while occupying a given status. 51

romantic stage: Burgess called this an early stage in a marriage where there is still passion in the relationship. 35

rule of distributive justice: Prescribes that rewards for each person in a relationship will be proportional to their respective costs and that the net rewards for each person will be proportional to their investments in a relationship. 112

sanctioned: Reactive responses from others that reward conformity to norms and punish deviance from norms. 45

sandwich generation: People usually aged 45–65 who are sandwiched between two financially and psychologically dependent generations of elderly parents and children. 185

scapegoat: In a chemically dependent family, another label for the rebel. In symbolic interaction theory, the person upon whom family members place the blame for all the family's problems and troubles. 63

scarce resources: In families, scarce resources include money, attention, affection, time, and space. Conflict theorists believe all social systems exhibit conflict over scarce resources. 87

second generation immigrants: Children of first generation immigrants; they were born and raised in the United States; they seek to assimilate into the culture of their peers and usually reject their cultural roots. 98

self-revelation: Second stage of Reiss's Wheel Theory of Love in which partners communicate their thoughts and feelings to each other. 34

self: In structural-functional theory, a norm governing values in interaction that permits people to behave out of self-interest. In symbolic interaction theory, the ability of people to step outside themselves and see and relate to themselves as objects in their own environment. 67, 132

sensei: Third generation Japanese immigrants. 98

shock: First stage in Hendrix's model depicting the demise of romantic love in a relationship. This involves realizing that one's internal image of the other is incongruent with how they "really" are. 36

sibling subsystem: Within a nuclear family, the brothers and sisters. 48

social group: For Mead, a collectivity of people who share common definitions of objects and events in their environment. 137

social stratification: Existence of power and status differential in a social system; all social systems exhibit social stratification, which can be a source of conflict. 87

socialization: Lifelong process of learning what we need to know to be considered competent adult members of a society. Cultural values, social norms, skills, language are all taught in this process. 45

socially isolated: Frequently, condition of single parents who do not have the time or energy to nurture friendships. 168

specific evolution: Notion that societies do not follow the same path toward urbanization and industrialization. 41

specificity: Norm governing interaction that permits the content of conversation to focus only around topics of a narrow range. 65

spousal subsystem: Within a nuclear family, the husband and wife. 17

stabilization: Wallerstein's third stage in a divorce in which interactional patterns become regularized, patterned, and predictable. 39

statistical norms: Measures of what people in fact do in their behavior. 164

stem family: Household consisting of parents, their unmarried children, and their eldest son and his wife and their children. 30

stepfamily: A family created by the marriage of two people, at least one of whom has children from a previous marriage. 167

stigmas: Facts about people that have the potential of discrediting them, of spoiling their identity in the mind of others. 139

structure of conflict: Description of who sides with whom against whom in conflict. 86

subordinate: Those people with the least power. 89

superordinate: Those people with the most power. 89

symbol: Anything that is capable of assuming multiple meanings. 139

synthesis: From Hegel, the integration of ideas that arises when a thesis and antithesis are in conflict; a synthesis becomes a new thesis. 86

system: Boundary-maintained unit composed of interrelated and interdependent parts. 46

taking the role of the other: Stepping inside the mind and heart of another, trying to understand how this other thinks and feels to comprehend why the other behaves as he or she does. 136

thesis: From Hegel, a widely accepted truth. 86

third generation immigrants: Children of second generation immigrants; they usually seek the cultural identity they share with their grandparents; they find identity in their ethnic roots. 98

tradition-directed: Concept used by Riesman to depict people who get cues for how to behave from traditional practices. 11

transitional stage: Wallerstein's second stage in divorce in which, in search of stability, the divorced family experiments with different kinds of living arrangements and coping styles. 38

triad: Three-person system. 23

universalism: In structural-functional theory, a norm governing interaction that encourages people to be treated equally. 68

value-orientations: In Parson's theory, desirable or preferred patterns of interaction. 64

value: Any quality, characteristic, or object that is deemed to be desirable, for which it is worth striving. 46

verstehen: German word for understanding. 136

Bibliography

Adams, B. N., & Adams, D. (1990). Child care and the family. In *2001: Preparing families for the future* (pp. 18–19). Minneapolis, MN: National Council of Family Relations Presidential Report.

Adams, G., Adams-Taylor, S., & Pittman, K. (1989, April). Adolescent pregnancy and parenthood: A review of the problem, solutions, and resources, *Family Relations, 38,* 223–229.

Adams, J. (1965). Inequity in social exchange. In L. Berkowitz (Ed.), *Advances in experimental social psychology* (Vol. 2, pp. 8–62). New York: Academic Press.

Ahrons, C., & Rodgers, R. H. (1987). *Divorced families: A multidisciplinary developmental view.* New York: W. W. Norton.

Albee, E. (1978). *Who's afraid of Virginia Woolf?* New York: Atheneum.

Aldous, J. (1990). Family development and life course: Two perspectives on family change. *Journal of Marriage and the Family, 52,* 571–583.

Aries, P. (1962). *Centuries of childhood* (R. Baldick, Trans.). New York: Knopf.

Aulette, J. R. (1994). *Changing families.* Belmont, CA: Wadsworth Publishing.

Bach, G. R., & Deutsch, R. (1970). *Pairing.* New York: Peter H. Wyden.

Bach, G. R., & Goldberg, H. (1974). *Creative aggression.* Garden City, NY: Doubleday Press.

Bach, G. R., & Wyden, P. (1968). *The intimate enemy: How to fight fair in love and marriage.* New York: William Morrow.

Banton, M. P. (1961). *Darwinism and the study of society, a century symposium.* Chicago: Quadrangle Books.

Basow, S. A. (1986a). Relationship consequences. *Gender stereotypes: Traditions and alternatives* (2nd ed.). Pacific Grove, CA: Brooks/Cole.

Basow, S. A. (1986b). Societal consequences: Prejudice and work. *Gender stereotypes: Traditions and alternatives* (2nd ed.). Pacific Grove, CA: Brooks/Cole.

Bauman, Z. (1988). Is there a postmodern sociology? *Postmodernism* [Special issue]. *Theory, Culture & Society, 5* (2–3); 217–238.

Bell, D. (1973). *The coming of post-industrial society: A venture in social forecasting.* New York: Basic Books.

Bell, D. (1989). The third technological revolution. *Dissent, 36,* 164–176.

Belsky, J. (1986, September). Infant daycare: A cause for concern. *Zero to Three.*

Belsky, J. (1988). The "effects" of infant daycare reconsidered, *Early Childhood Research Quarterly 3,* 235–272.

Belsky, J., & Rovine, M. (1988). Non-maternal care in the first year of life and the security of infant-parent attachment. *Child Development, 59,* 157–167.

Bem, S. L. (1983). Gender schema theory and its implicationsfor child development: Raising gender-aschematic children in a gender-schematic society. *Signs, 8*(4), 598–616.

Bengtson, V. L., & Allen, K. R. (1993). The life course perspective applied to families over time. In P. G. Boss, W. J. Doherty, R. LaRossa, W. R. Schumm, & S. K. Steinmetz (Eds.), *Sourcebook of family theories and methods, a contextual approach.* New York: Plenum.

Benokraitis, N. V. (1993). *Marriage and families.* Englewood, Cliffs, NJ: Prentice Hall.

Berk, R. A., & Newton, P. J. (1985). Does arrest really deter wife battery? An effort to replicate the findings of the Minneapolis Spouse Abuse Experiment. *American Sociological Review, 50,* 253–262.

Berkner, L. K. (1978). Inheritance, land tenure, and peasant family structure: A German regional comparison. In J. Goody, J. Thirsk, & E. P. Thompson (Eds.), *Family and inheri-*

tance. Cambridge: Cambridge University Press.

Biddle, B. J., & Thomas, E. J. (1966). *Role theory: Concepts and research.* New York: John Wiley.

Bielicki, T., & Waliszko, H. (1992, November). Stature, upward social mobility and the nature of statural differences between social classes. *Annals of Human Biology, 19*(6), 589.

Bierstedt, R. (1957). *The social order.* New York: McGraw-Hill.

Blau, P. M. (1964). *Exchange and power in social life.* New York: John Wiley.

Blood, P. D., & Wolfe, D. M. (1960). *Husbands and wives: The dynamics of married living.* New York: The Free Press.

Blum, E., & Blum, R. H. (1993). *Alcoholism: Modern psychological approaches to treatment.* San Francisco: Jossey-Bass.

Blumer, H. G. (1969). The methodological position of symbolic interaction. *Symbolic interactionism: Perspective and method.* Englewood Cliffs, NJ: Prentice Hall.

Blumstein, P., & Schwartz, P. (1983). *American couples: Money/work/sex.* New York: William Morrow.

Bock, K. (1963, April). Evolution, function and change. *American Sociological Review, 28,* 229–237.

Bowen, M. (1974). Toward the differentiation of self in one's family of origin. In F. Andres & J. Lorio (Eds.), *Georgetown Family Symposium* (Vol. 1). Washington, DC: Department of Psychiatry, Georgetown University Medical Center.

Brannigan, A. (1992). Postmodernism. In E. F. Borgatta & M. L. Borgatta (Eds.), *Encyclopedia of Sociology* (Vol. 3). New York: Macmillan.

Braun, J., & Chao, H. (1978, Spring). Attitudes toward women: A comparison of Asian-born Chinese and American Caucasians *Psychology of Women Quarterly, 2,* 195–201.

Brown, E. M. (1990). *Patterns of infidelity and their treatment.* New York: Brunner/Mazel.

Brown, S. (1985). *Treating the alcoholic: A developmental model of recovery.* New York: John Wiley.

Bulcroft, R. A., & Bulcroft, K. A. (1991, June). The nature and functions of dating in later life. *Research on Aging, 13*(2), 244–260. Newbury Park, CA: Sage Publications.

Burgess, E. W., Locke, H. J., & Thomes, M. M. (1963). *The family from institution to companionship.* New York: American Book.

Burr, W. R. (1973). *Theory construction and the sociology of the family.* New York: John Wiley.

Burr, W. R., Leigh, G. K., Kay, R. D., & Constantine, J. (1979). Symbolic interaction and the family. In W. R. Burr, R. Hill, F. I. Nye, & I. L. Reiss (Eds.), *Contemporary theories about the family* (Vol 2). New York: The Free Press.

Caldwell, B. M., & Richmond, J. B. (1968). The children's center in Syracuse. In L. L. Dittman (Ed.), *Early childcare: The new perspectives.* New York: Atherton Press.

Cancian, F. (1960). Functional analysis of change. *American Sociological Review, 25*(6), 818–826.

Carroll, J. B. (Ed.). (1956). *Language, thought, and reality: Selected writings of Benjamin Lee Whorf.* Cambridge: MA: The Technology Press of Massachusetts Institute of Technology; New York: John Wiley.

Carter, B., & McGoldrick, M. (1989). *The changing family life cycle: A framework for family therapy* (2nd ed.). New York: Allyn & Bacon.

Chafetz, J. (1988). *Feminist sociology: An overview of contemporary theories.* Itasca, IL: Peacock.

Cherlin, A. J. (1981). *Marriage, divorce, remarriage.* Cambridge, MA: Harvard University Press.

Cherlin, A., & McCarthy, J. (1985). Remarried couple households: Data from the June 1980 Current Population Survey. *Journal of Marriage and the Family, 47,* 23–30.

Chilman, C. S. (1980, November). Social and psychological research concerning adolescent childbearing: 1970–1980. *Journal of Marriage and the Family, 42,* 793–805.

Clarke-Stewart, K. A., & Feinn, G. G.(1983). Early childhood programs. In N. P. H. Mussein (Ed.), *Handbook of child psychology.* New York: John Wiley.

Clarke-Stewart, K. A., & Gruber, C. P. (1984). Daycare forms and features. In R. C. Ainslie (Ed.), *The child and the daycare setting.* New York: Praeger.

Clausen, J. (1986). *The life course: A sociological perspective.* Englewood Cliffs, NJ: Prentice Hall.

Coleman, M., & Ganong, L. H. (1990). Remarriage and stepfamily research in the 1990s: Increased interest in an old family form. *Journal of Marriage and the Family, 52,* 925–940.

Collins, R. (1975). *Conflict sociology: Toward an explanatory science.* New York: Academic Press.

Collins, R., & Coltrane, S. (1991). *Sociology of marriage and the family: Gender, love and property.* Chicago, IL: Nelson-Hall.

Comte, A. (1855). *The positive philosophy of Auguste Comte* (H. Martineau, Trans.). New York: Calvin Blanchard.

Comte, A. (1877). *System of positive polity. General appendix: Early essays* (Vol. 4). London: Longmans.

Cooley, C. H. (1964). *Human nature and the social order.* New York: Schocken Books.

Cooper, J. P. (1976). Patterns of inheritance and settlement by great landowners from the fifteenth to the eighteenth centuries. In J. Goody, J. Thirsk, & E. P. Thompson (Eds.), *Family and inheritance.* Cambridge: Cambridge University Press.

Coser, L. A. (1956). *The functions of social conflict.* Glencoe, IL: The Free Press.

Cromwell, V., & Cromwell, R. E. (1978, November). Perceived dominance in decision making and conflict resolution among black and Chicano couples. *Journal of Marriage and the Family, 40,* 749–759.

Cuber, J. F., & Harroff, P. B. (1968). *The significant Americans: A study of sexual behavior among the affluent.* Baltimore, MD: Penguin.

Dahrendorf, R. (1958a). Out of Utopia: Toward a reorientation of sociological analysis. *American Journal of Sociology, 64,* 115–127.

Dahrendorf, R. (1958b). Toward a theory of social conflict. *Journal of Conflict Resolution, 2.*

D'Amico, R. (1992). Defending social science against the postmodern doubt. In S. Seidman & D. G. Wagner (Eds.), *Postmodernism and social theory.* Cambridge, MA: Blackwell.

Darwin, C. (1859). *Origin of species.* London: J. Murray.

Davis, K. (1940, August). The sociology of parent-child conflict. *American Sociological Review, 5,* 523–535.

Davis, K. (1949). *Human society.* New York: Macmillan.

Davis, K., & Moore, W. E. (1945, April). Some principles of stratification. *American Sociological Review, 10,* 242–247.

Davis, W. (1983). *The rich: A study of the species.* New York: Franklin Watts.

De Shazer, S., & Berg, I. (1988, September/October). Constructing solutions. In *The Family Therapy Networker.*

Demos, J. (1986). *Past, present and personal: The family and life course in American history.* New York: Oxford University Press.

Dore, R. P. (1961, December). Function and cause. *American Sociological Review, 26,* 843–853.

Durkheim, E. (1893/1964). *The division of labor in society* (G. Simpson, Trans.). New York: The Free Press.

Durkheim, E. (1895/1964). *The rules of sociological method* (S. A. Solovay, Trans.). J. H. Mueller & G. E. G. Catlin (Eds.). New York: The Free Press.

Duvall, E. M. (1957). *Family development.* Philadelphia: Lippincott.

Duvall, E. M. (1977). *Marriage and family development* (5th ed.). New York: Lippincott.

Duvall, E. M., & Hill, R. (1948). *Report to the committee on the dynamics of family interaction.* Washington, DC: National Conference on Family Life.

Duvall, E. M., & Miller, B. C. (1985). Stage-critical family development tasks. In *Marriage and family development* (6th ed.). New York: Harper & Row.

Earle, A. M. (1889). *Child life in colonial days.* New York: Macmillan.

Eckenrode, J., & Gore, S. (1990). *Stress between work and family.* New York: Plenum.

Ehrensaft, D. (1990). *Parenting together: Men and women sharing the care of their children.* Urbana & Chicago: University of Illinois Press.

Elder, G. H. (1974). *Children of the Great Depression: Social change in life experience.* Chicago: University of Chicago Press.

Elnett, E. (1926). *Historic origin and social development of family life in Russia.* New York: Columbia University Press.

Emerson, R. (1962). Power dependence relations. *American Sociological Review, 27,* 31–40.

Emerson, R. (1972a). Exchange theory, Part I: A psychological basis for social exchange. In J. Berger, M. Zelditch, & B. Anderson (Eds.), *Sociological theories in progress* (Vol. 2, pp. 38–57). Boston: Houghton Mifflin.

Emerson, R. (1972b). Exchange theory, Part II: Exchange relations and network structures. In J. Berger, M. Zelditch, & B. Anderson (Eds.), *Sociological theories in progress* (Vol. 2, pp. 58–87). Boston: Houghton-Mifflin.

Emerson, R. (1976). Social exchange theory. In A. Inkeles, J. Coleman, & N. Smelser (Eds.), *Annual review of sociology* (Vol. 2, pp. 335–362). Palo Alto, CA: Annual Reviews.

England, P. (1989). A feminist critique of rational choice theories: Implications for sociology. *The American Sociologist, 20,* 14–28.

England, P. (1993). *Theory on gender: Feminism on theory.* New York: Aldine de Gruyter.

Etzioni, A. (1964). *Modern organizations.* Englewood Cliffs, NJ: Prentice Hall.

Etzioni, A. (1975). *Comparative analysis of complex organizations.* Glencoe, IL: The Free Press.

Falicov, C. J. (1988). *Family transitions.* New York: Guilford Press.

Faludi, S. (1991). *Backlash: The undeclared war against American women.* New York: Crown.

Farson, R. (1974). Why good marriages fail. In *Annual Editions: Readings in Marriage and Family, 1975/76.* Guilford, CT: The Dushkin Publishing Group.

Featherman, D. L., & Lerner, R. M. (1985). Ontogenesis and sociogenesis: Problematics for theory and research about development and socialization across the lifespan. *American Sociological Review, 50,* 659–676.

Fiala, R. (1992) Postindustrial society. In E. F. Borgatta & M. L. Borgatta (Eds.), *Encyclopedia of Sociology* (Vol. 3). New York: Macmillan.

Finkelhor, D., & Yllo, K. (1983). Rape in marriage: A sociological view. In D. Finkelhor et al. (Eds.), *The dark side of families* (pp. 119–130). Beverly Hills, CA: Sage Publications.

Flax, J. (1982). The family in contemporary feminist thought: A critical review. In J. Elshtain (Ed.), *The family in political thought* (pp. 223–253). Amherst, MA: University of Massachusetts.

Flax, J. (1987). Postmodernism and gender relations in feminist theory. *Signs, 12,* 621–643.

Forest, K. B., Moen, P., & Dempster-McClain, D. (1994). Depression and stressors across women's life course: The trigger effect hypothesis. *Journal of Family Issues* (forthcoming).

Foucault, M. (1980). *Power/knowledge: Selected interviews and other writings, 1972–1977.* New York: Pantheon Books.

Framo, J. L. (1981). Love and marriage. In *Helping families change.* New York: BMA Audio Cassettes, Guilford Publications.

Frank, A. (1990). Postmodern sociology/postmodern review. *Symbolic Interactionism, 14*(1), 93–100.

Freedman, E., & Thorne, B. (1984, Autumn). Introduction to feminist sexuality debates. *Signs, 10,* 102–105.

Freud, S. (1961). *Civilization and its discontents.* New York: W. W. Norton.

Fried, B. (1967). *The middle-age crisis.* New York: Harper & Row.

Fried, M. (Ed.). (1991). *From abortion to reproductive freedom: Transforming a movement.* Boston: Southend Press.

Friedan, B. (1963). The feminine mystique. New York: Dell.

Gelles, R. J. (1987). *Family violence.* Newbury Park, CA: Sage Publications.

Gelles, R. J., & Straus, M. A. (1988). *Intimate violence.* New York: Simon & Schuster.

Gerstel, N., & Gross, H. E. (1989). Women and the American family: Continuity and change. In J. Freeman (Ed.), *Women.* Mountain View, CA: Mayfield.

Giddens, A. (1984). The constitution of society: Outline of the theory of structuration. Berkeley, CA: University of California Press.

Giddens, A. (1990). *The consequences of modernity.* Palo Alto, CA: Stanford University Press.

Gilder, G. (1973). *Sexual suicide.* New York: Quadrangle Books.

Glick, P. C. (1992). American families: As they are and were. In A. S. Skolnick & J. H. Skolnick (Eds.), *Family in transition* (7th ed.). New York: HarperCollins.

Goffman, E. (1959). *Presentation of self in everyday life.* New York: Doubleday, Anchor Books.

Goffman, E. (1963). *Stigma: Notes on the management of spoiled identities.* Englewood Cliffs, NJ: Prentice Hall.

Goffman, E. (1974). *Frame analysis: An essay on the organization of experience.* Cambridge, MA: Harvard University Press.

Goldenberg, I., & Goldenberg, H. (1991). *Family therapy: An overview.* Pacific Grove, CA: Brooks/Cole.

Goldner, V., Penn, P., Sheinberg, M., & Walker, G. (1990). Love and violence: Gender paradoxes in volatile attachments. *Family Process, 29,* 343–364.

Goode, W. J. (1959, February). The theoretical importance of love. *American Sociological Review, 24*(1), 38–47.

Goode, W. J. (1963). *World revolution and family patterns.* New York: The Free Press.

Goodrich, T., Rampage, C., Ellman, B., & Halstead, K. (1988). *Feminist family therapy: A casebook.* New York: W. W. Norton.

Goolishian, H., & Anderson, H. (1987). Language systems and therapy: An evolving idea. *Journal of Psychotherapy, 24,* 529–538.

Greer, G. (1970). *The female eunuch.* London: MacGibbon & Kee.

Greif, G. (1985). Children and housework in single father families. *Family Relations Journal of Applied Family and Child Studies, 34*(3), 353–357.

Gresham, J. (1989). White patriarchal supremacy: The politics of family in America. *Nation, 249*(4), 116–121.

Gubrium, J. F., & Holstein, J. A. (1990). *What is family?* Mountain View, CA: Mayfield.

Haley, J. (1980). *Leaving home.* New York: McGraw-Hill.

Haley, J. (1986). The power tactics of Jesus Christ. In *The power tactics of Jesus Christ and other essays* (2nd ed.). New York: Triangle Books.

Hall, E. T. (1959). *The silent language.* Greenwich, CT: Fawcett.

Hall, R. A. (1960). *Linguistics and your language.* New York: Doubleday.

Haraway, D. (1985). A manifesto for cyborgs: Science, technology, and socialist feminism in the 1980s. *Socialist Review, 15.*

Harding, S. (1986). *The science question in feminism.* Ithaca, NY: Cornell University Press.

Harvey, D. (1989). *The condition of postmodernity.* Oxford: Blackwell.

Havighurst, R. J. (1953) *Human development and education.* New York: Longmans, Green.

Hawkes, G. R., & Taylor, M. (1975, November). Power structure in Mexican and Mexican-American farm labor families. *Journal of Marriage and the Family, 37,* 807–11.

Hegel, G. W. F. (1972). *Hegel's philosophy of mind.* Freeport, NJ: Books for Library Press.

Hegel, G. W. F. (1974). *The essential writings.* New York: Harper & Row.

Heitler, S. (1990). *From conflict to resolution.* New York: W. W. Norton.

Hemp, M. (1979). *Threshold.* Pleasanton, CA: M. K. Hemp.

Hempel, C. G. (1959). The logic of functional analysis. In L. Gross, (Ed.), *Symposium on Sociological Theory.* New York: Harper & Row.

Hendrix, H. (1988). *Getting the love you want: A guide for couples.* New York: Henry Holt.

Henley, W. E. (1970). In memorium: R. T. Hamilton Bruce (Invictus). *Echoes: The Works of Henley,* 1875 (Vol. 1, No. 4, p. 125). New York: AMS Press.

Hill, M., & Ponza, M. (1983, Summer). Poverty and welfare dependence across generations. *Economic Outlook, USA,* 61–64.

Hill, R., & Rodgers, R. H. (1964). The developmental approach. In H. Christensen (Ed.), *Handbook of marriage and the family* (pp. 171–211). Chicago: Rand McNally.

Hochschild, A. (1989). *The second shift.* New York: Viking.

Hoffman, L. (1990). Constructing realities: An art of lenses. *Family Process, 29*(1), 1–12.

Hoffman, S. D., & Duncan, G. J. (1988, November). What are the economic consequences of divorce? *Demography, 25*(4), 641–645.

Hofstadter, R. (1959). *Social Darwinism in American thought.* New York: G. Braziller.

Homans, G. (1958). Social behavior as exchange. *American Journal of Sociology, 63,* 597–606.

Homans, G. C. (1961). *Social behavior: Its elementary forms.* New York: Harcourt Brace.

Homans, G. C. (1964, December). Bringing men back in. *American Sociological Review, 29,* 809–818.

Homans, G. C., & Schneider, D. M. (1955). *Marriage, authority, and final causes: A study of unilateral cross-cousin marriage.* New York: The Free Press.

Hsu, F. L. K. (1970). *Americans and Chinese.* Garden City, NY: American Museum of Natural History.

Hunt, M. (1974). *Sexual behavior in the 1970s.* New York: Dell.

Ihinger-Tallman, M. (1988). Research on stepfamilies. In W. R. Scott (Ed.), *Annual Review of Sociology* (Vol. 14). Palo Alto, CA: Annual Reviews.

Ingelhart, R. (1977). *The silent revolution: Changing values and political styles among western publics.* Princeton, NJ: Princeton University Press.

Isajiw, W. W. (1968). *Causation and functionalism in sociology.* New York: Schocken.

Johnson, D. P. (1981). *Sociological theory: Classical founders and contemporary perspectives.* New York: John Wiley.

Kain, E. L. (1990). *The myth of family decline: Understanding families in a world of rapid social change.* Lexington, MA: Lexington Books.

Kain, E. L. (1993). Family change and the life course. In P. G. Boss, W. J. Doherty, R. LaRossa, W. R. Schumm, & S. K. Steinmetz (Eds.), *Sourcebook of family theories and methods.* New York: Plenum.

Kamerman, S. (1991). Parental leave and infant care: U.S. and international trends and issues, 1978–1988. In J. Hyde & M. Essex (Eds.), *Parental leave and children: Setting a research and policy agenda* (pp. 11–23). Philadelphia: Temple University Press.

Kaverman, S. B. (1980). *Parenting in an unresponsive society.* New York: The Free Press.

Kenkel, W. F. (1977). *The family in perspective.* Santa Monica, CA: Goodyear.

Kerckhoff, A. C., & Davis, K. E. (1962). Value consensus and need complementarity in mate selection. *American Sociological Review, 27,* 295–303.

Kett, J. (1977) *Rites of passage: Adolescence in America: 1790 to the present.* New York: Basic Books.

Kikumura, A., & Kitano, H. (1973, Spring). Interracial marriage: A picture of the Japanese Americans. *Journal of Social Issues, 29,* 67–81.

Kirkendall, L. A., & Gravatt, A. E. (Eds.). (1984). *Marriage and the family in the year 2020.* New York: Prometheus Books.

Komarovsky, M. (1962). *Blue-collar marriage.* New York: Random House.

Krissman, K. (1992, August). Single parenting: Interventions in the transitional stage. *Contemporary Family Therapy: An International Journal, 14*(4), 323–353.

Kübler-Ross, E. (1969). *On death and dying.* New York: Macmillan.

Kuh, D. L., Power, C., & Rodgers, B. (1991, December). Secular trends in social class and sex differences in adult height. *International Journal of Epidemiology, 20*(4), 100–101.

Lauer, R. H., & Lauer, J. C. (1991). *Marriage and family: Quest for intimacy.* Dubuque, IA: William C. Brown.

Lederer, W. J. (1961). *A nation of sheep.* New York: W. W. Norton.

Lederer, W. J., & Jackson, D. D. (1968). *The mirages of marriage.* New York: W. W. Norton.

Lee, G. (1979). The effects of social networks on the family. In W. R. Burr, R. Hill, F. I. Nye, & I. L. Reiss (Eds.), *Contemporary theories about the family* (Vol. 1). New York: The Free Press.

Lee, G. (1992). Family & household structure. In E. F. Borgatta & M. L. Borgatta (Eds.), *Encyclopedia of sociology.* New York: Plenum.

Lemert, C. (1992). General social theory, irony, postmodernism. In S. Seidman & D. G. Wagner (Eds.), *Postmodernism and social theory.* Cambridge, MA: Blackwell.

Lengermann, P. M., & Niebrugge-Brantley, J. (1992). Contemporary feminist theory. In G. Ritzer (Ed.), *Sociological theory* (3rd ed.) (pp. 447–496). New York: McGraw-Hill.

Lerner, G. (1986). *The creation of patriarchy.* New York: Oxford University Press.

Levy, M. J., Jr. (1949). The family revolution in modern China. Cambridge, MA: Harvard University Press.

Levy, M. J., Jr. (1955, September). Some questions about Parsons' treatment of the incest problem. *British Journal of Sociology, 6,* 277–285.

Lipman-Blumen, J. (1984). *Gender roles and power.* Englewood Cliffs, NJ: Prentice Hall.

Lipset, S. (1976). *Rebellion in the university.* Chicago: University of Chicago Press.

Loseke, D. (1992). *The battered woman and shelters: The social construction of wife abuse.* Albany, NY: State University of New York Press.

Luepnitz, D. A. (1988). *Feminist theory in clinical practice.* New York: Basic Books.

Lyotard, J. F. (1984). *The postmodern condition.* Minneapolis: University of Minnesota Press.

Macklin, E. D. (1987). Nontraditional family forms. In M. B. Sussman & S. K. Steinmetz (Eds.), *Handbook of marriage and the family.* New York: Plenum.

Markman, H. J. (1989). Constructive marital conflict is NOT an oxymoron. *Negative communication in marital interaction: A misnomer?* [Special issue]. *Behavioral Assessment, 13*(1) 83–96.

Marx, K., & Engels, F. (1885/1932). *Manifesto of the Communist Party.* New York: International Publishers.

McGoldrick, M., & Pearce, J. K., & Giordano, J. (1982). *Ethnicity and family therapy.* New York: Guilford Press.

McGoldrick, M. (1989). Women and the family life cycle. In B. Carter & M. McGoldrick (Eds.), *The changing family life cycle: A framework for family therapy.* Boston, MA: Allyn & Bacon.

McMorrow, F. (1974). *Midolescence.* New York: Quadrangle/New York Times Book Company.

Mead, G. H. (1934). *Mind, self and society.* Chicago: University of Chicago Press.

Meerlo, J. A. M. (1952). *Conversation and Communication.* New York: International University Press.

Merton, R. K. (1957). Manifest and latent functions. In R. K. Merton (Ed.), *Social theory and social structure* (pp. 19–82). Glencoe, IL: The Free Press.

Merton, R. K. (1968). Social structure and anomie. In R. K. Merton (Ed.), *Social theory and social structure.* New York: The Free Press.

Mies, M. (1983). Toward a methodology for feminist research. In G. Bowles & R. Klein (Eds.), *Theories of women's studies* (pp. 117–139). London: Routledge & Kegan Paul.

Mindel, C. H., & Habenstein, R. W. (1981). *Ethnic families in America: Patterns and variations.* New York: Elsevier.

Minuchin, S. (1974). *Families and family therapy.* Cambridge, MA: Harvard University Press.

Minuchin, S., Rosman, B. L., & Baker, L. (1978). *Psychosomatic families: Anorexia nervosa in context.* Cambridge, MA: Harvard University Press.

Mitchell, J. (1984). *Women: The longest revolution.* New York: Pantheon.

Monbeck, M. E. (1974). *The meaning of blindness.* Bloomington, IN: Indiana University Press.

Mott, F. L. (1986, January/February). The pace of repeated childbearing among young mothers. *Family Planning Perspectives, 18,* 5–12.

Mulroy, E. (1988). Women as single parents. Dover, MA: Auburn House.

Nagel, E. (1956). *The structure of science: Problems in the logic of scientific explanation* (pp. 520–535). New York: Harcourt Brace & World.

Naisbitt, J. (1984). *Megatrends.* New York: Warner Books.

Newman, K. S. (1988). *Falling from grace: The experience of downward mobility in the American middle class.* New York: The Free Press.

Nichols, W. C. (1988). *Marital therapy.* New York: Guilford Press.

Nicholson, L. (1992). On the postmodern barricades: Feminism, politics, and theory. In S. Seidman & D. G. Wagner (Eds.), *Postmodernism and social theory.* Cambridge, MA: Blackwell.

Norton, A. J., & Moorman, J. E. (1987). Current trends in marriage and divorce among American women. *Journal of Marriage and the Family, 49,* 3–14.

Nye, F. I. (1979). Choice, exchange, and the family. In W. R. Burr, R. Hill, F. I. Nye, & I. L. Reiss (Eds.), *Contemporary theories about the family* (Vol. 2). New York: The Free Press.

O'Neill, G., & O'Neill, N. (1972). *Open marriage.* New York: Avon.

Pagelow, M. (1981). *Woman-battering: Victims and their experiences.* Beverly Hills, CA: Sage Publications.

Parsons, T. (1937). *The structure of social action.* New York: McGraw-Hill.

Parsons, T. (1951). *The social system.* Glencoe, IL.: The Free Press.

Parsons, T. (1954, June). The incest taboo in relation to social structure and the socialization of the child. *British Journal of Sociology, 5,* 101–117.

Parsons, T. (1959). The social structures of the family. In R. Anshen (Ed.), *The family: Its function and destiny.* New York: Harper & Row.

Parsons, T., & Bales, R. (1955). *Family, socialization and interaction process.* Glencoe, IL.: The Free Press.

Parsons, T., Bales, R. F., & Shils, E. A. (1953). *Working papers in the theory of action.* Glencoe, IL.: The Free Press.

Parsons, T., & Shils, E. A. (1951). *Towards a general theory of action.* Cambridge: Harvard University Press.

Pittman, F. S., III. (1987). Turning points. New York: W. W. Norton.

Piven, F. F. (1990). Ideology and the state: Women, power and the welfare state. In L. Gordon (Ed.), *Women, the state and welfare* (pp. 250–264). Madison: University of Wisconsin Press.

Pizzey, E. (1974). *Scream quietly or the neighbors will hear you.* New York: Penguin.

Reich, C. A. (1970). *The greening of America.* New York: Random House.

Reiss, I. (1960, May). Toward a sociology of the heterosexual love relationship. *Marriage and Family Living, 22*(2), 139–145.

Rex, J. (1961). Key problems of sociological theory. London: Routledge & Kegan Paul.

Riesman, D., Glazer, N., & Denney, R. (1953). *The lonely crowd.* New Haven: Yale University Press.

Rodgers, R. H. (1962). *Improvements in the construction and analysis of family life cycle categories.* Kalamazoo: Western Michigan University.

Rollins, B. C., & Cannon, K. L. (1974). Marital satisfaction over the family life cycle. *Journal of Marriage and the Family, 36,* 271–284.

Rossi, A. S. (1985). *Gender and the life course.* New York: Aldine de Gruyter.

Rossi, A. S., & Rossi, P. H. (1990). Of human bonding: Parent-child relationships across the life course. New York: Aldine de Gruyter.

Rothman, S., & Marks, E. (1989). Flexible work schedules and family policy. In F. Gerstel & H. Gross (Eds.), *Families and work* (pp. 469–477). Philadelphia: Temple University Press.

Rowntree, B. S. (1906). *Poverty: A study of town life.* London: Macmillan.

Rubin, G. (1984). Thinking sex: Notes for a radical theory of the politics of sexuality. In C. Vance (Ed.), *Pleasure and danger* (pp. 267–320). Boston, MA: Routledge & Kegan Paul.

Sacks, N. E., & Suitor, J. J. (1992). Remarriage. In E. F. Borgatta & M. L. Borgatta (Eds.), *Encyclopedia of Sociology* (Vol. 3). New York: Macmillan.

Safilios-Rothschild, C. (1977). *Love, sex and sex roles.* Englewood Cliffs, NJ: Prentice Hall.

Sahlins, M. D., & Service, E. R. (1960). *Evolution and culture.* Ann Arbor: University of Michigan Press.

Sanik, M., & Mauldin, T. (1986, January). Single vs. two parent families: A comparison of mothers' time. *The single parent family* [Special issue]. *Family Relations Journal of Applied Family and Child Studies, 35*(1), 53–56.

Scanzoni, J. (1972). *Sexual bargaining: Power politics in the American marriage.* Englewood Cliffs, NJ: Prentice Hall.

Scanzoni, J. H. (1977). *The black family in modern society.* Chicago, IL: University of Chicago Press.

Schoen, R., Woodrow, K., & Baj, J. (1985). Marriage and divorce in twentieth-century American cohorts. *Demography, 22,* 101–114.

Schvaneveldt, J. D., & Young, M. H. (1992, October). Strengthening families: New horizons in family life education. *Family Relations, 41,* 385–390.

Seidman, S., & Wagner, D. G. (1992). *Postmodernism and social theory.* Cambridge, MA: Basil Blackwell.

Sewell, W. H., Jr. (1992, July). A theory of structure: Duality, agency, and transformation. *American Journal of Sociology, 98,* 1–27.

Sherman, L. W., & Berk, R. A. (1984). The specific deterrent effects of arrest for domestic assault. *American Sociological Review, 49,* 261–272.

Sluzki, C. (1985). Terapia familiar como construccion de realidades alternativas [Family therapy as a construction of alternative realities]. *Sistemas Familiares, 1,* 53–59.

Spanier, G. B., & Furstenberg, F. G. (1987). Remarriage and reconstituted families. In M. Sussman & S. Steinmetz (Eds.), *Handbook of Marriage and the Family.* New York: Plenum.

Spencer, H. (1852/1972a). A theory of population deduced from the general law of animal fertility. In J. D. Y. Peel (Ed.), *On social evolution: Selected writings* (pp. 33–37). Chicago: University of Chicago Press.

Spencer, H. (1857/1972b). Progress: Its law and cause. In J. D. Y. Peel (Ed.), *On social evolution: Selected writings* (pp. 38–52). Chicago: University of Chicago Press.

Spengler, O. (1926). The decline of the west. New York: Knopf.

Stack, C. (1974). *All our kin.* New York: Harper & Row.

Stanton, M. D., & Todd, T. C. (1982). *Family therapy of drug abuse and addiction.* New York: Guilford Press.

Staples, R., & Mirande, A. (1980). Racial and cultural variations among American families: A decennial review of the literature on minority families. *Journal of Marriage and the Family, 33,* 119–135.

Starr, A. M. (1989, June). Recovery for the alcoholic family: Family systems treatment model. *Social Casework, 70*(6), 348–354.

Steinem, G. (1986). *Outrageous acts & everyday rebellions.* New York: NAL/Dutton.

Steinem, G. (1992). *Revolution from within: A book of self-esteem.* New York: Little, Brown.

Sternberg, R. J. (1988). *The triangle of love.* New York: Basic Books.

Steward, J. H. (1956). Cultural evolution. *Scientific American,* CXCIV, *5,* 70–80.

Straus, M. A., & Gelles, R. J. (1988). How violent are American families? Estimates from the national family violence resurvey and other studies. In G. T. Hotaling, D. Finkelhor, J. T. Kirkpatrick, & M. Straus (Eds.), *Family abuse and its consequences.* Newbury Park, CA: Sage Publications.

Straus, M. A., Gelles, R. J., & Steinmetz, S. K. (1980). *Behind closed doors: Violence in the American family.* New York: Doubleday.

Strobel, F. R. (1993). *Upward dreams, downward mobility: The economic decline of the American middle class.* Larhan, MD: Rowman & Littlefield.

Stryker, S. (1959). Symbolic interaction as an approach to family research. *Journal of Marriage and the Family, 21,* 111–119.

Stryker, S. (1967, November). Identity salience and role performance: The relevance of symbolic interaction theory for family research. *Journal of Marriage and the Family, 30,* 558–564.

Stryker, S. (1972, Spring). Symbolic interaction theory: A review and some suggestions for comparative family research. *Journal of Comparative Family Studies, 3,* 17–32.

Sue, S., & Kitano, H. (1973, Spring). Asian American stereotypes. *Journal of Social Issues, 29,* 83–98.

Sztompka, P. (1969). Teleological language in sociology. *The Polish Sociological Bulletin, 3*(2), 56–69.

Sztompka, P. (1974). *System and function: Toward a theory of society.* New York: Academic Press.

Tannen, D. (1990). *You just don't understand: Men and women in conversation.* New York: Ballantine.

Thibaut, J. W., & Kelley, H. H. (1959). *The social psychology of groups.* New York: John Wiley.

Thirsk, J. (1976). The European debate on customs of inheritance, 1500–1700. In J. Goody, J. Thirsk, & E. P. Thompson (Eds.), *Family and inheritance.* Cambridge: Cambridge University Press.

Thomas, W. I. & Znanecki, F. (1958). *The Polish peasant in Europe and America* (Vols. 1 & 2). New York: Dover.

Tillmon, J. (1976). Welfare is a woman's issue. In R. Baxandall, L. Gordon, & S. Reverby (Eds.), *America's working women: A documented history, 1600 to the present* (pp. 354–356). New York: Vintage Books.

Toffler, A. (1970). *Future shock.* New York: Bantam Books.

Toffler, A. (1984). *The third wave.* New York: Bantam Books.

Toffler, A. (1990). *Powershift: Knowledge, wealth and violence at the edge of the 21st century.* New York: Bantam Books.

Tönnies, F. (1957). *Community and society—Gemeinschaft und gesellschaft* (C. P. Loomis, Ed. and Trans.). East Lansing, MI: The Michigan State University Press.

Toynbee, A. (1946). *A study of history* (Vols. 1–6, abridged by D. C. Somervell). New York: Oxford University Press.

Tumin, M. M. (1985). *Social stratification.* Englewood Cliffs, NJ: Prentice Hall.

Turner, J., & Maryanski, A. (1979). *Functionalism.* Menlo Park, CA: Benjamin/Cummings.

Tylor, E. B. (1871/1958). *The origins of culture.* New York: Harper.

Uhlenberg, P. (1980, Fall). Death and the family. *Journal of Family History.*

U.S. Bureau of the Census (1989). *Fertility of American women: June 1988.* Current Population Reports (Series P-20, No. 436). Washington, DC: U.S. Government Printing Office. Table 2, p. 17, and Table 10, pp. 46–47.

U.S. Bureau of the Census (1989). *Household and family characteristics: March 1988.* Current Population Reports. (Series P-20, No. 437). Washington, DC: U.S. Government Printing Office.

Vanderpool, H. (1973). *Darwin and Darwinism: Revolutionary insights concerning man, nature, religion, and society.* Lexington, MA: D. C. Heath.

Veevers, J. E. (1988, April). The "real" marriage squeeze: Mate selection, mortality, and the mating gradient. *Sociological Perspectives, 31*(2), 169–189.

Visher, E. B., & Visher, J. S. (1988). *Old loyalties, new ties: Therapeutic strategies with stepfamilies.* New York: Brunner-Mazel.

Visher, E. B., & Visher, J. S. (1990). Dynamics of successful stepfamilies. *Journal of Divorce and Remarriage, 14*(1), 3–12.

Vogel, E. G., & Bell, N. W. (1960). The emotionally disturbed child as the family scapegoat. In N. W. Bell & E. F. Vogel (Eds.), *A modern introduction to the family* (pp. 382–397). Glencoe, IL: The Free Press.

Von Senden, M. (1960). *Sight and space.* Glencoe, IL: The Free Press.

Walker, L. (1979). *The battered woman.* New York: Harper.

Wallerstein, J. S. (1982). Impact of divorce on parents and children. In *Separation, divorce and beyond.* New York: BMA Audio Cassette Publications.

Wallerstein, J. S., & Blakeslee, S. (1990). *Second chances: Men, women and children a decade after divorce.* New York: Ticknor & Fields.

Wallerstein, J. S., & Kelly, J. B. (1980). *Surviving the breakup: How children and parents cope with divorce.* New York: Basic Books.

Walsh, F. (1989). The family in later life. In B. Carter & M. McGoldrick (Eds.), *The changing family life cycle: A framework for family therapy* (2nd ed.). New York: Allyn & Bacon.

Walster, E., Walster, G. W., & Traupmann, J. (1978). *Equity: Theory and research.* Boston: Allyn & Bacon.

Weiss, R. S. (1979, Fall). Growing up a little faster: The experience of growing up in a single-parent household. *Journal of Social Issues, 35,* 97–111.

Weiss, R. S. (1981). *Going it alone: The family life and social situation of the single parent.* New York: Basic Books.

Weiss, R. S. (1985) Men and the family. *Family Process, 24*(1): 49–58.

Weitzman, L. (1985). *The divorce revolution: The unexpected social and economic consequences for women and children in America.* New York: The Free Press.

West, G. (1981). *The national welfare rights movement: The social protest of poor women.* New York: Praeger.

Wharton, C. (1987). Establishing shelters for battered women: Local manifestations of a social movement. *Qualitative Sociology, 10*(2), 146–163.

White, A. E., & McLennan, J. P. (1987, November). Single parents and social support networks: The contribution of parents of "parents without partners." *Australian Journal of Sex, Marriage and the Family, 8*(4), 164–172.

White, B. B. (1989, March). Gender differences in marital communication patterns. *Family Process, 28,* 89–105.

Wilson, B. F. (1989). Remarriages and subsequent divorces. *National Vital Statistics* (Series 21, No. 45). Hyattsville, MD: National Center for Health Statistics.

Wilson, W. J., & Necherman, K. M. (1986). Poverty and family structure: The widening gap between evidence and public policy issues. In S. H. Danzinger & D. H. Weinberg (Eds.), *Fighting poverty: What works and what doesn't.* Cambridge, MA: Harvard University Press.

Winch, R. F. (1958). *Mate-selection: A study of complementary needs.* New York: Harper & Row.

Winch, R. F. (1963). *The modern family.* New York: Holt, Rinehart & Winston.

Winch, R. F. (1967). Another look at the theory of complementary needs in mate selection. *Journal of Marriage and the Family, 29,* 756–762.

Winton, C. A. (1970, January). On the realization of blindness. *The New Outlook for the Blind,* 16–24.

Winton, C. A. (1971, June). The beautiful blind. *American Foundation for the Blind Research Bulletin, 23,* 9–37.

Winton, C. A. (1974). *Theory and measurement in sociology.* Cambridge, MA: Schenkman.

Winton, C. A. (1975, May). Stresses among university students in Hong Kong. *San Jose Studies, 1*(2), 17–27.

Winton, C. A. (1981). *Family therapy: Etiology and treatment of illness.* Novato, CA: Applied Medical Training.

Witt, D. D. (1987, December). A conflict theory of family violence. *Journal of Family Violence, 2*(4), 291–301.

Wolf, P. A., & Mast, E. (1987, January–February). Counseling issues in adoptions by stepparents. *Social Work, 32*(1), 69–74.

Wolff, K. H. (1950). *The sociology of Georg Simmel* (K. H. Wolff, Trans.). Glencoe, IL: The Free Press.

Ybarra, L. (1982, February). When wives work: The impact on the Chicano family. *Journal of Marriage and the Family,* 169–178.

Yorburg, B. (1993). *Family relationships.* New York: St. Martin's Press.

Zimmerman, S. (1992). *Family policies and family well-being: The role of political culture.* Newbury Park, CA: Sage Publications.

Zinn, M. B. (1982, Summer). Qualitative methods in family research: A look inside the Chicano families. *California Sociologist,* 58–79.

Index

Page references in **bold** indicate glossary terms.

Staff

Editor Dorothy Fink
Production Manager Brenda S. Filley
Art Editor Pamela Carley
Designer Charles Vitelli
Typesetting Supervisor Libra Ann Cusack
Typesetter Juliana Arbo
Proofreaders Diane Barker and Howard Battles
Editorial Assistant Marion Gouge